SAGE was founded in 1965 by Sara Miller McCune to support the dissemination of usable knowledge by publishing innovative and high-quality research and teaching content. Today, we publish more than 750 journals, including those of more than 300 learned societies, more than 800 new books per year, and a growing range of library products including archives, data, case studies, reports, conference highlights, and video. SAGE remains majority-owned by our founder, and on her passing will become owned by a charitable trust that secures our continued independence.

Los Angeles | London | Washington DC | New Delhi | Singapore

Why You Must Know This Man

Thank you for choosing a SAGE product! If you have any comment, observation or feedback, I would like to personally hear from you. Please write to me at contactceo@sagepub.in

—Vivek Mehra, Managing Director and CEO,
SAGE Publications India Pvt Ltd, New Delhi

Bulk Sales

SAGE India offers special discounts for purchase of books in bulk. We also make available special imprints and excerpts from our books on demand.

For orders and enquiries, write to us at

Marketing Department
SAGE Publications India Pvt Ltd
B1/I-1, Mohan Cooperative Industrial Area
Mathura Road, Post Bag 7
New Delhi 110044, India
E-mail us at marketing@sagepub.in

Get to know more about SAGE, be invited to SAGE events, get on our mailing list. Write today to marketing@sagepub.in

This book is also available as an e-book.

Why You Must Know This Man

The Life and Times of Amit Dutta Gupta

Edited by
ARJUN MALHOTRA
SUSHMITA SENGUPTA

www.sagepublications.com
Los Angeles • London • New Delhi • Singapore • Washington DC

Copyright © Arjun Malhotra and Sushmita Sengupta, 2015

All rights reserved. No part of this book may be reproduced or utilized in any form or by any means, electronic or mechanical, including photocopying, recording or by any information storage or retrieval system, without permission in writing from the publisher.

First published in 2015 by

SAGE Response
B1/I-1 Mohan Cooperative Industrial Area
Mathura Road, New Delhi 110 044, India

SAGE Publications Inc
2455 Teller Road
Thousand Oaks, California 91320, USA

SAGE Publications Ltd
1 Oliver's Yard, 55 City Road
London EC1Y 1SP, United Kingdom

SAGE Publications Asia-Pacific Pte Ltd
3 Church Street
#10-04 Samsung Hub
Singapore 049483

Published by Vivek Mehra for SAGE Publications India Pvt Ltd, typeset in 11/14 pts Bembo by RECTO Graphics, Delhi and printed at Sai Print-o-Pack, New Delhi.

Library of Congress Cataloging-in-Publication Data

Why you must know this man : the life and times of Amit Dutta Gupta / edited by Arjun Malhotra and Sushmita Sengupta.
  pages cm
  1. Gupta, Amit Dutta. 2. Computer engineers—India—Biography. 3. Businesspeople—India—Biography. 4. Information technology—India. 5. HCL Technologies. I. Malhotra, Arjun, editor. II. Sengupta, Sushmita, editor.
  QA76.2.G87W49   621.39092—dc23   [B]   2015   2014028544

ISBN: 978-93-515-0038-4 (PB)

The SAGE Team: Rudra Narayan, Vandana Gupta, Rajib Chatterjee, and Rajinder Kaur
Cover image courtesy: Purnima Dutta Gupta.
Khorkaai image courtesy: Arnav Dutta Gupta.

CONTENTS

INTRODUCTION   ix

HIS LIFE AND TIMES   **1**

1. The Beginning   5
2. Friends Forever   25
3. Coke before Computers   37
4. Game Changer   45
5. Profiting by Design   89
6. Soft Turn to Success   107
7. Amit—The Leader and Mentor   125

KHORKAAI   **179**

ABOUT THE EDITORS   310

INTRODUCTION

Cicero, the great politician and orator of Rome, in the Ist century BC, may have inspired the Cicero Pizza restaurant in Cupertino (home of Apple) California—Cicero Pizza was the "watering hole" for many Indians who were working in the Silicon Valley in the IT Offshore Services Industry in 1998. These Indian engineers participated and inspired the rapid growth of the industry that blazed the hallmark of the first global industry out of India.

Indian IT Industry gave respect to Indians all over the world. This industry fulfilled thoughts, wishes, hopes, desires of many young men and women in India who did not have too many options with them to start a rewarding career. This became the industry where both "Logical" and "Intuitive" were recognized and rewarded. This industry spun out leaders who later became movers, stimulators, and adapters in different sub-industries—BPO, IT infrastructure, and so on as well as in other emerging industries as the Indian economy started to pick up.

> "'Inflection Point' is defined as an event that results in a significant change in the progress of a company, industry, sector, economy, or geopolitical situation. An inflection point can be considered a turning point after which a dramatic change, with either positive or negative results, is expected to result. Companies, industries, sectors, and economies are dynamic and constantly evolving. Inflection points are more significant than the small day-to-day progress that is made and the effects of the change are often well known and widespread." (Dictionary meaning of Inflection Point)

Why You Must Know This Man

The moment of Inflection Point—dramatic change in the development of Indian IT Industry happened when HCL launched their System-2 mini computer in 1981 through a well thought-out advertisement campaign that resulted in an overwhelming response that stimulated the latent IT and computer market in India and sowed the seeds for the IT revolution that all of us talk about today.

This is the story of one of the "Stimulators" of that Inflection Point.

The rest is history!

Arjun Malhotra

IDEA

Let Me Tell You a Story ...

There was a Tamilian boy, Shiv, with an Electrical and Electronics Engineering degree from PSG College of Technology, Coimbatore ... and his own dream ... *Chaand taaro ko chhune ki aasha, Aasmaan me udane kee aasha ... Dil hai chhota sa chhotee si aasha.*

And then this Punjabi *munda* ... Arjun with an Electronics and Electrical Communication Engineering degree from IIT Kharagpur ... and his own dream ... *Har lamhe ko khul ke jeeta tha woh, Behti hawa sa tha woh, Udti patang sa tha woh.*

And a romantic intellectual Bengali Amit with a mechanical engineering degree from NIT Durgapur ... and his own dream ... *Woh aasman jhuk raha hai zameen par, Yeh milan humne dekha yahin par, Meri duniya, mere sapne milenge shaayad yahin ...*

It was a hot Delhi summer in 1981—there was no power in the office (typical load shedding of Delhi)—four young executives (Shiv, Amit, Arjun, and Raman) had been cloistered in my (Shiv Nadar) cabin of Siddhartha Building in Nehru Place for the past eight hours. In fact, we had been doing this for the past three months ... for 12 hours a day. We were strategizing the launch of "System-2" in India and were betting our 'Company' in this launch. It was a start-up atmosphere, and we didn't know then that we were laying the foundation of something that would make India mainstream someday.

I used to have this table that was used as the conference table. I remember when we were drafting the advertisement, I was sitting on one side of the table and Amit was sitting next to me, when Arjun came in,

He said, "Full-page ad?"

I said, "Yes."

"Okay," he said and then asked, "how many?"

I said, "Four of them."

He asked, "National?"

I said, "Yes."

He said, "I hope you have worked out your cost right. Finally advertisement karane ke baad koi ayega toh nahi, it's an 8-bit machine" (After publishing this ad, no one will come, it's an 8-bit machine).

Amit just winked at Arjun and said, "Arjun, you will get your enquiries."

Then Arjun caught hold of Amit and said, 'kitna lagaya paisa? barbad ho jayega.' (What's your budget on this account? You will rock the company upside down.)

I said, "Arjun your enquiries will come. Now can we concentrate on how we will close it?"

He said, "Yaar tu aadmi ko mere samne khada kar, uske bad mai paise ko liye bagair usko chodunga nahi" (My friend, just get me prospects, I won't leave them till I make a hole in their pocket).

He was so hungry. We all were very young and shared a very special bond that you don't find these days.

At this time we didn't realize that what we were planning would revolutionize the Indian IT industry. And it did ... the launch of HCL System-2 computers turned the Indian IT industry upside down, and it exploded the myth that computers were complex, scientific machines, and treated it like any other consumer product, like a typewriter, for example. It was the beginning of consumerism in computers, and it also gave birth to what is today—the only industry that came out of India and became global ... Shiv Nadar, Founder, HCL; Chairman, HCL Technologies and Shiv Nadar Foundation

They had IT background except one—Amit Dutta Gupta—his last experience was in Coca-Cola. The role that Amit Dutta Gupta played in that launch has not been forgotten but articulated in this book by Shiv Nadar and Arjun Malhotra, who were in the room strategizing the launch of System-2 with Amit on that hot summer day.

A few evolved IT professionals under the leadership of Arjun Malhotra banded to create a "leadership journey" for young professionals. In this narration of an intellectual, romantic Bengali, the group has brought out an individual's passion for life. This passion enabled the person to rise above limitations, leaving remarkable footprints that have become concrete reminders of extraordinary leadership.

Amit Dutta Gupta left irreversible imprints in the lives of several people. These permanent watermarks on the lives of Bikram Dasgupta, Founder and Executive Chairman, Globsyn Group; Co-Founder, PCL; C.P. Gurnani, Managing Director and CEO, Tech Mahindra Ltd; Pradeep Gupta, Chairman, Cyber Media; Sujit Baksi, Chief Executive, Business Service Group, Tech Mahindra Ltd; Sumit Bhattacharya, SVP and Head of Global Marketing, Sutherland Global Services; Neelam Dhawan, Managing Director, Hewlett-Packard India; Subroto Bagchi, Chairman, MindTree; Raj Sirohi, Ex-President and CEO, HCL Technologies America Inc; Pradeep Sen, Ex-Managing Director, NCR Corp and Senior Director, SAP India; Mohan Rao, Founder Director, Spatik Consultants; Rajeev Sawhney, Former President, HCL Europe and Global Public Services; R.K. Gupta, President, Neilsoft; Ex-Country Manager, Autodesk India; Ravi Thumboochetty, Ex-CEO and Director, International Operations, HCL Infosystems; R.P. Singh, Founder, Corporate Value Add; Shravani Dang, Group Vice President, Avantha Group; S.V. Sriram, Senior Vice President, Tech Mahindra Ltd and many more give you a sense of the leadership he influenced. In a sense, Amit arguably influenced a type and section of technology services leaders that helped create a critical global wave in technology and technology services.

The prime movers of Amit's life were WHY and WHAT FOR, and his existence was not dependent on the subordination of the metaphysical to the man made. On the contrary, it was always driven by the rational—where the principle of rational was moral. His actions never demanded any betrayal or sacrifices of his values; neither did they transform his values into threat to his own moral worth. He was chiefly interested in human nature, environment, and their interplay.

Many in HCL believed that apart from creating the pathbreaking strategy that launched the indigenous PC revolution in India, he was also THE "Go To" person in the company. Arjun Malhotra thinks, "Every company has a soul in some person and Amit was that soul in HCL."

My relationship with Amit da was like that of the seven colors of the rainbow. Each important on its own, but fading into insignificance before the grandeur and sublime of the whole. He was my mentor, then friend, and like an elder brother.

Amit da was a great storyteller who could easily generate a child-like excitement in others. He would effortlessly teach me the most difficult lessons in life and business by his interesting teaching technique, and also make the learning process memorable and enjoyable. I have learned my management lessons from him, be it—brand building, securing, and converting leads in emerging markets—his great "Cook & Kill" strategy or process around decision making. The best thing about him was that he could always create a flawless process around the principle he would teach. Much of what I am today has been imbibed from his infinite depth of knowledge and philosophy.

The day Purnima, Amit da's wife, broached the subject of the unfinished book that Amit da was writing, I felt that publishing a book for our younger generation on this inspirational leader and the "quiet changer," who conveyed the spirit that you don't need the corner office to make changes, would be my fitting tribute to the great man, not for the reason that it would make him happy wherever he is, but for the fact that the world would be left much poorer if they missed out on his profundity of life.

I sincerely hope that our readers enjoy this story and get motivated by this inspirational leader with "Ma Saraswati resides in him" (as his friends would remember Amit) and learn a lesson that would help them in life.

Amit and Arjun—A Unique Camaraderie

When does casual office banter, while sipping tea in an office cabin, develop into a friendship? When does synergy in office transgress into a friendship? When do you help each other out in situations outside a professional context? Each friend represents a world in us, a world possibly not born until they become friends.

The friendship between Amit and Arjun was of thoughtfulness and care.

Professionally, Amit viewed Arjun as the most charismatic global IT Leader we have from Indian IT industry today. At a personal level, he had the highest regard for Arjun. In many conversations, he often addressed Arjun as "Devtullya" which virtually means saintly, or, in other words, "he is of the purest mind and heart" in Bengali.

Arjun first met Amit in HCL although both started their careers as senior management trainees in DCM. Over the years, relationship between Arjun and Amit evolved from office colleagues to friends, to Arjun becoming Amit's mentor and guide in Amit's life at HCL and after HCL. Arjun did not share business responsibilities with Amit while Amit was trying to achieve his goals after leaving HCL, but the positive relationship that they shared gave Amit the enrichment, which is required to enjoy the sense of fulfillment that accompanies such an undertaking.

The day before he passed away, Amit was restless and asked his wife Purnima for Arjun's telephone number—Arjun was on an international travel schedule—Amit wanted to reach out to his friend. Purnima, Amit's wife, recalls—"Amit never asked anything from anyone, except from Arjun."

Arjun and Amit were the greatest influencers in the formative years of HCL. Now that we look back and try to recall the relationship between Amit and Arjun—there were a number of common traits in their personality, their working style, and personal philosophy. They had a lot in common in their value systems.

Arjun and Amit's "out of the box" thought process, combined with their contagious and attractive personality, left none of the HCLites untouched. Today, we speak of "charisma" of certain leaders—Arjun and Amit moved HCLites to follow. The idea of helping people by matching them to situations where they can thrive (motivation) was what Amit and Arjun did best. Arjun and Amit never gave instructions on what to do—they gave options, and let the individual decide what to do as long as the individual took responsibility for it.

I recall it were those many late evenings (both Arjun and Amit liked working late) we spent watching Amit and Arjun interact, (wow) and respect and honor each other. The mutual trust they had for each other was amazing. They made hard work and long hours into exciting and interesting fun. Above all, they showed us how to respect a human being.

The humor that both Arjun and Amit brought to the workplace—whether it was in the jokes that Arjun shared or Amit's unique style of describing a business situation—was possible because of their ability to make friends easily. Arjun and Amit retained the freshness, humor in all the situations.

Arjun and Amit were always in sync—they knew each other's habits, stress points. When business situations did not pan out as planned, they would take the blame on themselves—never expose the subordinates. Arjun's pugnacious style on addressing business challenges was matched by Amit's Bengali courtesy on personal matters. Both Arjun and Amit were adored by executives and respected by even those who profoundly disagreed with them.

Read the employee handbook of any company and it is likely to see the company's workforce described as a "family," an inspiring thought, but that may not ring true in most of the companies. The relationship that Arjun and Amit had with the employees in HCL took the "family" word seriously. In one of the instances, as recalled by Purnima, Amit's wife—Arjun and Amit (with their spouses) made it a point to attend the wedding of the daughter of a tenured office helper. The wedding was in a remote village. All four of them stayed throughout the ceremony, ate with family, and left only after the *vidai*.

The single most important element of business friendship is not only the company of others, but the opportunity to give unselfishly, receive feedback, support each other, and work together to reach goals unattainable on our own. We tend to view other people's actions as reflections of their characters. The friendship of Arjun and Amit personified this.

Amit passed away on August 17, 2010, leaving his own creation (Khorkaai) unfinished—when he was about to write his professional journey through IT. While Purnima trusted me completely with Amit da's manuscript, I approached Arjun (Arjun Malhotra) who was in the United States to complete this unfinished work of Amit, as he was the most suited person and Amit's confidant to take this project forward. His confirmatory reply came in a few seconds. Without Arjun's whole-hearted support and his personal contribution, this book would not have been written and published.

Sushmita Sengupta

His Life and Times

Arjun Malhotra
Sushmita Sengupta
Purnima Dutta Gupta
Narasimham Koti
Bharat K. Singh
Dilip Kumar Basu
Arnav Dutta Gupta

01

1

THE BEGINNING

The prime movers of Amit's life were "WHY" and "WHAT FOR," and it was always driven by the rational—where the principle of rational was moral. Foundation of one's value system first commenced at home under the guidance of parents and then in school by your teachers. Amit's minute "sense and sensibilities" also commenced very early in life under the guidance of his spiritual parents and untiring fathers of Loyola School.

1946–1968

Life around Khorkaai

Arjun Malhotra and Sushmita Sengupta

I was from the 9th batch of Senior Management Trainees (SMTs) in DCM, and Amit was from the SMT 7th batch. Both Amit and Shiv (Nadar) were batchmates in DCM, and he had already left and was working with Coca-Cola when I joined DCM. I met Amit in HCL for the first time where we began our journey of a long-lasting "treasured" friendship ... "Each friend represents a world in us, a world possibly not born until they become friends."

"Khorkaai" is the main tributary of the river Subarnarekha. It originates from the Chota Nagpur Plateau and meanders through the districts of West Singhbhum, Bokaro, East Singhbhum, Ranchi, and merges with Subarnarekha at Sankchi. Jamshedpur is situated at the confluence of the rivers Khorkaai and Subarnarekha, a place where Amit spent his childhood and perhaps developed the art of thinking, of systematic study of human thoughts and feelings, and his love for wisdom. This story of Amit's "journey through life" began around Khorkaai, and we will witness where it finally reached as the story unfolds.

Parents

Amit was the eldest amongst the three children of Shri Madhabendra Nath Dutta Gupta and Smt Bela Rani Dutta Gupta, a younger sister (Arundhati Chakraborty), and then a younger brother (Dr Subhashish Dutta Gupta). His father was Deputy Director of Inspections DGS & D, Government of India, posted in Jamshedpur, while his mother was a devoted homemaker. Amit's father was a spiritual soul, who devoted his entire life to the teachings and philosophy of Shri Ramakrishna, Sharada Ma, and Swami Vivekananda. He also encouraged Amit's mother to do the same. Amit's father was also a prolific writer and his years were spent on the pursuit of spirituality, yoga, reading, and writing. Needless to say, the foundation of Amit's unfaltering value system commenced at home under the guidance of his spiritual parents.

Literary Sweethearts

Amit was a voracious reader since his childhood. His father was responsible in a way for Amit to develop his love and passion for reading, as Amit would say, "My father had been forced, owing to circumstances, that he couldn't control to start going to school at the age of 3 in an era and in a village where you didn't even think 'school' until you reached the ripe age of 7. This left a life-long scar on my father's psyche, and an intense revulsion towards the formal school process." So for Amit, he announced to the world at large that Amit would bypass the entire school education scene, sit as a private candidate for matriculation, and thence on to college.

This was an excellent arrangement, as far as Amit was concerned, since it freed him completely from any regimen, and empowered him to continue with his innovations on every kind of prank possible and unchecked hours of play on the Khorkaai sand banks and fruit trees in the neighborhood. But more lastingly, it opened the floodgates of reading literature—first Bengali and then English.

Values

At the appropriate ripe age, Amit went to Loyola School at Jamshedpur. He was a great scholar and orator. The sparks of sheer intelligence and caliber of Amit could be noticed from his early childhood. However, Amit would give this credit to the untiring commitment of those good fathers of Loyola School, first, for having built in him a solid foundation of good, strong, and enduring value systems and then for imparting knowledge. To Amit, school was not just a medium for transferring doses of learning and knowledge. It was, rather, a meeting place of intellects for constant interaction and pondering on basic issues of strength of character, courage, eternal curiosity about life all around him, social responsibilities, and healthy competitiveness.

Love for Writing and Theater

From his very infant days, Amit had been greatly intrigued by the science and art of writing, of the strange magic by which a group of words is made to communicate whole stories, a picture, thoughts, and feelings—to be captured forever in a unique lattice of profound meaning. The English and Hindi texts, of course, were picked up in school, along with the Bengali learnt at home.

Amit remained indebted to his English teacher, Father Power, who taught the language with Teutonic military discipline and unfolded the true majesty of the written English language to him.

Amit learnt similes and metaphors from him in his own inimitable style. He first taught Amit the elements of literary criticism. This led naturally, and causally, to the whole art of acting, first without any words and then with words and a definite script. And it's the beginning of Amit's another passion, along with his studies .... That is, *theater*.

Sense of Humor

Another important trait of Amit's character was his sense of humor. He believed that the one thing which we could practice with ease, with no need for accessories, discipline regimens, or gurus, and is yet the most effective, is plain old humor.

He would often say,

> Nothing takes away all the wrinkles and stressful premonitions than a break-out humorous session, even if it lasts only for a moment. It's like one's sweating out the mind toxins that are so corroding our peace. The other great thing about humor is that it doesn't depend on the size of anyone's pocket to indulge in. It only calls for an ability to not just see, but actually observe and assimilate the ludicrous, the deviant, and the mirthful in an otherwise dull, prosaic, or indeed even a painful situation. And the quicker the response, the more productive it is.

Being Amit's colleague in HCL, I have personally experienced this throughout his tenure. He had mustered and skillfully used this art with great ease in his professional and personal life.

Going to College

Amit finished his school with marks that broke all previous records of the school in Senior Cambridge. He joined IIT Kharagpur and then moved to NIT Durgapur, from where he completed his Bachelor of Engineering in mechanical stream.

Amit spent five of the happiest years of his life at NIT Durgapur. It was exciting purely because of the collection of different characters and the unique characteristics that each one had. According to Amit, college life would have become utterly dull and boring if all you had to do was to attend classes, do assignments, prepare for exams, and ad nauseam, and therefore he continued with his passion for debating and elocution throughout his college days with great élan.

When Amit came out of engineering college, the job situation was really bad in Bengal and the Naxalite movement had already begun. Amit had one standing job offer—in Durgapur Steel Plant—but he didn't want to remain cooped up in a small industrial town like Durgapur for the rest of his life. So he started looking out and applying everywhere, and was extremely fortunate in getting through, after several rounds of tests, into the prized—SMT program at DCM Delhi. He was the only candidate from Bengal to get selected that year. Amit also got selected in IIM Calcutta. He had to choose. Family responsibilities prevailed, and he joined DCM as SMT.

Naatyakaal

The start point of Amit's association with Naatyakaal (era of plays) was Mihir, who was Amit's first friend in Karol Bagh, Delhi.

In the 1970s, the group created many plays and performed them right up to Calcutta at various forums—play competitions, *puja* festival, sponsored visits, and also a Hindi translation of the very popular play on the all-pervasive impact of advertising. They performed Chaalchitra and Auho! Bignyapan at CLT, in 1975, and the audience was spell bound. It included Nirmalya Acharya, Editor of Soumitra Chatterjee's magazine *Ekh khon* (Soumitra Chatterjee and Satyajit Ray are among the finest pairs of director–actor in the world of cinema, and both are honored with the Dadasaheb Phalke Award for lifetime contribution to

Indian cinema.), and the legendary theater and film personality of Bengal, Bijon Bhattacharya, whose house they visited the next day at Bhawanipur. He was delighted with their performance and gave them his whole-hearted blessings.

Purnima

I remember attending Amit's registered marriage with Purnima (a postgraduate in English literature) in Kolkata, and also being one of the main witnesses to sign the marriage papers. Amit was blessed with two healthy handsome boys, Anirudh and Arnav, and he remained a most loving and doting father to them. Both his sons pursued engineering, and are also bright students.

Amitava—The Infinite Light of Purnima's Life

Purnima Dutta Gupta (Wife)

Amit's father assiduously shunned the consumerist material world in thought and deed. There was always a glow on his face and a smile, which can only be defined as the Mona Lisa smile. I never saw him angry, irritated, or impatient. He was an authority on yoga and tried his best to inculcate the practice in each one of us. In his spare time, he would indulge in his passion of treating the colony children with various ailments, and distributing German homeopathic and biochemic medicines for free. After a time, the neighborhood children and their mothers refused to visit an allopath. He never, in all his life, touched an allopathic medicine. The only time I saw him filled with quiet rage was when my gynecologist recommended caesarean operation for my first delivery. He told me that the gynecologist was unscrupulous.

Amit's mother had a unique passion. Every morning, the neighborhood working mothers would drop their children onto her lap and vanish. They would come back in the evening, smiling from ear to ear, thank her profusely, pick up their children, and vanish again till the next morning. Amit's mother spent the whole day juggling with cooking, household chores, playing all kinds of games with the children, and taking care of them hands-on. She would herself become a child while playing all kinds of games with the children. This life-long hobby of hers continued till her old age. These children spent some of their most joyous days with her, and when they grew up they became her, devoted friends.

When Amit was born, his father had his horoscope made by a well-known astrologer, which was by itself a work of Bengal folk art. The language was pure Sanskrit. It was predicted that at the age of 18, Amit will renounce the material world and become a monk. When he got admission into IIT Kharagpur and started attending classes, his father developed cold feet. Simultaneously, he also got through NIT Durgapur entrance test. His father asked his son to come back home saying he was unwell.

Amit's parents had mastered the art of getting him to agree to an arranged marriage. They were going to meet a girl for the 200th time with a lot of trepidation in their hearts. The last proposal their son rejected was when the girl's father made an indecent offer (indecent according to Amit). The girl's father offered to gift him a house, a fat bank balance, and the ownership of a well-known pharmaceutical company. Moreover, Amit found the girl too fair and too affected. There were many a time when his poor father had to escape from his own house, or hide in the store room at the back of the house, or crawl back into his own house through the backdoor, while Amit's mother was being subjected to sit in front of some girl's father in the drawing room who was keen on having their son as a potential son-in-law.

So, here was this young 21-year-old girl sitting on a divan swinging her legs which sort of blew his mind, given the delicate circumstances. After the initial introduction, he got into a deep conversation with her on *Kramer vs. Kramer* (which he had just seen), and further into the books she was reading at that time. Somehow he found this girl to be totally different from other Bengali girls and might be somewhere in that first meeting their ideas and their souls connected.

Given his pre-conditions of No Dowry in cash or kind, no gold jewelry, a simple registered marriage, his parents were definite that this marriage proposal is not going to materialize.

In the girl's house, deep into the night, there was a round table conference among her aunts, uncles, and parents. The girl was of course pretending to sleep. They were totally at a loss on what decision to take. They finally decided to ask her. She sprung up from the bed and announced to everyone present that it's either this boy or none at all.

A seven-hour marathon debate ensued at Amit's place the night before the D-day (*Ashirbad* and formal engagement) between the girl's father and his potential son-in-law. The topics of the debate—Amit's beliefs, ideas, and value systems of the traditions of a conventional marriage, practice of dowry and gifts, and various other profundities. His potential father-in-law returned home at 3:00 a.m. dazed with a puzzled look on his face and scratching his head. But he had already become Amit's life-long devoted friend.

So it was a simple registered marriage after all. All of Amit's near and dear ones came from far and wide. The main witnesses to sign the marriage papers were the concerned court authority, the bride and the groom, the bride's father, the groom's brother-in-law, Arjun (Arjun Malhotra), Amit's friend and mentor.

A special mention has to be made about the journey back to Delhi.

On the deluxe coach, none of the co-passengers seemed to mind that a steady stream of sugar syrup was flowing from one end of the coach to the other. They were busy relishing the wedding sweets (the size and look of which reminded one of the raining of sweets *handi*s [sweets in big earthenware pots] from the sky in

Ray's *Goopy Gayeen Bagha Bayin*) which the bride's family insisted on loading onto the train and which Amit happily distributed to one and all.

The rest of the time he was secretly singing Rabindra Sangeet to his bride in his mellifluous voice. Purnima never ceased to wonder, throughout her life, at the magical qualities of Amit.

Amit to his wife, Purnima, embodied pure romance and the spirit of romanticism and the purest of souls. The collection of his letters to his wife whenever he was away from her would surely comprise pure literary work. He never, throughout his life as he often told her, thought of his wife as a wife but always as a lover. He often recited Tagore's famous poetry to her.

In fact, Purnima often wondered secretly how he managed to survive in this wicked world and yet remain as pure as ever. Is it possible? Though he often thought that Purnima would not be able to survive without him, the same applied to him. What never ceases to amaze her is never once in action, thought or deed, she ever saw Amit seek or pursue personal interest, gain, or personal advantage in any sphere of life. She wondered, "Has he achieved nirvana?"

Amit—My Friend from Childhood

Narasimham Koti
Country Manager for L&T Group in Americas

My association with Amit goes back to the time when we were next door neighbors in Jamshedpur. His dad and my dad were working for Government Metallurgical Lab which came under DGS&D, and they were colleagues probably for about 35–40 years. My early memories go back to the children's recitation contests held annually in our colony, where he used to walk away with top honors in Bengali poetry (Rabindranath Tagore), and I used to land up with similar honors in Hindi poetry. He had that modulation and sensitivity in his voice, which I can never forget.

I remember there was a death in his house (one of the grandparents) and while all the ceremonies were going on, he would sit quietly in one corner and concentrate on his studies. It was an example, which my father always gave to all of us (similar to the one about the boy on burning deck).

Snippets of Our Lives Together with Nostalgia

Bharat K. Singh
Chairman, SBRC Aditya Birla Group

I share with all of you who knew him and loved him, a few incidents that bring back a smile to my lips and fill my heart with love and affection for my childhood friend, debating partner in college, and friend throughout my life.

Amit and I had been to the Marine Engineering College in Calcutta. We were returning victorious after winning the All-India Intercollegiate Debating Contest Trophy. The trophy was a big one—the cup itself was about 3 feet tall on a wooden base. We were triumphantly returning to college in Durgapur and while carrying it in a crowded bus on the way to Howrah Station, a fellow passenger seriously enquired, "Is it the trophy won by Mohan Bagan Team in football?" Amit quipped, "Not exactly, but for a similar competition." When we got back to the campus hostel that night and shared the highlights with friends, there was prolonged "ganjano" on this quip!

By 1964–1965, several intellectuals had their names etched in the debating trophies of Calcutta—Jayashree Ghosh, Aparna Sen (Actor, Director), Amit Mitra (Finance Minister, West Bengal), Dhritiman (Sundar), Chatterjee (Actor)! Loreto House, Calcutta, was a reputed and sophisticated battleground for intercollegiate competitions. Prof. S.M. Chanda wanted Amit and me to go for the Loreto House Trophy. Amit won the toss and chose to speak against the motion "It's a Woman's World," and I was left to speak in favor. With the "who's who" of the debating world present in the college auditorium, I made a serious opening and closed with a light-hearted jibe at the house to stroll down Park Street and see for themselves that it is, indeed, a woman's world. Opposing the motion, Amit was in great form. He explained that the hallmark of advanced civilizations is having men and women in balanced roles; and the concept of Ardhanarishwar. The audience sat spellbound. Needless to say, we won—and it was one of the most beautifully designed trophies.

On the way back, Amit said, "SMC will be particularly happy ... and, sure enough, Prof. S.M. Chanda was beaming with joy as he admired the trophy." He wouldn't leave us until he had heard every detail. I glanced at Amit and he winked at me as if to say, "I told you so."

Amit and I qualified to represent Burdwan University at the All-India Inter-university Debating Championship at Benares Hindu University on January 9, 1966. We arrived there on the 8th of January and were told that 48 university teams were participating. Our distinct disadvantage was that we were from an unknown university in the circles of extracurricular activities in English medium. For some unknown reason, our turn to speak came towards the end by which time everyone was bored stiff with a two-day continuous spew on the dry subject of "Co-operativisation of the Indian Economy ...." The topic had been flogged to death!

Amit and I did some quick thinking and decided to depart from our planned content. We spiced up our presentation with light-hearted humor. We were chosen as the Winning Best Team! When our names were announced, we jumped with joy and hugged each other as we made our way to the stage of the auditorium. The BHU students carried us in a procession around the campus, saying that we had won their hearts.

Then tragedy struck. Before day-break, the news of Prime Minister Lal Bahadur Shastri's demise in Tashkent due to heart failure spread a pall of gloom over everyone. Tearful stories of the young Shastri who had grown up in that city; who swam across the Ganges to school as a little boy; the gentle person who led the nation bravely in the war against Pakistan; and how the Nation gave up the Monday night meal to conserve food grain were on everyone's lips. That morning, we chose to visit the Holy shrines of Benares and offer flowers with prayers in Shastriji's memory. When we returned to Durgapur, we were happy to see a large number of our college mates, led by Sudhanshu Chakraborty, at the station to receive us. Our joy was boundless. It was our hour of glory. We felt like two heroes who had put the college and university names on the Youth Map of India! In spite of the gloom due to Shastriji's demise, an all-night celebration in the hostel had us narrating the previous three days' "Ganjano," flavored with fun.

I could go on and on writing about my dear friend, Amit, but must end by writing .... Always cheerful, full of life, spontaneous and witty—that was my friend, Amit. I was privileged to have grown with him, and studied in school and college together. For 10 years, we ate lunch together in school, argued about everything under the sun, from King Elvis' style to Pat Boone's melody, such as, the Russian Growth Model, Khruschev-Bulganin visit versus Chou En-lai's, doted about John Kennedy's swearing in ceremony as the US president, moaned over his assassination theories, lamented China's betrayal of India's friendship as we munched together. Then, to my pleasant surprise, we both got into college, he on lead! Five long years in college turned enjoyable thanks to his wit and humor at *rockbajy* leading to debating on topics, such as, "It is a Women's World" and "Flirtation as an art should be encouraged!!" The shock was, when both of us got into IIM

Calcutta and he didn't join!!! In more recent times we enjoyed the movie *Fiddler on the Roof* together ....

Amit in Life and in Theater

Dilip Kumar Basu
Retired Professor of English Literature, Delhi University

I first met Amit in 1970. By that time, I had come to know of his mother who had travelled from Durgapur to join her son, who had started working in Delhi. Some new acquaintances, a few old friends and I, were meeting practically every evening at Amit's flat, in Delhi, to work on a theater script for our recently formed group, Naatyakaal. In those days, Amit was hardly ever in Delhi as he was travelling all over eastern India, serving the Coca-Cola Empire. Of my new acquaintances, quite a few were Amit's friends, and that was how we could walk into Amit's flat at WEA, Karol Bagh, and into his mother's life. We, in Delhi, were also travelling east—the play was to be an inquiring into the nature of our relatedness, if any, with Bengal where lately there was supposed to be a prairie-fire raging, and some expecting a spring to come soon. The script was to be the result of a collective effort, improving and debating things happening in and around Kolkata. Amit was already curious about those happenings, had previous stage experience, and thus mentally in tune with this effort. The play was staged in the last week of April. Amit could not be amongst the cast because he had no chance to rehearse, but he could watch some rehearsals when he was for a few days in Delhi. His mother, our Bela masima, whose handwriting was excellent, made the fair copies of the script, and took the pains of crossing out in medink the word "Revolution," printed in 500 copies of our brochure as part of a sentence—a quote—"Revolution is not a dinner party." As per plan, crossing out that word, she, in its place, wrote "Theater."

This theater group was young, and so were all the actors. In December 1969, the group had staged its first play, written by Satrajit Majumdar, one of the founder members. They staged yet another play in December 1970. Amit could remain in Delhi for a longer time only in 1971, and it was in that year that the group could shake off a lot of clumsiness that attended our earlier productions and could find the direction; our very experimental theater was to take on. As far as getting rid of clumsiness was concerned, I have always felt that Amit's intervention, more than anyone else's, did the trick. His penchant for organizing things with neatness and clarity was evident here. So, the next play "Natak" was cleanly projected, it communicated magnificently with the audience, and Amit did a marvelous job as an actor too, especially when on behalf of all of us he addressed the audience seeking to build a bond between the auditorium and the actors on stage. The quality of that voice, calm, tranquil, intimate, yet reaching the farthest row of audience in the main hall and even the still more distantly seated people in the balcony of AIFACS Theater in all clarity, was something to savor. The play's two utterances, Amit's unexcited one soliciting friendship of the audience close to the play's beginning, and the mock-excited, sardonic voice of another actor Mihir Dasgupta at the end of the play were absolutely crucial in achieving the effect we wanted.

Amit, even offstage, was calm and tranquil then, with an expression of amused tolerance and kindness hovering around his eyes and lips. His gentle demeanor exuded an assurance of generosity. There was virtually no need to appeal to that soft, unassuming helpfulness one felt. My amateurish understanding of psychology leads me to believe that this quality in him made that remarkable in the aforementioned play easily possible. At that moment, in the production of the play, he had only to be himself that sufficed.

From 1971, Amit became very essentially a Naatyakaalite, working to give shape to the plays (all written and directed collectively) that followed. In the 1970s, of the last century, like many others, Amit and friends thought that they were contributing in a small way to the creation of a dream country where soon there will be no saving people and that shelter and clothes, medicine, and education will be available to all. Amit was not spending his evenings with his office colleagues or going to parties where perhaps delicate adjustments are made in preparation of ascending the economic ladder. He, instead, was seriously trying to find out a way to study things, such as, econometrics, for he thought it was necessary for him to understand properly what *Das Kapital* speaks of. The romantic young person who had adored Bibhutibhushan Bandyopadhyay, author of *Pather Panchali*, *Aparajito*, and *Aranyak*, was now giving his dream a direction shared by many who were young in the 1970s.

Various political groups tried to establish close relations with Naatyakaal; there may be different interpretations of why the group did not choose to associate itself with any of them, but we ourselves thought that we maintained our distance with them because of our valid objections regarding their tactics and such.

Amit, while still working for Coca-Cola & Co., was once in Kolkata doing a market survey, and he hired the service of his cronies, Shyamal Guha, Pradip Bose, and Mihir, for his work. During those days, a contact was made with a theater group that was staging their plays at a particular point in Kolkata Maidan every Saturday afternoon. They made a friendly gesture by asking us to take their place in the Maidan on a particular Saturday. Since only a few of us were in Kolkata at that time, we could not produce a play but decided to sing some songs from our plays connecting them with a commentary. Amit, one of our most correct singers, together with Naatyakaal males, available then in Kolkata, sang the songs. After the performance, the audience asked many questions that we answered. It occurred to us a whiff too late that one curious gentleman amongst them, very emphatically expressing his wonder at the political courage of the group in the national capital, in all probability was a police informer ...! A few months later, at that very spot, Probir Dutta, a theater person, was killed while watching a play in performance. Amit and friends, Delhi people, had little idea of the risk they were running.

It should be clear from the way this piece is getting written that in writing about Amit, the life pattern of a group is being written, for it was a period of that kind in our history and it was how Amit lived then: part of a group of cultural workers, sharing a dream of liberation of a billion people. Certain values imbibed during the period must have remained with Amit and his friends in a quasi-permanent manner, a few shadows "obscuring the onlookers" view of it.

He changed jobs, got married, had a family; he was building "Hope," his own organization, doing good work there. *The Economic Times* carried an article on the young entrepreneur with a photograph of him inset there—I saw it and preserved it in my files.

My Father

Arnav Dutta Gupta (Son)

As a 5-year-old, I remember taking walks with my father around the neighborhood complex, and all along the boundary wall there used to be large trees standing passive witnesses to the meanderings of father and son. Each day my father used to point out the trees to me and explain how they were living beings just like us. He would pick up seed pods off the ground, and break them open with infinite care and tenderness, and show me the small hard seeds inside. He would compare these seeds to the human equivalent of babies. He would explain to me how, if these seeds were planted, they would grow into the very same large trees standing by our side. The concept of such a tiny seed transforming into such a large tree in the course of a few years would enthrall me and I would inevitably gape and gasp with all the appropriate wonder and innocence of a 5-year-old. Together we would bend down, each holding a handful of seeds and embed them in the ground. We would then stand up and my father would say a small token prayer, with myself repeating after him, and then we would continue on our way.

Sometimes, in certain situations, my father seemed to have a very methodical bent of mind. When faced with certain situations or problems, he used to proceed in a very matter-of-fact, step-by-step manner using utmost logical care and analytical finesse, but beneath this mantle of superior intellect used to flow a very strong current of all encompassing love and altruistic spirit.

Normally as a child, I used to hate listening to Indian classical music, but some days in the late evenings when my father used to switch off the lights in his room, take up a glass of ice-cold scotch, put on some soothing Indian classical music, and just sit and listen to it, I would sit by his side. On such occasions, whether I wanted or not, my mind would invariably be attuned to the calming waves of the music, and I would feel an inescapable, inexplicable bliss.

As a child, I remember my father bringing many exciting toys and games for me either from the local markets or from abroad. On each such occasion, a certain "protocol" would be followed. Before simply handing over the gift to me, he would unwrap and open the box or container himself despite all my vain protestations. He would then take out all the different parts, fiddle with them for a while, and start assembling them before my impatient eyes. If I tried to intervene or help, he would get excited, brush my wrist away, and say, "Let me do it first." On such occasions, we were both hopelessly restless and impatient children, each trying to put his brain into the assembly of the toy. After he had done playing with it for a while, he would hand it over to me saying, "Now you can play with it all you want."

Arjun Malhotra
Shiv Nadar
Amol Redij
Sushmita Sengupta

2

FRIENDS FOREVER

There are only two means by which men can deal with one another: guns or logic, force or persuasion. Two reasonably intelligent minds would always win each other by means of logic, and such relationships will always last forever, sometime staggering and sometime running. As Shiv would say, "We never killed each other's ideas, we always won each other's ideas by means of logic." "Shiv and Amit" are one such example of friendship, they remained in each other's heart ... where love and compassion run deep beneath their calm exterior like ever-flowing stream of water beneath the dry Falgu riverbed.

1968–1970

DCM Days: Initiation into the Business World

Arjun Malhotra

While I never met Amit in DCM, I did hear a lot about him because Amit had built a reputation of being a "quiet intellectual," having attention to detail, and opening his mouth only when he had something to say, instead of talking all the time. In our time, if you grew up in Bengal, like I have, you are exposed to a very socialist kind of leaning; you read and follow Marx, Engels, and Ann Rand, as part of your "growing up." All of us have discussed these ideas and some of us actually tried and thought more deeply about these, and took the discussions and thoughts to the next level. "A lot of folks think that's the way life should be—somewhat idealistic, and Amit was one of those thinkers."

Shiv and Amit ... Friendship Unlimited
Part I (DCM Days)

Shiv Nadar
Founder, HCL; Chairman, HCL Technologies and
Shiv Nadar Foundation
Amol Redij
Sushmita Sengupta

16th of September, 1968, two young men, Shiv (Nadar) and Amit (Dutta Gupta), both part of Senior Management Trainee Programme of the same batch of DCM, met and embarked onto an expedition of their career and friendship.

Amit and I joined DCM on the same day as senior management trainees, in Jhandewalan, Head Office Personnel Department (HOPD), a very small function, only meant for elite force being created for DCM. Therefore, we have trained together, we have worked together, and we have drunk together. Actually, I don't know of another person like him.

Background

In 1889, Rai Bahadur Ram Kishen Das Gurwale started the Delhi Cloth & General Mills Company by establishing a spinning mill in Delhi. In 1909, Lala Shri Ram joins the company, and eventually acquires it and changes its name to Delhi Cloth Mills. In his formative years in DCM, Lala Shri Ram took the responsibility of managing the company's ginning mill which utilized facilities within to produce yarn. World War I for the first time brought the business acumen of Lala Shri Ram to the fore. It was around that time, Lala Shri Ram decided to divert the *dosuti* (generally used for making coarse garments) and *niwar* (generally used for making cots) for making tents and supply the same to the Indian Army. Lala Shri Ram, in 1923, put up another proposal to set up a bleaching plant and a dyeing plant with state-of-the-art facility. His idea was to transform the company from a 19th-century outfit to a modern 20th-century company. The two plants, which went on stream in 1924, made DCM self-sufficient in yarn.

This was an unbleached cloth that closely resembled khadi, a very coarse material. At that time, simplest tools were used to build the harshest cotton and make products out of them, which the Britishers sold at very low prices. One way to ensure that Manchester runs into losses, and thus cripple the British regime's control over the textiles was to produce in India. India's gain was Manchester's loss. It was when the Boycott Movement was being practiced. So the Independence movement also closely ran parallel to them. As they said, any cloth that came from Britain they burnt—the Boycott Movement.

Lala Shri Ram's original vision to venture out in the textile business was to create a retail network in India so that the people could buy the material (cloth) at a reasonable price. For DCM, this was the principal objective, which came from a fairly benevolent and far-reached thinking of Lala Shri Ram, whose brothers were the cofounders of the company. DCM Group was founded on the robust principles to sustain itself during the formative years. At that time, DCM was analogous to Delhi like what Birla and Tata were to Bombay (present-day Mumbai).

Until 1857, the First War of Independence in India, there existed a system of "joint-stock" companies, which had no legal impositions on the structures of its memberships or ownerships. After 1857, all companies required registration, thereby making all "joint-stock" companies into legal entities. It, thus, gave a structure to the companies, making them a limited-liability company that separated the owners and the management. The entire structure was slowly progressing towards delegating technical and business intelligence operations to an agency, which came to be known as a "managing agency." The model of managing agency took birth in the milieu to expand and strengthen the Indo-British business relationship.

The managing agency system meant the British could take a major chunk of the profit, around 10 percent, as the managing agency commission. The British did not put all their money in the company itself, they raised money in England. And when the family businesses came up, such as, Bharat Ram and Charat Ram Private Limited—they would be the managing agency of DCM.

Senior Management Trainee Programme

When eventually the next generation took over the DCM operations, Bharat Ram and Charat Ram coined a strategy to change the age-old model of management style to upgrade their management force. Aligned to their tactic, Bharat Ram planned to hire Narayan Thadani (N.R. Thadani) from Hindustan Lever. Thadani, that time, was considered to be the real management guru, who joined the DCM Group as the marketing controller, the only board member during those days when the system of "managing agency" was very much prevalent.

Bharat Ram, having discussed and thought well with N.R. Thadani, was convinced that one of the ways to strengthen the management force was to go through the old systems of Indian Administrative Service, Civil Service, and Indian Industrial Service. This was the same system that the British created in their companies as a part of the management training system, such as, the ICS created by the British.

Hindustan Lever had been already practicing that style of management training. The practice then was to pick up fresh talent from the engineering and management colleges, impart them with effective theory and practical training, and then put them on the job in the chosen fields of purchase, marketing, HR, and so on. The recruitment process made sure that only the best talent across the country was selected. This methodology promised an accelerated growth along with a fast-track career growth to their recruits, quite evident from the fact that most of the chairmen at Hindustan Lever were the ones who had once joined the company as a management trainee. DCM was almost a century-old company, and it was obvious that it wanted to leverage itself to the modern-day business practices. Bharat Ram and Thadani decided to borrow this system from Hindustan Lever and introduce it to give a fast-track growth along with polished management operation styles to their employees.

In 1968, when the seventh batch of management trainees was selected, Amit and I were a part of this batch among many other highly talented people across the country. What perhaps sparked off between Amit and me in the first meeting was the diverse personalities. I was an introverted person while Amit a highly extrovert, who was a person from the theater and, hence, was more outgoing and exceptionally good at communication skill. Not only did Amit possess these sociable qualities, but also had outstanding English language skills. It was an unsaid rule that any input given to Amit would be transformed into the best possible English. I came from a rural Tamil Nadu region and had a heavy Tamil-laden English accent, which often made me shy away from the group that came from a very good English background. However, it was perhaps the first conversation that I had with Amit that instilled some kind of confidence, and we went on to become very good friends.

Amit and I complemented each other in a way. I was an intelligent man with efficiency in application. For example, during the DCM management training days, the group was required to write project reports for every function. I was always very quick at completing the projects and usually completed more than one project. On one occasion, Amit, though being an intelligent guy himself, borrowed one report from me; I remember Amit asking me, "Can I copy yours?" And I would happily give it to him with a caution that Amit might lose an opportunity to go to the textile unit if their reports appeared any similar. Later on we often talked, joked, and laughed about the incident, and thus began a journey to a great friendship.

Amit was supposedly considered to be the second best in the team, after Bawajit Singh, an IIT Kharagpur graduate, who quit DCM within a month and went on to join Metal Box, and eventually went to the United States. Another member of the team with whom Amit shared a wonderful association was Paramjit Singh from Delhi, who had completed his Masters in history from Stephens. It was a great group at the DCM then. Those days of learning were mostly filled with fun activities, probably like any other hostel life days. Among the many memories that refreshed the group was the one when we had food at a roadside *dhaba*, the only thing around Jhandewalan then, next to Shiela Theater. The seniors had made us look shameful for our act of eating at a *dhaba*, for it was believed the management trainees of DCM should eat at so-called proper places, where soup and main course are served. However, the irony was that none had that kind of money to spend on those luxuries then.

Traversing many such episodes at DCM and being a part of a highly intellectual group, Amit and I completed the training. We both were posted in a place called Kota. Unfortunately, Kota was a place that had high temperatures all-round the year. It was a region that had semi-arid climate with long summers from March to June, with temperatures typically going above 40°C. Amit and I arrived in Kota during that time, the month of May, when it was blistering hot because of the pure desert heat.

DCM was in a phase of expansion at that time. Their first expansion plan was into fertilizers. Unfortunately, the company wasn't doing well at that time and, therefore, the expansion plan was a tightly driven project for obvious reasons.

Amit was posted in Shriram Rayons. I got a placement with Vinyls & Chemicals. However, both were stationed at the same location. We obviously decided to share a room as it would have meant saving some money, then a primary objective of all 20 something working people. The comradeship that had grown since the DCM days continued to nurture when we both stayed together in Kota—similar days of scholarly discussions and days of having merriment. Survival, except the temperature, wasn't an issue. As Amit knew Hindi, going around places and interacting with people wasn't a hassle. However, fighting the temperature was a daunting task. The heat was terrible. Also, Amit and I smoked and drank at times. In that weather, these habits would add to the ill effects of scorching heat, which made it very dry. However, both of us stuck to the plan and continued to work there in such dire conditions. Air conditioners weren't affordable then. Fortunately, the room we shared had electricity supply. To add to our luck, we had a fan in our room that worked too. Nonetheless, every so often, the fan wasn't of much help. At such occasions, the intelligent duo devised an arrangement. Dip a towel in water, put it over yourself and sleep under the fan. The only challenge in this trick was to fall asleep before the towel dried or else the exercise had to be repeated all over again. It indeed was a fun. Amit and I thoroughly enjoyed our foremost days of employment.

Among the many other fun-filled incidents those we had together, an episode after a late-night movie show, which perhaps, till day, vividly reverberates on my mind. The cycle rickshaw was the only means of transportation that we could afford those days. And it used to be fun riding on those cycle rickshaws. The cycle rickshaw was required to be pulled with hands which was a strenuous task to do, especially in that hot dry weather. Amit and I were sitting behind in a cycle rickshaw. The puller was doing his job of taking these two gentlemen to their destination. Suddenly, I told the rickshaw puller to sit behind and allow me to pull the cycle rickshaw. Amit was quick to caution me about not attempting to do so, as it was a very difficult job to accomplish. However, I was far from heeding to Amit's admonition. I requested the driver, addressing him as a friend, to sit on the back foot and to handover the cycle rickshaw to me. Amit, a compassionate friend, advised me again to not do it saying, "Don't try it, it is a tough task." I dodged it away smilingly, "If you think it is a hard job then I am a tough guy. I will smoke, and I will do it rather easily." Within a few steps, I had begun gasping and wheezing like almost breathless. Amit sat behind laughing quietly, though not making it look like he was mocking at my state. Amit then stated that one of them, either he or the cycle puller, will get down and push the cycle rickshaw from behind. So one of them got down from the cycle rickshaw. It wasn't Amit though. He remained there sitting behind while still continuing to laugh silently. The liberty of the late-night hour made Amit and I enjoy the moment to the core. Perhaps, there was no one who would witness it, except the cycle rickshaw driver, to make us feel embarrassed. It was our moment of merriment. I came towards the backside of the cycle rickshaw and took his seat. Amit asked the rickshaw puller to proceed. Both headed back home laughing to heart's content.

Amit and I shared several interesting incidents of humor and discussions on intelligent topics, one of which was Communism. Intelligence was one of the basic necessities that one should possess to be in Amit's company. He was very idealistic in his mental formation. In DCM days, he would often tell me that to be eligible for being in his company, he or she would know all, Shakespeare, literature, history, politics, Communism, Marxism—these were the basic minimum to qualify, unless you are a very intelligent guy who went and did engineering, didn't read much and still have a long way to go—and that was me. I told him always, "If you want to compete with me in studies, why don't you compete with me in physics, math, I am very good in those subjects." Engineering, hesitantly, he will give but he will never compete with me in physics and math. I was much better. We used to test each other. You know, when two reasonably intelligent people get together, they always test each other, not for the sake of competition but for pure fun and joy, and of course it can only happen between two very close friends. So I asked one day, "What you want me to read?" He asked, "Have you read anything on Communism?" He further added, "You are illiterate as far as Communism is concerned but you have a very good mind, you waste your time, hours and hours, why don't you read the basics of what Marxism has to say?" I took his books, they were all paperbacks. I read all of them and I was fascinated by Communism, Marxism and later on I used to discuss a lot of it with him. Some of my business principles are greatly influenced by this philosophy, thanks to Amit, a friend who will always remain very special in my heart.

As the days progressed, conceivably Amit could sense that being in the textile industry wasn't his long-run dream and had quit to join Coca-Cola Export Corporation (CCEC) in 1970.

Sushmita Sengupta
R. Narayanan

03

3
COKE BEFORE COMPUTERS

One should never restrict learning, making it unidirectional, though the myth remains to develop domain expertise, for example, industry or domain specific. It's up to you to find applicability of your learning, irrespective of industries and market. Amit's learning on coke marketing equipped him enough to be able to bring a paradigm change in the mindset of computer industry in the late 1970s and early 1980s.

1970–1977

Coke Days ... A Different Learning Experience
Sushmita Sengupta

The credit of the first international soft drink brand to enter India goes to Coca-Cola. Until then, Indian brands dominated the country's market. However, soon Cola drinks overpowered the soft drinks market by capturing a market share of around 40 percent. In 1970, Amit quit Shriram Rayons to join Coca-Cola Export Corporation (CCEC). Amit enjoyed working at Coca-Cola primarily because of his basic interest to get a hands-on consumer marketing. He wanted to work in a setup where you are not dealing with the consumer directly, but through advertising and other medium, and different channels, and thereby studying the behavioral patterns that impact consumer's buying behavior, etc.

The primary responsibility for Amit in Coke was to set up a distribution network, increase the product penetration, and hence the market reach. He spent seven and a half years establishing Coca-Cola, Fanta Orange, and Fanta Soda all over eastern India, and then also in other parts like Bangalore, Meerut, Madurai. Amit would start from the bottling plant with other personnel as aides and head to small towns in search of potential distributors. He charted this strategy since the larger towns already had distributors. The next step would be to zero in an already existing distributor of other well known soft drink brand, irrespective of his capacity. He specifically chose to approach existing distributors as they already understood the product distribution methodology; thus, a lot of time in explaining the basics could be saved.

Understandably, summer was the time when soft drink sales would be at the peak. It was discernible that to achieve the targeted sales in summer, the ground work would be accomplished during the pre-summer period. They were initially supplied with ice boxes. Later, with passage of time and technologies, ice boxes were replaced with electric-bottle coolers. However, the electric-bottle coolers turned out to be a big disaster—especially the ones from Blue Star. In areas of Durgapur, Dhanbad, and Sindhri, the electric supply was erratic which caused heavy-voltage fluctuations, thereby blowing the compressors. This not only caused problems to the retailers in terms of sales, but also to the company for they had to get the compressors replaced as urgently as possible to keep the business steady.

While replacing the compressors was one daunting task, the other major problem in coke marketing was mitigating the possibilities of smuggling of Coke bottles. The sales tax structure, then, was such that the rates varied from state to state. Thus, the cost of coke bottles changed for every distributor and dealer or retail outlet with every change in the state boundary. Obviously so, in order to reap higher profits, the dealers from the areas where the cost price was high would smuggle the Coke bottles from the areas where it was available at a lower cost. Amit and his team had a tough time keeping an eye on such activities.

Coca-Cola Exit from India
Sushmita Sengupta

Morarji Desai government with George Fernandes as the union minister for industry made it difficult for multinationals, asking them to leave their source code or generic formulae back in India. Mr Fernandes made this a key point to rigidly press the enforcement of FERA. This did not go well with the two multinationals Coke and IBM. Mr Fernandes cited the example of Japan, where the entities wishing to set up their operations were required to give the source code, and also questioned the adamant behavior of multinationals operating in India and further insisted them to give their source code to India. Coca-Cola staunchly disagreed to hand over the generic formulae, which they obviously considered to be their intellectual property. Finally, sensing that the union minister for industry wasn't ready to budge from his stance, Coca-Cola shut down its operations in India in 1977, and as a consequence, Amit lost his job.

The Case of the Missing Fanta

R. Narayanan
Co-Founder, Xcode Life Sciences Pvt Ltd

Year 1977

George Fernandes fired his salvo to rid India of one of its biggest enemies, namely Coke. Most of the 21 execs in Coke and who could think knew that our days were numbered and had started our quest for an alternate job. "Blame to None If This Is Done" was the title of an internal manual which specifically stated what all should NOT be done in a country. With great diligence, the 21 of us had collectively figured out that management at Coke had violated without exception, every single clause. Indeed our days were numbered.

Frustration was building among the 21 execs, as there were few signs of a job materializing.

There were barely any private sector jobs in Delhi in those days. Amit and I had already visited two of them, including Coke. Situation looked bleak. On a cold November overcast morning, I exclaimed to Amit, "Dottie jee, my heart bleeds for thee, but 1977 looks real bleak." And so I would greet him every morning, and Amit would figuratively respond with a "drip, drip, drip," reflecting solidarity with a bleeding heart.

The drip accelerated into a flow, when eight of us received interview letters from the same company at our office address. Indeed those were bleak days. Around the same time, the management of Coke determined that visible signs of frugality were called for (the jury is still out on whether this call for frugality was triggered off by George). One management missive to the 21 execs stated that there had been considerable "investigation" at the high consumption of Coke/Fanta within the company, and if the declaration of the 21 execs were to be accepted at face value, then there would remain unsolved the case of the missing Fanta. Where were they disappearing?

Amit defined this behavior in one word—"Nero," he kept muttering. Given the gravity of the George Fernandes broadside, there appeared an element of truth to this profound comparison. Meanwhile, I was determined to assist the company in its quest for truth and provide some entertainment for 20 frustrated execs.

One morning, while I was opening a Fanta, I observed Amit navigating his way to the washroom.

"I have solved the mystery of the missing Fanta," I bellowed, and 19 Coke executives jumped out of their seats and spilt onto the corridor. "Show me your pocket, quick," I told Amit.

He innocently held his jacket pocket open for me, and I poured the Fanta into his pocket. He continued to hold his pocket open exclaiming, "What are you doing?"

"I have just solved the case of the missing Fanta." I informed 19 giggling execs.

You laughed the loudest, Amit. I will miss you, my friend. Now, 2011 looks real bleak. Drip, drip, drip ...

Arjun Malhotra
Sushmita Sengupta
Shiv Nadar
Ajai Chowdhry
Bikram Dasgupta
Late Yuvraj Bahadur
Mohan Rao
Sumit Bhattacharya
Neelam Dhawan
R.K. Gupta
Pradeep Sen
Subroto Bagchi
G.S. Sachdeva
R.P. Singh

04

4

GAME CHANGER

Fascinating story of a perfect team and of leadership demonstrating how you drive the best minds on fire, as you live in the world of fast changing technology. From being an underdog, they finally became the GAME CHANGER of the industry in early eighties. Charismatic story of India's world-class JUGAAD.

Amit ... The Game Changer

Arjun Malhotra and Sushmita Sengupta

HCL days—Part I (1977—1985)

"When HCL started, there were less than 100 computers in India. By 1988, computers were working in more than 300 towns. These things happened because a bunch of young people fanatically believed that you had to take the product to the market, and not sit pretty expecting the market to come to the product.

As one grows older and moves towards hanging up one's boots, there is great nostalgia about these events and phenomena, and a yearning to take a shot at yet another industry launch and nurturing." (Amit Dutta Gupta)

"He moves like a butterfly and stings like bee." This analogy written in praise of the incomparable pugilist Muhammad Ali may well be attributed to HCL in the microcomputer segment, as right from the beginning, HCL was prowling around, looking for the smallest gap in the market, and then springing into attack and finally controlling the very pulse of the lower end segment.

June 1, 1978 was a very significant day in the history of the Indian computer industry. On that fateful day, International Business Machine (IBM) closed down its operations in India, though the winding up operations had begun much earlier. In August 1977, in a preemptive move, we launched our 8C and 8C/R machines, country's first microcomputer designed for commercial use. Around that time, Amit moved from a structured MNC life to HCL, the new entrant in Indian computer industry that itself was in its infancy.

Let's go back few more years to look at the global environment and its impact on the computer industry, back in India, then. This will not only give you an idea as to how the industry and the technology were progressing at that time, but also will help you to relate to the time and the story of this marketing genius in its own perspective.

Dawn of a New Era

My dear readers, some of you would perceive the computer industry today as just a cacophony of machines, factories, and offices. However, in reality, it is an outpouring of dreams and passions, hope, hard work, and striving perseverance of a group of people who pioneered the products and companies of your times. And the least we could do is salute the minds that have shaped the Indian IT industry.

US President, Lyndon Johnson (November 1963–1968, following the assassination of J.F. Kennedy) cut down a lot of programs at NASA. He threw out hundreds and thousands of engineers out on the streets, mainly around Silicon Valley. Engineers who came out of NASA were too overqualified to be employed by the traditional technology companies of those days.

Most of them had worked on technologies that were far beyond what commercial technology companies were doing then. Thus, most of them started garage start-ups and small companies that designed and manufactured chips. A lot of these chips were computational chips, which were widely used in the initial electronic calculators. I know this because, when I was with DCM in 1971, we had decided to get into electronic calculators. We actually had to scrap a couple of designs because the companies, from whom we were buying chips sets, went out of business. That was how life was at that time. These garage operations are big names today, such as, Fairchild, Intel, National, etc.

Now, this particular technology morphed itself into what we call microprocessors today. In India, DCM started with calculators as their business in the field of technology. The first one we designed used a seven-chip set and had simple functionalities of addition, subtraction, multiplication, and division. By the time DCM (the division was called DCM Data Products [DCMDP], and I will use DCM and DCMDP interchangeably throughout this narrative) launched it, that company back in the United States had failed. Another new company Varadyne was doing it with four chips, and it had an added a square root function. DCM did not have a percentage (%) key until their next calculator was designed, which was a two-chipset design from a company called Electronic Arrays. Every few months, there would be more integrated chips and less real estate on the printed circuit boards, therefore more new models, so we could make smaller, better, and faster machines.

What DCM did was really interesting. They formed their own R&D unit. So we, at DCM, took some standard chips, integrated those with some PROM (programmable read only memory) chips of our own, and made our product somewhat unique. While competition would sell only standard calculators made of "off the shelf" standard chips, DCM would integrate these standard chip sets with additional PROMs and give single key press functions that were required by the customer—a product far more customized. We had a product called MOSCAL 1402, which was a great statistical calculator. It did all sorts of statistical calculations, such as, finding mean, sigma, multivariate regression analysis, etc., that statistical researches required. Our price was high, but it was immaterial because our product had a lot of required functions with single keystroke as compared to other calculators which required tens or hundreds of keystrokes, thus increasing the chances of making errors while entering so many keys. Our calculator was very convenient and much more accurate. This research by the DCM Data Products, R&D group progressed from there to then develop microprocessor-based microcomputers. It was an exciting prospect, and we were convinced that microprocessors were going to change the world.

In India, those were the strict License Raj days, a nightmare for any businessman. Unfortunately, as India was a socialist country, in those days, our country had an act called Monopolies & Restrictive Trade Practices (MRTP) Act, which was pretty tough and it essentially tried to restrict private sector, especially large private sector companies, from getting into new areas. As a philosophy, for growth in socialist economies, such as India, where we practiced Fabian socialism, nearly all of those new business areas were reserved for the public sector as per Five Year Plans that reflected the country's vision in those days. DCM had a plan to get into microprocessor-based computers as a progression from programmable desktop calculators. However, unfortunately, the DCM management, which was worried about the government displeasure by going against the MRTP Act, decided against doing this.

As a result, under the changed circumstances, a number of people from DCM Data Products, actually six of us (Shiv Nadar, Ajai Chowdhry, D.S. Puri, Yogesh Vaidya, Subhash Arora, and myself), convinced about the future potential and the power of microprocessors, decided to move out and do something in this area on our own.

We all actually felt very strongly that microprocessors would be a real paradigm shift in technology in the years to come, and they had arrived to "change the world." The thought processes behind setting up our own company was that we had a fair amount of knowledge about this technology while at DCMDP, and also had a good feel of the market, then why not just go ahead and do it on our own, especially when DCMDP had already made their decision against it?

Starting a company was an "accident" and purely a "spur-of-the-moment" decision and we thought that, "If companies like IBM could sell junk in this country, then obviously we could do much better." Lots of bravado, no business plan, just the thought that we had a good grasp of the technology, and we had a sense of the market. Also the fact that our major competitors, whether it was ECIL (public sector) or IBM (who also moved out in 1977) or ICL (later morphed into ICIM), were selling older generation computers and older technology, also because of foreign exchange restrictions, imports were very difficult and limited in those days.

In 1975, we founded Microcomp Limited and set up our office in my grandmother's *barsati* (room on the top floor of the house) in the lanes of Golf Links, New Delhi. The company tried to cut down on as many expenses in the beginning as it could. Within a year, the company premises had expanded into the bedrooms. The drawing room served as a waiting area and reception, and very soon the office took over the entire house. My grandmother was greatly involved in the company from the very beginning. She undertook the tasks of meeting people, receiving guests throughout the day, and making something to eat. Eventually, the company got so big that we finally had to move out from there.

We started Microcomp to trade in electronic calculators so that we could make some money, which we wanted to invest in R&D to develop our own microprocessor-based computer. We had started only in October 1975. By January 1976, we were able to allocate funds for this development. It later came to our knowledge that we needed a manufacturing license to make computers and that these licenses were reserved for state sector and public sector organizations only. The UP Electronics Development Corporation (UPTRON) was one such company who had the computer manufacturing license. We (Microcomp) spoke to UPTRON and signed an agreement with them to set up a joint sector company, of which UPTRON held 26 percent. Thus, in August 1976, a new joint sector company was formed which was named as Hindustan Computers Limited (HCL). This was the first joint sector company that UPTRON had set up and was the only 1 out of some 20 odd companies that they (UPTRON) ultimately formed which did not have UPTRON in its name. Since our manufacturing license was for UP, we set up HCL's manufacturing in Noida, which is where HCL is headquartered even today.

In those days, a decision to buy those old technology computers also brought along with it a consideration for additional cost involved towards the infrastructure, such as, special flooring, special air conditioning. Remember, those were the days when you even had to take off shoes before you entered the computer room, so that you could avoid dust and consequent damage to the disc drives. On the other hand, microprocessor-based machines were very much like today's PC. All you required was a good earth connection for your power supply, a good voltage stabilizer, a normal window air conditioner, and the machine pretty much worked. So, basically, the industry in the late 1970s was at that stage.

MICRO 2200

When we, six kids (we were all in the age bracket of 23–28 years), came out of DCM in 1975, we initially made programmable calculators, based on the 4-bit microprocessor-based CPU (PPS-4 from Rockwell), which had its own memory and supported peripherals, such as, magnetic card reader. We called this a "microcomputer" in those days. This MICRO 2200 (named for its 200 memories and 2,000 program steps) was launched in 1976 for scientific, educational, and research establishments. For all scientific and statistical work, it gave you a fairly powerful machine on your desktop to do your analysis work. It was like a personal microcomputer on your desktop.

Here again, to give you an idea as to how life was in those days, let me give you an example. If you needed to invert a 10 × 10 matrix and suppose you were in a city, such as, Madras (now Chennai), you had to either punch the data on punch (Hollerith) cards (remember them from the earlier computer days) or send a person with the program and data to the IIT Madras IBM 370 computer center where they would punch the cards, if you had not punched them earlier. Then they would feed these cards through a card reader into their computer. The computer would run the program and do the inversion and give you the answer on a printout. Then you have to take the printout and go back to your research unit. The computer CPU process might take a few seconds but by the time you would go to IIT Madras, get into the job queue, get your job done, get printout at the computer window, you probably had to wait there for couple of hours, so the whole day was gone. In short, you spent most of the day in getting a 10 × 10 matrix inversion done and get the answer back. Imagine, for many users in those days problems of this size were 50 percent or more of their actual computational work.

What our HCL MICRO 2200 machine did was that it gave you the result in a minute, maybe in 2–3 minutes, right on your table and even gave you a printout. So if you look at the work you are doing, and if 80 percent of your calculations are done automatically by this microcomputer right on your table, most people became far more productive as they did not have to wait the whole day for their result. This computer came in an affordable price of ₹20,000–25,000 and with it, for a little more (₹10,000), you could buy a magnetic card reader which meant that once you wrote the program, let's say 10 × 10 matrix inversion, you need not key in 1,400–1,500 program steps again. What you can do is feed the program into this magnetic card reader and every time you wanted to load this program, the magnetic card reader would load the program into the memory automatically for you. So, HCL was able to get a pretty nice efficient machine to researchers/statisticians on their desktop.

Another nice promising feature of that machine was the availability of four user definable keys (UDK). If you had a specific function that you needed to do very often then you just needed to press the appropriate program keys once and store them in the UDK. After that, one press of that particular key would automatically get that function done for you. It could be something as simple as a percentage calculation (scientific machines did not have a % key then) or something more elaborate, such as, Hyperbolic Sine (Sinh).

Competition

At that time, our competition was DCM. After six of us had quit, DCM changed their mind and decided to get into this microcomputer business as well, thus, posing a real competitive threat for us. Furthermore, a company called ORG from Baroda, part of Sarabhai Group, better known for market research, also decided to get into hardware business and that too into computers.

There was a company in Bombay called National Radio, which the Tata acquired and it became NELCO. At a later date, NELCO too entered into this business.

So the startup, Hindustan Computers Limited (HCL), had to compete with three large industrial houses—Sriram (DCM), Sarabhai (ORG), and Tata (NELCO). All this in a market where buyers are traditional and conservative, who prefer buying a computer kind of a product from a "safe and stable" company, which, you are sure, will be there tomorrow to service your computer.

8C and 8C/R Mini Computer

In 1977, we announced 8C and 8C/R, first full-fledged microprocessor-based system, based on the new Rockwell PPS-8 chip. The operating system was ROM-based which not only supported a ROM-based commercial basic interpreter, but also supported both 8" and 5¼" floppy drives. Our 8C, as it was branded, had memory (both RAM and ROM), a printer, and a display. In the earlier version, it had a single-line display, the big display (video display unit [VDU]) that you know of today had not come out at that time. It had a small JCL (job control language), a small 40-column printer that printed out the small display. Thus, the operator would be aware of which jobs are being run on the computer and how they stacked up. It had a number of floppy drives, one or two or three or four 8" floppy drives and a 5¼" floppy drive, which were called mini floppies. We used the mini floppy in our offline data entry devices KTMF (key to mini floppy), branded as Data 7400, Data 7500, and Data 7600. The data entry could be done and verified offline as these machines ran a number of batch jobs. The data was entered on the 5¼" floppy which was fed into the machine through a mini floppy drive. It also had a very unique feature called PSAR (power shut auto restart). Our, innovatively built, own stabilizer with a truck battery (take into account, resources were really scarce then) drove the power through this to the computer. What it did was, when the power failed or the power fluctuated (that happened all the time), the machine would switch to the auxiliary power of the battery. This battery could hold all the programming pointers as well as the memories' status where they were. After the power supply resumed and the machine started, it would start the job from where it stopped, rather than going back to the beginning, thus saving the operator's efforts and time in sorting out what went wrong or which memories got corrupt, etc. Therefore, it was a very powerful and probably essential feature those days. Please remember, in those days, even if you had an auxiliary power source, you did not have automatic backups that you have now. The alternative power source took you 15 seconds, 5 minutes, 15 minutes, whatever time it took you to switch, during that period it could hold the computer. Now if you were in a city, where you had 8-hour power cuts and would like to use the computer, you put an additional battery. It may look like an ugly setup, but it worked perfectly for the system to hold the computer memory for a longer time. It was a unique feature that we had designed for our computers, in India, that made our products unique compared to all competitors as well as any imported machine. People who worked on computers those days still remember the PSAR unit with lot of affection even now. I think it really was one of the earliest examples of "Jugaad," a word that is now part of every MBA curricula around the world. Again, I am giving you this background because I just wanted to give you an idea of the market at that time, and also who were our competitors in the initial years.

The computer database in India at that time comprised some old "mainframes," such as, the IBM 360 and 370 in research institutions with some IBM 1620s. The commercial users had the IBM 1401s. ICL had their 2904s and ECIL had the TDC 312, TDC 316, and TDC 332. Most of the companies had something called a unit record machine (URM) to do their stock ledgers, etc. This basically was a patch board-based system which sorted and collated punched cards, and once that was done it printed out the results. You also had rows of card punchers and verifiers to punch and then repunch the cards to ensure the correctness of the punched data. A patch board that had holes and patch cables handled all the logic functions. Depending on how you had to sort/collate the cards, you set up the cables on the punch board and that did the sorting and collating. Absolutely no programming of any kind was needed.

Everyone's initial thought was to replace the URMs. These URMs replaced manual ledgers for accounts, for stores, etc., and gave you the printed ledgers. Again, you needed elaborate air conditioning, voltage stabilizers, special flooring, and stuff like that.

All of us were quite unsuccessful, as everyone in those days was trying to sell the computers which needed programming to URM managers, who unfortunately did not know programming and were somewhat threatened by these new machines. At that time, there were three or four companies in the market and each one managed to sell about 200 computers nationally every year. That was the size of computer industry in India then.

Our 8C and 8C/R minicomputers were targeted for commercial establishments, business houses, industry, and data centers having turnover of medium-range industry. Folks who have been around, since those days, have never forgotten that full-page advertisement and the timing of 8C launch. Our campaign immediately spurred a virtually inactive, though latent industry into action. Introduction of a commercial computer was revolutionary at that time, and each of these companies began to create their own distinct niches.

The real battle for supremacy was in the lower-end markets, where both HCL and DCM were strong. HCL came out to be the winner primarily because we had better and newer technology, all owed to our R&D. Also, we were nimbler in the market, and we were very aggressive when it came to marketing and advertising. In some ways, our KTMFs were the pioneers in virtually opening up the electronic data entry market in India.

Amit Joins HCL

The first phase of HCL, between 1976 and 1980, was one of the establishing credentials in the marketplace, and also of consolidation. Amit joined HCL during this period and made significant contribution towards that.

In 1977, when Coca-Cola shut their doors in India, fortunately, for HCL, Amit was available. He was one of the people

Shiv identified for HCL. Amit joined HCL as the head of the eastern region, based in Calcutta. Amit was an exception, as one of the things we had initially experimented with was the lateral recruitment from outside and had experienced a 100 percent failure rate. We had, therefore, decided to go to the best schools—engineering and management schools, pick up the sharpest, brightest minds who fitted our profiles, and also the HCL work culture as that would help the company in achieving growth much faster. We did this very successfully. The only people we took laterally were the ones who were known to some of the founders who felt that these people understood our culture and the fast changing high technology world we lived in.

Amit went to Kolkata after he joined HCL and embarked his journey in IT from a small room, sitting on a newspaper spread on the floor. He used to write proposals by hand and get them typed by roadside typists in Dharmtolla Street. He never flinched from going up and down the 17 stories many times a day, as the never-ending power cuts of Kolkata stalled the elevators of Chatterjee International building very often. The eastern region at that time contributed some 33–35 percent of HCL's national revenue. East was a fairly large potential market for computers then, and in 1977 and late 1970s it was still a potentially large market, though it had started facing some of the slowdown owing to the problems that exist in that region even today.

HCL had couple of older people working there in Calcutta. Also, Amit did recruit a number of freshers from IITs and IIMs; therefore, he had an adequately nice team. In fact, most of the members of his team of that time are today either successfully running their own companies or have become very successful CEOs of large companies. We did manage to give Amit a great group of people and, to his credit, he was able to mentor them. A lot of their initial mentoring, the initial knowledge, and "GYAN" (if I can use that term) came from Amit when he was their boss. Pradeep

Gupta of Cyber Media, known as PG to the IT world, was one of the recruits from IIMC and also Bikram Dasgupta, Founder and Executive Chairman, Globsyn Group, and Co-Founder, PCL were amongst them.

Coming of Age

In 1980, we forayed into international markets by setting up Far East Computers in Singapore, a bold move for an Indian company in those days. The venture was a hit. We got the software developed in India, and provided both software and hardware solutions to clients in Singapore. Chennai was chosen as the location for the Software Export Division.

By 1981, we firmly entrenched as a market leader in the micro segment in India. We opened up new segments, such as, data centre bureaus, distributors, traders, etc., and had more installations than the rest of the companies put together.

This is the time when Amit was back in Delhi corporate office as the head of marketing. During this time, he contributed significantly towards HCL's vision by creating path-breaking strategies for our products and markets. As you know, Amit had worked with DCM and then joined Coca-Cola. The reason behind joining Coke was that he wanted to get an exposure to consumer marketing where you don't deal with your consumer directly, but through advertising and other different channels/medium and then learn customer's behavioral patterns that impact buying behavior, etc. This kind of viral stuff was of a lot of interest to him and armed with his in-depth retail experience at Coke, Amit created a strategy in 1981 that positioned HCL effectively in the small and medium markets. This strategy was totally a game changer at that time, a concept never tried and heard before in computer industry. His understanding of retail marketing coupled with his extra sensory perception (ESP)—the rare insight into what could happen tomorrow, Amit crafted THE marketing strategy to energize HCL sales hordes to take on the bigger players, who had by standards of those days' better products. In short, by the early 1980s, HCL took the lead and never looked back.

> He was a brilliant strategist. His biggest success was his strategy, because '81 campaign his strategy won, '85 more strategy won, '86—strategy won. Sumit (Sumit Bhattacharya) will tell you the same thing, Arjun (Arjun Malhotra) will tell you the same thing, Dadan (Late Dadan Bhai), he also passed away, would have said the same thing, Bikram (Bikram Dasgupta) would have said the same thing.
>
> Shiv Nadar
> Founder, HCL; Chairman, HCL Technologies and
> Shiv Nadar Foundation

"Even your typist can operate it."
Amit's Path-breaking Campaign for System-2—A clear winner right from the time it took off

In 1981, at HCL, it was a start-up atmosphere and Amit and the team didn't know that they were laying the foundation of something that would make India mainstream someday.

We got some MBA students to do a market study to look at how computer purchase decisions are taken, and they came back with few decision models. One of them was what we called the "entrepreneurial" model where basically one person took the decision. If you hit this need (hot button), the sale was made.

Technology moved, and we had sturdy machines and sealed Winchester disc drives that could work in less stringent, controlled climate conditions. Basically, we could use computers in rooms where people normally worked.

The mouse and visual display units were commercially available, so we could write programs and give menu-based options on

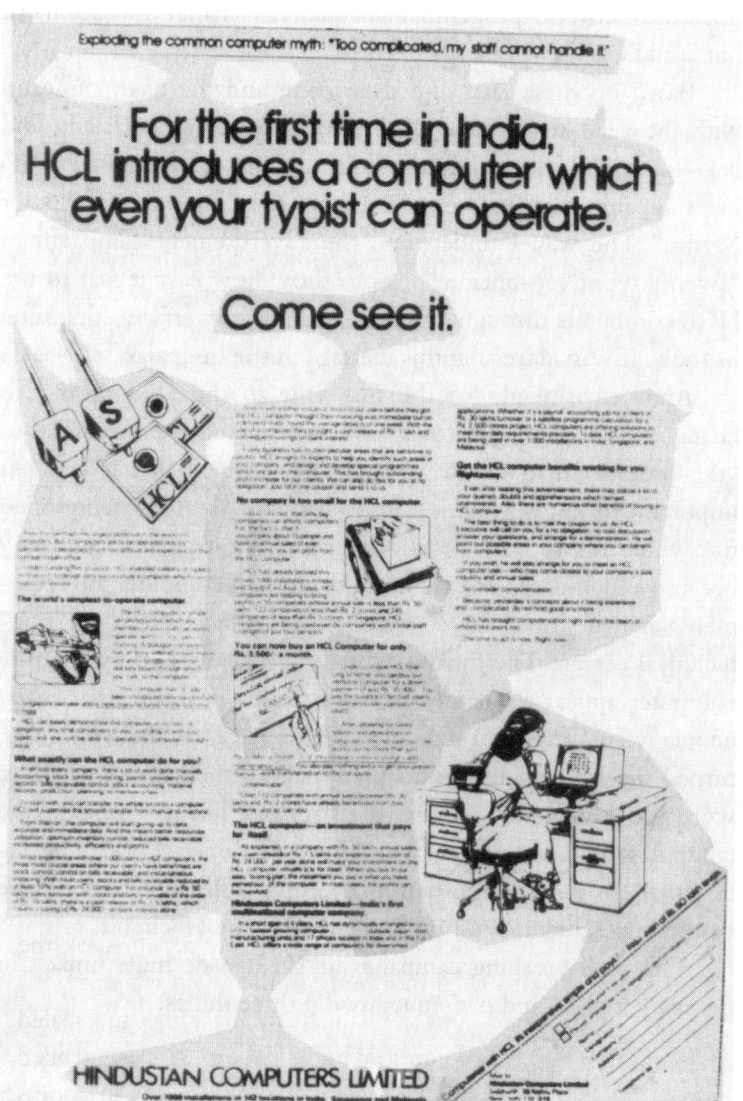

Source: HCL Archive.

the screen, and the user could now use the machine even if he did not know how to program. He could not change the program, but could use it (typist can operate).

Based on these facts and data, Amit and the team came up with the very successful HCL System-2 campaign. What he did was—packaged this technology together and created an advertising campaign that we were "Breaking the Common Computer Myths." The way I understood the advertisement campaign of "Even a typist can operate" was to show how easy it was to use HCL computers through "menu-based" user interface—first time in India. It was addressing this message in the campaign.

Amit envisioned, for the first time in the IT industry, to change the marketing focus away from the EDP professional to "the ordinary man in the street," and assumed that it was less important to know what it will do for you. So Amit demystified the whole thing. This process of demystification was necessary because a high degree of technical content in computer advertisements at that time kept computers at a distance from the non-technical person. The thrust of the campaign came in making the computer appear a friendly machine. Amit, realizing that many people were scared of the high-tech image of the computer, turned the advertising line to user-friendly applications, such as, word processing. This led to the strongest line yet seen in the computer industry, "Even your typist can operate it." The tag line that has been immortalized by Amit still circles around the marketing segment, and not limited to just the IT circuit.

This path-breaking campaign in 1981 made huge impact in the market place and consequently did three things:

- Launched the indigenous "PC" revolution in India
- Created the Indian computer industry
- Built the brand of HCL as market leader in SMEs

Those were the days when HCL really grew rapidly. A lot of these ideas came out of Amit's head. Everything that came out had to have his approval. Very often, Amit personally sat and detailed the plans so that we could roll those out successfully. Amit would call it "idiot proofing," in the sense that the plan would be so detailed that anyone can execute it without any brief. This is what we know as Program Management. Today "advertisement" is something even the big IT Services companies are struggling to get right. Amit actually did that 30 years ago. I have not seen anyone who has a better eye for the details than Amit.

Amit advised HCL to focus their sales on this new emerging market and not on the traditional market, as the URM users were very difficult customers to convert. As a strategy, Amit focused sales more on the First-Time User (FTU) and really when he said FTU, he meant the small user, not the retail shop; although lots of shops bought it, his focus was the small business units who had never thought of using computer and never knew the utility of a computer.

The way you could sell the computer to this emerging market was to understand the customer's business. As a salesperson, you don't really need to know how to run his business, but understand what were its hot buttons, problem areas, what gave him headaches, and what could change his productivity, profitability dramatically. Based on these assimilations, try and tell the customer how the computer would help, give all the information required to solve the problems, and show a prospect of enhancing the business profitability.

Amit recommended the sales team at HCL to just sell the solution by justifying the need of the customer, instead of going for an aggressive hardware sale. Thus, the USP was to give one application free along with the hardware and everything was bundled in the total price. It is worthwhile to note that in those days, there were good margins on the hardware. Good application programmers were not considered expensive and were available. The real risk was the application program dragging on longer than estimated, especially in the market where FTU would not know how to specify applications, etc. The strategy had to cover the risks of all these and more.

It was amazing when we went to the market, and it was fantastic how the market reacted. I remember talking to Amit and saying that what we ended up doing with this campaign was what I call Primary Marketing. That is like being pioneers and opening up a completely new market. Not too many of us have that opportunity. You saw it with the iPad. Therefore, think of our level of excitement when we did it with the S/2 in India back in 1981. I think Amit realized that when he was doing the planning, with his extra sensory perception, and I realized it only after we went into the market and saw the reaction. He and Shiv also worked together at that time on the plan. Shiv too did a lot of work on thinking through this. In fact, we all worked together to see how we could position the product so that we could get the buyer's interest. It actually changed the whole dynamics of the market. Marketing and advertising had been one of our biggest cornerstones of success. We actually taught the Indian IT industry the art of marketing and promoting computers. It exploded the myth that computers were complex, scientific machines, and treated it like any other consumer product, such as, a typewriter, for example.

"Muhammad Goes to the Mountain"
Strategy behind road show

Amit was not content with marketing their "easy-to-use" concept through the printed media alone. He thought of getting other methods into the armory. The greatest fun we had with this concept was with the road shows. It was again the first time that had been tried in the Indian computer industry. We realized that the lack of regional offices was restricting HCL's growth. "So, if the mountain won't come to Muhammad, let us take Muhammad to the mountain," as Amit would say. The road show consisted of a three-pronged attack on the potential customer bases. We started with Ludhiana; for seven days we literally combed the streets.

The three-day road show was set up in a major hotel in the city. In each location, the potential customers were greeted with an audiovisual presentation. The customers comprised the owners of small businesses: a *pan masala* producer, a cloth trader, and a small transport company from Orissa. Most customers visiting the road show came in with a lot of anxiety and angst. Our first task was to cool them down with normal hospitality and so on, then give them a demonstration of the computer systems, and then eventually try to find out what was the main pain point of the customer.

There was only one way in which you break the apprehension of the average visitor and that was to ensure that they got hands-on experience. It was no use getting the number two or number three "person" to have a go, it had to be the boss himself so that the decision making can be prompt, preferably on the spot.

This was easy to achieve, as Amit would claim, because all were equally scared of the machine and it was quite natural to defer to the boss because of his higher status.

Amit said, "Once he sat at the machine a sale was sure to be closed. You can talk till you're blue in the face, but if you can cross that bridge .... When you saw the guy work the machine to his will; you could visibly see him grow."

Some More Marketing Strategies

For Amit, pricing was a means to create a market and broaden the base. He believed that a time would come very soon when generic advertising will give a way to brand-specific advertising.

The fundamental barrier to sales at that time, of course, was the high cost of computers. Amit believed that the secret to higher sales would be to spread this cost. To this end, we set up a personal financing scheme. We went to the Industrial Development Bank of India (IDBI), which gave the softest financing scheme at that time. This enabled a full 55 percent write-off after the first year, with deferred payment over five years.

We then channelized the IDBI money, enabling purchases to be made on easy terms. This finance scheme reached the customer through our advertisement as "a computer for just ₹3,500 a month." Amit designed this ad campaign to break the myth that only large corporations could afford a computer, and as a strategy, perhaps, the hardest hitting ad campaign in the history of the Indian computer industry. It was the beginning of consumerism in computers. This was followed by another ad campaign proclaiming "even if your sales are ₹50 lakh, computers can bring you profit."

One more occasion I remember when Amit's pricing was a big hit. That was the time when HCL had failed to recognize a potential market at the beginning of 1984. Very quickly we realized that Wipro had snatched the initiative from us in terms of multi-terminal machines. Their image in the computer market was superb, their support was excellent, and they were raking off the high prices. So Amit decided, rather than take on Wipro, we would come out with a completely new strategy and repackage the Workhorse. The result was the desktop Workhorse II. Initially priced at a hefty ₹3–9 lakh, Amit and his marketing manager, Ashok Jain, decided to look at how low they could drop the price of the repackaged machine. The new price structure they put before Shiv and the other members of the board was just ₹1.5 lakh to ₹4 lakh. To their surprise it was accepted. Amit said, "Ashok Jain and I proposed blue murder and we got away with it."

Remembering the Campaign

One of the many folklore that are still sung amongst the HCLites of this never to be forgotten hero is the impeccable and inimitable approach pursued by him for the marketing campaign centered to create a need and ease of usability of computers. "A computer is so simple, even a typist can operate it." But then again, this was nothing new for the man who was always a great orator, and juggled words with ease, only one of his capabilities could.

Ajai Chowdhry
Co-Founder, HCL Group

In 1981, when the famous HCL's campaign "Even your typist can operate the computer" hit the market, Amit da was excitement personified. I was lucky to be a part of the process first as the Regional Sales Manager in HCL, Kolkata, and then as the Market Development Manager at head office reporting to Amit da.

Bikram Dasgupta
Founder and Executive Chairman Globsyn Group;
Co-Founder, PCL

For Indian IT industry and for HCL, Amit da started the road show concept to generate leads, his famous "cook and kill" strategy.

Late Yuvraj Bahadur
Ex-Director, JK Technosoft

Amit, the Wizard capable of successfully marketing Coke or Computers with equal ease.

Mohan Rao
Founder and Director, Spatik Consultants Pvt Ltd

Until you sat for a while and listened to Amit talk, nothing gave you a clue what a mind and imagination the man possessed. He made the extraordinary seem commonplace and could extract amazing insights from the seemingly mundane—all without breaking stride and in between puffs of an ever present cigarette and switching from English

> to Hindi to Bengali within the space of a sentence. This was the man who created path-breaking campaigns like "Head on Fire" and "Even a Typist Can Use It."
>
> Sumit Bhattacharya
> SVP and Head of Global Marketing at
> Sutherland Global Services

Amit's people skill
Train hard and fight easy ... as Amit would often say ...

Ajun Malhotra and Sushmita Sengupta

One of the crucial factors of HCL's success story is its people. The company had always believed in employing go-getters, result-oriented executives, especially in the sales and marketing departments. We had developed our own unique training modules and recruitment methodologies, and this is primarily the reason why most young professionals see HCL as a great training ground. HCL also deviated from the unstated norm in the industry that only engineers from premier institutes could market computers, we had successfully deployed ordinary graduates as well in this function.

Earlier when you had to sell a computer, it was a seven-call process—you did system study, then gave a proposal, then see if you could justify the ROI in the proposal, and then try and close the order. Now with the advent of this new segment (SME) and HCL's positioning, the sales process became much simpler. Most of these FTUs were much more entrepreneurial and if you hit their hot button and justify their needs by providing a solution, they would give you the order across the table, as they held the decision-making powers. HCL started getting orders and soon they were pouring in. In fact, I remember, one of my salesmen complained to me that he had become an order-collecting machine.

What Amit used to do—he would train his salespeople from being just a salesman—someone who sold computers/hardware in the traditional sense, to being consultants who would understand customer's business, identify and understand their business issues while probing the prospects, and judge their hot buttons so to analyze things troubling the customer, and finally how those to be solved by having a computer. To our surprise, the customer would actually allot dedicated time period for the application development people. While, obviously, the application development person did not have the actual assessment of how much time it would require, but they had a broad idea of how much time it would take to write the set of programs to address the problem. Amit essentially trained the sales team to look at customer's process, decide how robust it was, whether systems people could automate it, and put it on the computer. Amit also made the team understand the importance of collecting right data so that the systems people can design a proper solution. You need to remember the first principle of the computer and that is GIGO (Garbage In Garbage Out).

Amit had to sit with his sales people across the country as he conducted this training countrywide, and actually gave them some pointers as to how they could judge or get some idea of what to look for while talking to the potential prospects. You are not always able to find the right set of questions you need to ask, to your prospects, and then what are the questions you need to have in mind when you return and discuss with your managers, colleagues back in office, as, if you addressed it right, you pretty much got the business.

I think it was an amazing experience, and I remember it vividly because it changed the entire work culture in HCL. I remember talking to Amit and he would say, "we are growing too rapidly, we need to slow down otherwise we will not be able to get our processes and back office support systems to catch up."

Source: HCL Archive.

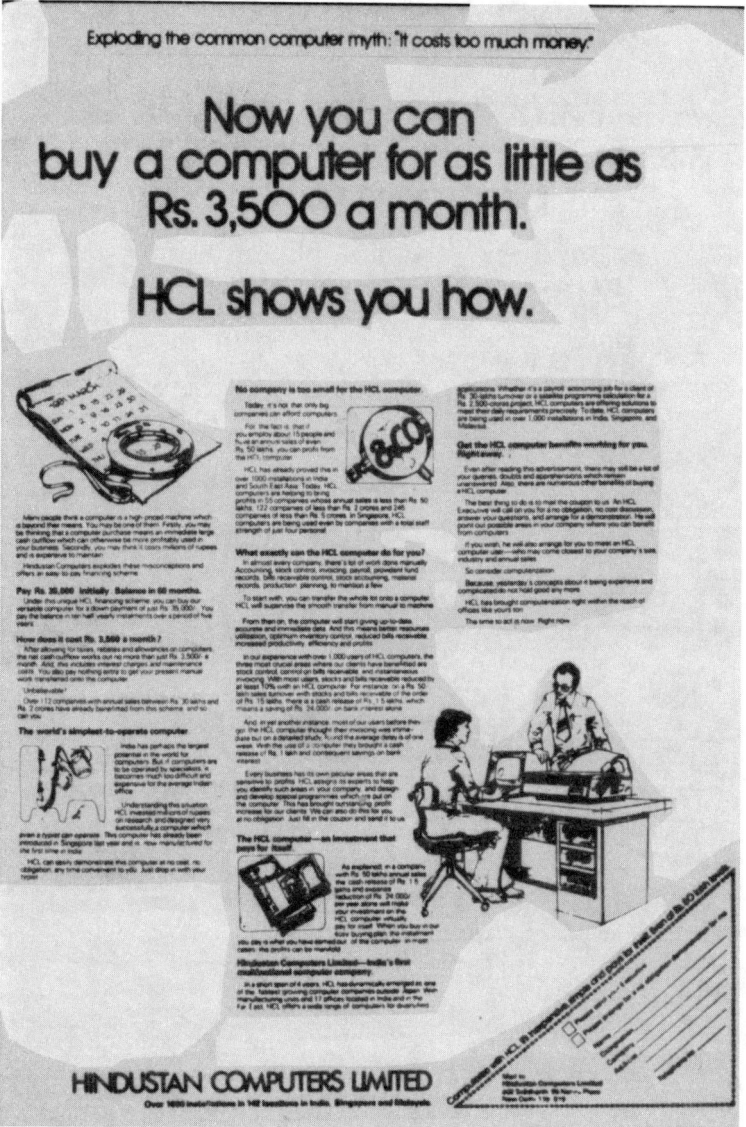

Source: HCL Archive.

Source: HCL Archive.

Amit and Shiv: Minds on Fire ... The HCL Way
Source: Purnima Dutta Gupta.

Amit and Arjun: Stimulators of Indian IT industry
Source: Purnima Dutta Gupta.

Training and Amit

Amit was the mentor for many people in HCL. The sales guys said "There is no point going to Arjun or Shiv, they would say ... come on yaar I'll tell you how to sell and they would take us to the customer, sell the product, and come back. We can't do that, they are very good." Therefore the sales team would go to Amit. They used to call him Amit da, he was Amit da to everyone and Amit would train them with endless cups of tea and cigarettes. He took mentoring very seriously. You see people who had worked in HCL those days, were the real intellectuals, best brains in the industry, and they got trained by Amit. They are the industry leaders today, all very aggressive people, intellectually very powerful, never afraid, completely fearless, technologically very competent, technically very competent, well, not competent to right a program, writing a program is something that Amit could have done if he could get more time ... not for any other reason but to keep his mind competitive. That was Amit's level of competence.

Shiv Nadar
Founder, HCL; Chairman, HCL Technologies and
Shiv Nadar Foundation

I learnt, most of what I know about marketing from him (Amit). Besides being a wonderful friend and person he was a great guru. He taught something every time I met him.

Neelam Dhawan
Managing Director, HP India

While at a philosophical level one always learns from everyone, but even after 35 years of professional career, I can say with ease that the two people or bosses who have influenced me and contributed the most in my life have been Arjun and Amit.

R.K. Gupta
President, Neilsoft;
Ex-Country Manager, Autodesk India

The HCL mantra was "Make It Happen"—and the man for the job was Amit.

Sumit Bhattacharya
SVP and Head of Global Marketing at
Sutherland Global Services

My first recollection of Amit da was when I met him in training in a hotel back in 1981 when I joined large systems division. We were very curious to meet the Marketing head honcho of a company that had a so much buzz going around. Amit da walked in brisk strides and spoke about marketing in HCL. We saw in otherwise a small frame a charismatic being, aggressive, passionate, and he spoke with unmatched eloquence. He sure made his presence felt.

Pradeep Sen
Ex-MD, NCR Corp, Senior Director
SAP India Private Limited

The Last Comrade

A common problem with the sales folks was the contempt they faced whenever they would meet a corporate buyer who was technology savvy and invariably questioned the pedigree of HCL. People who had glass-enclosed computer rooms did not think high of the HCL salesman, much less his technology. Companies like ICIM, ORG, DCM ruled the roost. HCL was the bastard in a British public school. It sometimes led the HCL hustlers to moments of self doubt. "Comrades," Amit would extoll everyone, "we must do as Chairman Mao has told us. Encircle the cities from the villages." The cultural revolution was brought about by the communist forces not fighting the incumbents in the cities. Mao wanted his bare feet army to go to the villages and progressively engulf the cities. Instead of trying to fight the big dogs in their "sophisticated dens," Amit da would tell us to go where none has gone before. Chandigarh and Udaipur, Bikaner and Agra, knocking on the doors of small traders and businessmen, telling them we could give him a

> *computer that his typist could operate. The messianic call had tremendous impact and HCL sales people fanned out, changing along the way, the norms of the industry until a day came when HCL became legitimate.*
>
> Subroto Bagchi
> Chairman MindTree, India's best-selling
> author of business books

> *Amit was a clear headed person and did not like ambiguity and equivocal opinions. Under such circumstances, he would elicit revised version by politely reminding in his typical stylized query, "ghoda bolo ya chatur bolo." This wording comes from a comedious song of a feature film, Padosan. The intention here is to highlight his politeness even in demanding a direct and specific answer.*
>
> G.S. Sachdeva
> Ex-HCL, Professor, JNU and NALSAR

> *Amit da did a prelaunch sales training when HCL launched the Workhorse range of products. He was so thorough in his preparations; I was amazed. He had, as if, put Philip Kotler (bible for all Marketing MBA students) in actual practice.*
>
> R.P. Singh
> Founder, Corporate Value Add

Shiv and Amit ... Friendship Unlimited Part II (HCL Days)

Shiv Nadar
Founder, HCL; Chairman, HCL Technologies and Shiv Nadar Foundation
Sushmita Sengupta

"Shiv is one of the finest precision managers we have in India, an entrepreneur with incomparable business acumen." (Amit Dutta Gupta)

"Earlier, Nadar was the leader of the commando unit called HCL. Today he is the General of the well-oiled infantry called HCL Corp." (Amit Dutta Gupta)

Amit was working in Coke, and I was working in DCM when I met Arjun. We (Arjun and I) founded Microcomp in 1975, and, in 1976, we founded HCL. In 1977, George Fernandes came up with throwing out two international giants, one was Coke and the other was IBM. A key thing Fernandes said was that the companies had to keep the source code in India. That was his fundamental viewpoint. Coke objected to this outright as that's their sole intellectual property. So Coke had to shut down, which resulted in Amit going out of job. Amit needed a job then, and we had the position of regional manager in Calcutta. I thought he would be a perfect fit.

Those days whenever I wanted to talk about a job opening in HCL to someone, really of that caliber, I would take him to Woodlands. Woodlands used to be where Lodi hotel was, there was a small Udipi restaurant. Woodlands came from Madras, South Indian vegetarian Tamil food. So we chatted, and I had described the job to him.

Amit said, "Thank God! I would be doing something connected with engineering now!"

Few days later, one day he said, "I need to talk to you Shiv."

"Sure," I said.

When we met, he enquired, "Can I ask, just for the sake of a norm, is there something called an 'employment letter' in your organization?"

I said, "Sure, but, forgive me, it did not occur to me. We'll generate one and I'll make sure you get one."

As we were leaving, he said, "Do you believe in concept of salary and things? Or, you guys work for fun? It seems great fun to start with. I would love to work there for nothing also, but we all set to food and things will have to go by" (Amit had a great sense of humor. Extremely dry humor).

And I said, "sure." When we met again to decide the joining date, etc., he was feeling very shy this time as he couldn't remind me that I hadn't given him the letter of appointment and told him to join the Calcutta office on a particular date.

He said, "I need to see the products and there should be some kind of induction process. Who do I meet there? Where is the office? And you were saying somewhere in Park Street. It seems some strange location," So I prepared the letter, gave it to him.

I said, "This is your letter."

He said, "May I read it?"

I said, "Of course, you can read it, it would be very simple and there will not be many terms and conditions, a two-page letter."

He read though the whole thing, he read it again, he closed it, and then he told, "Shiv, you didn't have to do this."

I said, "What?"

He said, "Do you know my salary in Coke?" (That was back in 1977, second half of 1977.)

I said, "Amit, I know your salary. Remember! We are friends from DCM days, I also know many people from Coke as we all know each other—all the friends, so I know exactly how much you were drawing."

He said, "I am without a job. I was drawing ₹2,000 salary. This job is 4,000 rupees, you know, it's not necessary. If you just have given me a place to live with my mother and something to eat, for the fun of the job, I would take it ... it would not cost me more than a thousand rupees. And I would have come with a discounted Coke salary."

"Don't think of it. Coke is Coke. Every job in India would be at a discount compared to Coke," I told Amit.

He said, "CITI, Coke are highest paying companies and you are paying me twice. I mean I am out of job."

I told him, "Amit, I read about Communism, thanks to you, and we'll have some touch of it here. I draw a salary of ₹4,000,

Raman draws salary of ₹4,000, Arjun draws a salary of ₹4,000, and you will draw a salary of ₹4,000, Pawar also draws ₹4,000. We all draw the same salary, some equity somewhere."

Then he said, "You know Shiv, I really like the way you are approaching this structure of the organization. So you are the managing director and I am the regional manager and we both draw the same salary."

I said, "Pretty much so. I work less and you work more, and that's the luck of the draw that you have."

So that's Amit for you, a man with highest level of integrity and fairness. We had loads of fun working with each other. Next, I want to talk about is "The first stock option program adopted by a corporate in India." It was conceived by me and Amit in the early 1980s, which no one in HCL knew then. We shared some common Marxist thinking and we decided employees must own stock options, shares. It was the first stock option, thought through by me and Amit in HCL. Also, we were the first to introduce the concept of employing directors in India. We would designate them as executive directors. Amit and Pradeep Mal were not only the first "executive directors" of the company, but also were the first beneficiaries of shareholding that was allotted to them.

What comes next to my mind is one of the most brilliant campaigns that we had created was the 1981 campaign. Sometime towards the end of 1979, we started working on our first overseas venture that was Far East Computer Limited (FECL). I had gone with Late Raman to Singapore to form the hypothesis. Our first hypothesis was "what people look for to buy?" We focused on businessmen who did work manually, which was prone to inaccuracy, very cumbersome at times, and also time consuming. These businessmen were struggling with such problems. So Amit suggested me to go to Singapore to study the problems. At that time, we relied on ourselves when we did this hypothesis. I discussed it with Amit only, called him over to Delhi before I went there, he helped me draw this entire paper. Then Raman and I went to Singapore. For our first advertisement in Singapore, I gave them a budget of million dollars, our first year revenue. When I was discussing all those aspects with Amit, he told me that I was a very courageous man to do something like this, and we had settled for a full-page advertisement.

Finally, there is a company that was not talking about computers, but computerization! It was August 1980 when that full page advertisement was out. I was sitting in the office expecting that someone is now going to come and say that this is what we have been looking for all the time. The only person, with whom I was discussing this, was Amit.

When the first call came we were all very excited. The first call was from an agency that placed receptionists which said, "You are a new company in Singapore and you might need receptionist." It was amazing. We received 11 calls, all from staffing agencies. I was a bit disappointed. However, I felt tomorrow the letters would come. So we waited for the next day, yes they came.

In India, around that time, we were struggling a bit. I was travelling between Singapore and India, spending 15 days in Singapore and 15 days in India. By then Amit had moved to Delhi to head marketing. The campaign took off and was hugely successful in Singapore; cash flow was no longer an issue because we took advance. Singapore was all set, working all right. However, we were struggling here, because our 16-bit machine, system-4 got delayed. It was very unsound engineering, and it did not have that rigor of the product or the robustness which was necessary. We could not identify whether it was the software hang which created the problem or was it the hardware.

One evening, Amit and I were sitting in my cabin; he said, "Shiv, you know how to do this but the field is not doing this right. Shiv, you can't reproduce yourself 40 times nor Arjun can reproduce himself 40 times. We have to finally give it to salespeople, something which they can sell."

Few days later, Amit just winked from a distance, so that he could come in. Then after sitting down, and while having a cup of tea and smoking a cigarette, he said, "Now I'll say something and then will run away from here."

I asked, "Now what? You want to say something and as a result I will lose my sleep and then you'll also run away and I can never catch you (he was a nimble person)."

"Why don't you repeat Singapore in India? Its valid here, computerization, you are addressing first time users in India. No one is going to look at whether it's an 8-bit machine or 16-bit machine. This is like, if you are going for ultrasound or any scan, if it says its certain mega frequency, I don't think, I would know the difference. What's important was—Does it lead you to the necessary findings? You are just trying to find out the problem, and you are not technically looking at precision level. So think about it," Amit told me.

I said I will think about it and then I thought about it. Amit and I shared the similar mental tuning on many things, and therefore it was absolute fun working together.

After I had thought about what Amit had said, I told myself, this time let me try out without Raman, in my own broken Hindi. So I went to Chandni Chowk, Nai Sarak, then some place in Madras, and Barabazar in Calcutta. It was Pakka Marwari area. English itself was a struggle for these guys, so to them, computer was a far cry. But I could make out that they were dying to get one because they never trusted that all their business transaction data are safe with the *munim* (accountant), for the day *munim* is gone, everything is gone, every data is gone, the account is gone, money is gone, and therefore, they would love a device which could manage all these data. All of them had untold amounts of money, so money was not the issue. The issue was whether it was possible to do it, so their data was safe and secured even without the *munim*?

We tested out and that entire construction of the testing was done by Amit. I wanted to be safe, so I went to the field. Amit accompanied me for some of these field meetings. Finally we wrote this. So here comes Amit. He said, "Shiv, we can write a beautiful copy for this, it is advertiser's delight to do something like this. An advertising agency will give you a wonderful copy, you would love it. I can give you a wonderful copy, and you would love it too, but that one won't do the job. The text needs to be written in very simple English to relate to these small time businessmen/houses. The person who can write this is you."

I said, "Are you trying to say that my English is that bad, so that a person in Chandni Chowk could only follow?"

"No, your English is understandable by most people, that's what I meant and that's what we need," said Amit.

I went to Singapore, took a few days off and wrote the copy, brought it back, and gave it to him. He read it through, he simplified it further, arranged it for the sequence of how the mind would read it. Then I went to IDBI, worked out the special schemes. My memory says it was between April and June 1981, it's 1981. "Even a typist can operate it" was spun by Amit and became an absolute winner. He said, finally the typist in the organization will see himself elevating to a very high level because he now can work on a machine. He will make sure that the boss reads it. He will make sure that the enquiry is sent to us. And my God! The market opened and how.

I used to have a table that was used as the conference table. I remember, when we were drafting the advertisement, I was sitting on one side of the table and Amit was sitting next to me. When Arjun came in, he said, "full-page ad?"

I said, "Yes."

"Okay," he said and then asked, "how many?"

I said, "Four of them."

He asked, "National?"

I said, "Yes."

He said, "I hope you have worked out your cost right. Finally advertisement *karane ke baad koi ayega to nahi*, it's an 8-bit machine."

Amit just winked at Arjun and said, "Arjun, you will get your enquiries."

Then Arjun caught hold of Amit and said, "kitna lagaya paisa? Barbad ho jayega."

I said, "Arjun your enquiries will come. Now can we concentrate on how we will close it?"

He said, "Yaar tu aadmi ko mere samne khada kar, uske bad mai paise ko liye bagair usko chodunga nahi." He was so hungry. We all were very young and shared a very special bond that you don't find these days.

Coming back to campaign, till then it was all push sales, not pull sales. This is the first time that a computer manufacturer used "pull sales" like the one used in the consumer-durable sales and marketing.

So first day we had some computation that we later continued every single day. We said first day multiply by 30 (Day 1) should be the life time number of enquires that you'll get. We had our own computation on how to take an annual one. At the end of first month, Amit said that he will shave off his moustache, if less than 10,000 enquiries come. And that meant we were going to grow by 100 percent that year. We were selling it at 85 percent gross margin and 10 percent we used to take as advance, delivery not less than a year later because the order book was so strong. Amit said, "Profit to pahele aa gaya!!"

Amit came from Coke. So to him any product which had 98 percent gross margin was perfectly legitimate, and he was a very firm believer of this marketing theory. Between marketing theory and its implementation, if you are not courageous you may bring down the price, when you bring down price it will work against you. The system-2 campaign was probably the most brilliant campaign that was ever done in the history of computer industry in

India. It has never been beaten till now. Ten thousand enquiries for a product and you must remember the price, ₹364,100 at that time. That number by itself will not mean anything to you, unless you find out the price of an ambassador car at that time, it was less than ₹20,000. So it's 18 times the price of a vehicle, being advertised and then pulled in and on a single call we closed, purchase order released.

So Amit said we are going to spend the money and we'll get that output. We broke the computer myths. "A typist can operate it"—a hypothesis which was an outright winner. Then, "At 3,500 rupees even small companies can buy this" was the next full-page advertisement. I remember about six months later, interviewing someone in the industry, he said, "I was scared when I went home on Saturday night and I hated the idea that I have to get up in the morning on Monday to see a full-page advertisement from HCL, because you just psyched us, frightened us with such mammoth advertising." Also when it came to pricing, Amit took the most perfect pricing decision, and I didn't allow anyone to interfere. "This is what should be the price," he said. "Let's see how to work it out," and he worked it out.

"Hamdard Dawakhana, Hamdard Dawakhana mein English mein accounting nahi tha, it's all in Urdu." So how do you convert this into English data? That was the part of our contract. When HCL was founded I turned 30, Amit was same age as me. And in the subsequent 10–12 years this industry was set. You know, we all worked together because we enjoyed the process. And all of us worked like equals. It was great fun. Lots of friendship, lots of bonding and warmth, and we were a bunch of guys who got together, the age group was similar, identical. And we were teaching this country a few things, in the process. Outsourcing, again for the first time it happened in India in 1979, and the first piece of outsourcing took place right from Madras. They were fun days, trying to do business in a completely unconventional way. Being a pioneer is fun if you have people like this, best brains, I would say guts, pure guts of doing this, audacity of doing this, and as we went—Bit-by-Bit-by-Bit. That's how the computer industry in this country was created.

Arjun, Amit, and Benu designed the first ever road show in India. Arjun one day came and said we want to have a meeting with you because we are conceiving a different method of selling. How we are selling is one-to-one. We go and meet the possible potential client and sell one-to-one. He said, we need to change this into, like, a manufacturing process. Here we would do it differently. We'll say, "aap cheque book le kar aa jaiye, pasand aa gaya to book kar lena, advance de dena, and nahi aya to check book wapas le jaiye." They said that the USP of giving the cheque is that you will get an early delivery. They went and took the entire ground floor at Oberoi, the conference room, the function room, and they go one-by-one—table by table, from the entry point and finally there was a place which was called the cooking place. That was the point at which the closure took place. I said, "Amit, finally you do something very good." This became so successful that it became nationally accepted new method of selling. Several new things were tried for the first time around that time by HCL in the history of Indian computer industry.

Amit was extremely aggressive yet a soft-spoken man. I found that his mind was aggressive and his strategy was completely aggressive. His aggression came from all of us, the managing team. I think most aggressive person in our team was late Raman. Technology wise, the kind of outrageous aggression that was shown by him at the first PC was out of the world, the most advanced Unix implementation of the world, the first multifunction UNIX implementation of the world, first relational database in the world, and to match that you needed an intellectual like Amit to do such technology aggression to the market in very simple words.

The highest profit for a hardware company to achieve is something like 40 percent profit pretax, which we had achieved in 1986–1987. That was the year we had done the worst, a very tough year, 1986–1987. In the same year, we launched our Unix product. Unix was a very sophisticated product and for the first time Amit floated the price. He gave the sales team a broad construct of the price and you could have variations—variation in memory. Amit gave many variations to the constructive price according to the budget of the customer. Amit said, "In the initial period, you can go and cream. Don't go and sell it at base price," and the sales team went all the way because it was the only Unix product in the market. It was his marketing strategy and the implementation in the field was done by Arjun.

Amit said, "If you see a distant radar signal, how would you pick it up and then how do you take the noise out and find the shape? You could shoot it down very quickly, but you need to have the patience of a very indulgent mother to let another person resolve and develop it." I have seen this with Amit. I was very blessed with a team, with whom, if we were brainstorming, we would never kill each other's ideas and in that the most important person was Raman because, if technically it is not possible, then the idea gets killed very quickly, or if someone like Amit came and said I don't think dimensionally marketing wise this could be done. So, for me, I always needed him to say if I can draw a boundary and if I have only three dots, will he think in complete synchronization of mind with me and see the shape whether it's a circle, or it is a triangle, whatever I want to see, will he be able to see it together with me? It needs tremendous synchronization of the mind, it's almost like running a relay race, I complete this and I hand it over to someone, he is running too, and Amit would do that extremely well. I always knew he would do it and knowing that he would do it, I tried something more audacious. So HCL did lot of things audaciously. Its a collection of best minds put together, not just one, not one or two, its Arjun, Amit, me, and Raman—the four pillars of HCL. In the process, I know for sure, Amit or I or Arjun or Raman would not have done it any different and we would have given anything to keep those days, same team.

Amit always insisted that I was a good precision manager. I always told him that I make a very good chairman, but I make a very lousy chief executive officer. Without you people I would have fallen all over the place. He said, "If we were not been there, you would still have found someone else to do that." Amit was a terrific guy. He was a brilliant strategist. Sumit will tell you the same thing, Arjun will tell you the same thing, Dadan, he also passed away, would have said the same thing, Bikram would have said the same thing. Bikram himself got a very vivid mind, very fertile mind.

I remember reading one of the books that Amit gave me. There was lot of writing about Air Marshal called Lim Piao of Mao Tse Tung, and I believe he was a superb planner. And the first bomb, when it went out, he would go to sleep. This is for every possible first day outcome. He would have planned everything and it's like I can now sleep it off, such a thorough planner. Amit was such a thorough planner, that if so much response comes up how do we do? If less comes, how do we do? And he could take a risk, risk of this nature. The face of this risk was always me, but the persons behind the execution of the risk, from the marketing side was Amit and from the sales side in the market place was Arjun.

Amit's 1986 campaign was marketing wise very cleverly thought out of bringing down the PC price. At that time, the threshold that we could think of was ₹20,000, and Amit completely unbundled the price. He, for the first time, introduced what we call three dimensional prices. Here, if you want to buy a PC and take it home and install there—the price would be ₹20,000 and a warranty in which you will bring the computer to the shop. Then you will get the machine fixed. And if you want installation then there was a price. Every service offering was separated out and unbundled. That was the USP and when you add it up, it probably came back to the same price. It looks very lucrative and if anyone wanted to buy that way, it was perfectly fine. If it is a distant location, such as, middle of Madhya Pradesh, then for the installation you have to take it there and install it there. You can't buy the machine in Bombay and ask to install this in your place (remote location). Each location has different price. The big advantage was that if someone wanted to compete, unless he competed with us in Jodhpur at the Jodhpur price, he could not compete, you can't take the Bombay price and compete in Jodhpur, as, then the price would be higher. If it was Shillong or some place, the price would be radically different. So it was completely adjusted to the intensity of the market and intensity of competition. There was also a real cash draw products, which was Intel 8086 based data card that cost us ₹400 and we priced it at ₹8,000. The salesman incentive was 400, so when the sales guy would sell a machine, immediately he would sell the card.

"The last few meetings we (Amit and I) had, when I suggested and told him that 'enough is enough, you left HCL, now come back to HCL,' and this is one part that I don't know whether anyone knows …. It should have happened, it should have happened …. Anyway destiny is destiny."

Arjun Malhotra
Sushmita Sengupta
G.S. Sachdeva
Manoj Deb

05

5

PROFITING BY DESIGN

CAD/CAM: Profiting by Design

Arjun Malhotra and Sushmita Sengupta

The next phase of Amit's HCL days that I would like to share with you now is the formation of CAD/CAM Division (CCD) in HCL.

As HCL had come a long way since 1975, in 1984–1985, we observed a marked change in our strategies and style of functioning. We entered the industry as an aggressive, abrasive company, hell bent on just swamping the market, though the aggression remained and it continued to drive the market, it had been tempered down with incisively strategic thinking and planning. We had constantly changed, adapted, and modified ourselves according to the needs of the Indian market. We always rejected the premise of marketing decisions based on "what is selling now and who the usual customers are?" But we, instead, looked at "what doesn't exist now but could sell and who are our potential new buyers?"

Although HCL had achieved a lot in the first 9–10 years, now the time had come to consolidate the gains while continuing our role as the market driver. By this time, we had realized that it would be a difficult task, especially when the awareness about computers was growing, coupled with the fact that competition was getting intense with others slowly coming to grips with the marketing game along with emerging standardization of products.

Technology was changing. Workstations were just coming out. For a long time, it had been a known fact that a visual display was far easier to comprehend than a written letter or a spoken word. The computer technology had begun to meaningfully exploit this fact now. One application area which extensively used visual display was Engineering Design. We saw the emergence of computer-aided design and computer-aided manufacturing (CAD/CAM). The areas which could utilize the concepts of CAD/CAM were endless. Since networking and graphics had also become easily accessible and affordable, all of a sudden you had networked workstations with a lot of engineering software coming on them—both for mechanical CAD and electronic CAD, as also for architectural design, for plant layout, for pipe layout, for ship building, etc. Lots of application software was available at somewhat affordable prices. There were many engineering applications, such as, drafting and AutoCAD, that were made available on PCs. However, applications that were more sophisticated in nature were still on engineering workstations. The prices of these workstations had come down, so had the cost of these applications that ran on those workstations. Networking had now become a "plug and play" model, thus making the price of the package on each of the workstations reasonably manageable.

So far, HCL had made a name in the microcomputer/minicomputer arena by focusing on SMEs. However, in the process, we had lost touch with the large corporates where companies, such as, Wipro, Tata Elxsi, DCM, ORG, and ICIM were the major players. Therefore, as a strategy, we decided that we would address this CAD/CAM business and quickly get back to the large customers. Consequently, armed with our new range of products, we now consciously took our focus off the FTU segment and gradually shifted our attention towards the medium and large corporate user.

We wanted to address this solution-based business with a separate internal group that would exclusively focus on this new engineering solution business. As an engineer with some interest in core engineering and with some field sales exposure, I was asked to head this division.

I decided to take people from within HCL, at least my core group had to be the people who had worked in the company for a while. Once I had them, I would be able to take fresh engineers, train them, and work around them.

Amit was one of the early people whom I identified for CAD/CAM, since he had been in marketing for a possibly long time. Also, he wanted a change and to do something different, so this worked out well. I basically had Amit run that whole business. So, Amit and I handpicked 13 professionals, all engineers, as they translate the high technology better, to initially run this division. Gradually, we recruited more people all over India, as per our requirement. In fact, Amit looked after the entire back office, the solutions, the entire agreements with the vendors, the support for the clients, and the solution team that we had set up to run this business.

We had a number of solutions in mechanical CAD, such as, SDRC, ANSYS, etc. We had a number of solutions in electronic CAD, Visula from Racal Redac, Mentor Graphics suite, GABLE in architectural CAD. We had some Norwegian ship building software (Autokon) and CALMA for plant design, and so on.

Strategic Consultative Selling

We had experts who could converse in detail with the designers in each of these areas, discuss their problems, and suggest solutions. These were consultants who knew engineering issues, understood the application software, and were able to train and help customers to solve their problems. It was not as simple as writing a business application program.

The biggest challenge to the team was how to address the potential of this market. The first question that Amit had in mind was: "Is CAD/CAM a strategic issue for a customer?" There were reasons in my mind as to why a customer/buyer should approach CAD/CAM from a strategic perspective, at that time. First, it was a significant investment for the company and then several companies had been able to turn CAD/CAM capabilities into an important competitive advantage by outperforming their competitors, as they say, "profiting by design," largely because of their effective management and utilization of this technology. CAD/CAM helped to fundamentally recognize:

- Greater flexibility in design and manufacturing
- Improved product cost or performance
- Reduced need for physical prototypes and, therefore, faster to market
- Better performance at the leading edge
- More efficient use of scarce expert knowledge
- Making the planning process more efficient

Therefore, the process for evaluating and planning for CAD/CAM started with a top management mandate to develop from an engineering and/or manufacturing point, a strategic profile of the business, to view its products' strength, weakness, and opportunities through the eyes of their customers. And to effectively justify that we had to get real experts who understood the business and could talk to the clients convincingly. It was amazing how Amit was able to learn a lot of it. He seemed like an expert in most of these fields. I knew he was not an expert in them, but he seemed like he could have this conversation at a reasonably deep level in terms of how do you approach a problem, what are the different ways of looking at the same problem, how to solve the problem, and so on. It was quite amazing when you went on customer calls with him because he would engage the customer in their actual work, have a look at it, then try and understand it, and finally suggest a possible solution. Some of the customers actually had a lot of respect for him in terms of what he did.

CAD/CAM was new. We had to educate a number of customers on how to use the solutions. We had to create a team of the best engineers, train them on both—engineering and commercial aspects of business. It was a model of learn and simultaneously educate. You had to learn yourself and educate, and then make sure that the people you educate, learn to share their knowledge when they went out to the field.

The biggest challenge we faced in this business was how to manage the customer relationship. To tackle this, Amit's guidance to his team was: "Since we are in a new business—CAD/CAM, we must service the prospect and not go for direct hard sale." We should go to the people who are experts in their chosen fields, like professors in IITs, RECs, etc., and meet them as they are consultants from whom we can learn. I would go to IIT Kharagpur, Yuvraj was ex IIT Kanpur, and he would go to IIT Kanpur and Madras while Amit would go everywhere.

> *Amit would advise his CAD/CAM sales team, "Never be afraid if you are not been able to answer a question, jot it down intelligently and tell the prospect that you would get back to them. You can never be a specialist in all the areas but always get back to the prospect. Then you develop relationship based on mutual respect and when the professors see the value, they will always acknowledge. Maintain a relationship of a teacher and student, tell them on the new technology and learn from them."*
>
> Late Yuvraj Bahadur
>
> Late Yuvraj Bahadur, Ex-Director, JK Technosoft, was a pass out from Indian Institute of Technology, Kanpur, reported to Amit in CAD/CAM division. He also held various leadership positions in HCL and HCL HP. Mr Bahadur shared a very special bond with Amit, professionally and personally.

Since we were selling a number of solutions in many different areas of engineering design and manufacturing, we had to manage a lot of partners. For the software solutions that we were selling, we had to ensure that we met every vendor's expectations, lean on them sometimes for support because when you come up with a problem with a new product that you can't solve yourself or never seen before, you would need to go back to the respective vendor specialist who obviously had much wider experience, as they supported their product globally and came across lot more problems, than we saw in India. What was interesting to observe was that over a period of time, as our experts grew in knowledge and confidence, some vendors would lean on us for advice to solve problems they had with their customers.

At that time, we used to import workstations which actually restricted the market considerably as the process of import approvals and the delivery lead time for the orders tended were very long and unpredictable. In view of this, we persuaded Apollo Computers, whose workstations we were selling as a part of our CAD/CAM solution, to allow us to manufacture these workstations in India. This strategy worked for us, as it allowed us to expand the market, and also gave them a larger market share.

I think that was an enormous breakthrough that time. Amit was one of the key movers behind this. I was the one to go to Chelmsford, Massachusetts, and sign the agreement, but a lot of work at the back end which allowed me to sign this agreement, was done by Amit. I was quite amazed, someone who left engineering right after the college became a management trainee in DCM, then worked in marketing in Coke, and then worked in marketing and field sales in HCL was able to get into engineering-based solutions and set up the CAD/CAM division. How well he adapted and how much his own engineering fundas came back that he was able to help understand the customer problems and help them with solutions, train them, and then do all that was associated with their engineering problem was indeed like a miraculous experience for us.

I also remember one particular incident that I would like to share with you that showed Amit's "out-of-the-box thinking" abilities while addressing a crisis situation. The way we had structured the CAD/CAM Division in HCL was that we would run it like a company within a company. So, CAD/CAM Division (CCD) had a business plan that had to be cleared by the Corporate Board as it had an "investment." I can't remember the exact number, but I think it was ₹25 lakh at that time. The understanding was that as long as you stay within that budget, you could draw cash from the central accounts, but the minute you need more than what you had budgeted, you needed to come back to the Board and explain why you need more money with proper justifications.

Now we were doing pretty well, we have got lot of orders and everything looked good, except that these high-technology machines needed specific clearance from the US Department of Commerce for import into India at that time and lot of these clearances were held up. In fact, none of the clearances had come, they were all in the process and were expected to come. However, it was already something like 8–9 months from the time we had booked these orders. Everyone knows that booking orders costs money, and when you actually deliver them and collect payments the money comes back into the system. Since we had booked the orders but not delivered them, there was no question of collecting the money and getting it back into the system. We were going to face a cash-flow problem, although we were doing quite well in terms of meeting our sales numbers. So we all sat down, had a meeting and I proposed that we should go back to corporate, explain the situation, and ask for some more money. I remember Amit saying, "No, No, we can't do that." In fact, he used the term "yeh Mooncho ka sawaal hai." It's our reputation that's at stake. We told the board that we would be able to run this division and that was all the cash we needed. He said we better find another way instead of just going back to corporate office. So we all brainstormed a little longer and it finally turned out that the solution was right there in front of us, but we had just not seen it.

We were representing Autodesk and selling AutoCAD in India. If we could just increase the sales of that, then our commissions and our margins from that would have taken care of our cash flow. At least the cash we needed for the next few months, till the delivery and clearances from US Department of Commerce, came in. That's exactly what we did. We went to the United States and tied up with Autodesk, got their software into India, and managed to do fairly well with it. In fact, it was so successful that it became a separate division in HCL.

Besides just the marketing strategy, Amit also had to handle numerous other back-office aspects, such as, compliance with US licensing requirements for usage of sensitive equipment and these could be very critical as the United States could put HCL on a blacklist if we had even a single deviation.

By the end of the tenure of CAD/CAM business, we enjoyed some 80 percent market share for workstations, as well as large market share in many niches like 90 percent market share in shipbuilding, where we had offered a package called Autokon from Norway.

CAD/CAM success was due to the team, which Amit headed efficiently. Some of the benefits that HCL got from the CAD/CAM Division were:

- HCL got back into many large corporates—the entire Padi belt of Madras, Pricol of Coimbatore, BHEL, SCL, and many more.
- Customers held the HCL team in very high esteem at that time, as "consultative selling to large corporates" was a paradigm shift from the earlier "box selling" to "intellectual property and solutions" selling. Our CAD/CAM team

did an excellent job and Amit, to his credit, groomed them methodically and trained them to be the finest samurai for these high end solutions sales.
- "Service" became even more important as part of HCL "work culture."
- In 1986–1987, the order value from Semiconductor Complex, Chandigarh was over ₹20 crore. They designed and manufactured integrated circuits (chips). Orders from BHEL, ICF, BEML, etc., were all over ₹1 crore each.

Indirect Benefit from HCL Apollo Tie Up

When we collaborated with Apollo Computers to manufacture their DN 3000 and DN 3500 workstations in India (we called them Nexus 3000 and Nexus 3500), we had hit a wall with some government regulations. One big problem was that the large color monitors that Apollo used which they sourced from Philips, who would assemble, test, and then ship these to Apollo. However, this was not an allowed import in India. Our regulations only allowed us to import the raw display. Then we needed to build the electronics to run the screen, and assemble and test it in India. Philips was unwilling to give us the "kit" for us to do the assembly locally. Amit with R.N. Dodeja (our R&D person in CAD/CAM), R.N. Lavania (our manufacturing person) and with the blessings of late S. Raman (director looking after R&D at HCL), and some of his software team (R. Arjun, R. Kumar, etc.) worked this magic. We got a monitor from Mitsubishi in Japan and built our own electronics to drive it and interfaced it with the Apollo box. In fact, the display was so good and so clear that Apollo talked to us about buying it from us for their own manufacturing unit.

HP bought Apollo Computers in March 1989. HCL had such a dominant position in the workstation market in India that HP agreed to let us be the India face for them and the Apollo workstations. This relationship and our performance as their partner in workstations subsequently lead to the formation of a more comprehensive joint venture between HCL and HP, and HCL-HP was born. HP was very clear that the JV, HCL-HP could not represent any specific software vendor. HCL-HP had to be neutral to a number of software vendors and so as the CAD/CAM Division of HCL HP; we had to give up some of the business that we had. Thus, Autodesk was one of the software vendors we had to give up.

When Amit parted with HCL, he was very clear that he did not want to compete with HCL. As a result, they could not get into PCs or computers and had lots of restrictions. Therefore, Amit and the group that split out from HCL started with the portfolio of two portable computers and subsequently diversified into the field of CAD/CAM services for distributing AutoCAD and multimedia tools in India, as HCL had already parted with Autodesk.

AutoCAD was run on PCs. At HCL, we all were excited about selling high-end software on high-end workstations, but we did not really look at this business opportunity, which had a huge market potential. When Amit obtained license from Autodesk for their venture, he effectively exploited this opportunity to the hilt.

Amit Was a Motivating Leader

G.S. Sachdeva
Ex-HCL, Professor, JNU and NALSAR

Amit was a motivating leader, amply supported by Arjun Malhotra, and he acted as a cohesive factor in the division. As head of the division, he marched his team to achievements and shared the laurels generously. He was ambitious, but with hardly any ego. He had the finis of a gentleman.

My association with Amit was while working in CAD/CAM Division, of which he was the executive director. I had come to join from the defense background, but we gelled well. He was, of course, conscious of my edges to adjust in civil working environment, but he highly regarded my sincerity, integrity, and loyalty to the organization.

Amit was a non-interfering boss and accorded full freedom to his staff to operate and act on their own style and wisdom. At the same time, he was non-compromising on tasks and targets.

CAD/CAM concepts were new at that time. There was very little awareness and still lesser knowledge about these new and advanced techniques. Amit and his marketing team pioneered this computer segment, and the thrust was on IITs and education institutions as well as the private R&D, and manufacturing industries. The marketing strategy worked well. It was a futuristic project with gestation period. The dedicated team, with good marketing vision, covered the flanks well and sowed good seeds of business development that were, in due time, to be reaped by later heads of the division, namely, Saroop Chand and Gupta ji.

The hardware for CAD/CAM applications was high-end product from the Apollo, United States, and even some of the software applications pertained to dual-use technologies and were treated sensitive. Therefore, most sales were subject to commercial licensing restrictions based on end use. I was involved in this process of justifying and vouching for the end use and ensuring licensing clearances. This middleman job was at times tricky; nevertheless, it had to be accomplished without glitches and was successfully achieved. The role of marketing services was well vindicated.

At that time, Indian computer users were not too familiar with elaborate copyright agreements for specialized software emanating from the West. This created misperceptions in the minds of the customers about consequences of alleged breaches. It was here again that my role became prominent to allay misapprehensions by explaining legal nuances of the agreements, and sometimes by offering back-to-back contracts to indemnify the buyers against actions, if any, initiated under foreign jurisdictions and other germane fears. I was mostly successful in supporting marketing efforts.

CAD/CAM Strategy

Manoj Deb
Consultant Design Using Electronice CAD

1980s saw the advent of low-cost, high-performance computers (Engineering Workstations). This resulted in the reduction of per seat cost and brought it within the reach of mid-size corporate houses.

- HCL's approach was to understand the need of the customer and suggest a solution to realize that need. This consisted of:

    – Study of client's existing design process and arrive at a solution in consultation with the client.
    – Study of client's existing design process and arrive at a solution in consultation with the client.
    – Sourcing of computer, application software, and special purpose peripherals.
    – Helping client in completing statutory formalities as per requirement.
    – Installation of hardware/software and completing task of integrating them.
    – Training of client in usage. This sometimes consisted of doing a complete design in close collaboration with client engineers.

IMPACT: Perception regarding HCL changed from a hardware supplier to a solution provider. This also impacted the industry as a whole, as other suppliers also started following this. However, HCL was perceived as a leader in this concept.

- As CAD/CAM systems proliferated, a large number of application specific solutions were available. Each application was complex and was support intensive, and hence needed technical expertise. HCL took a focused approach and concentrated on the following areas:

    - Mechanical CAD (MCAD)
    - Electronic CAD (ECAD)
    - GEOMATICS
    - Plant data solution (PDS)
    - Artificial intelligence (AI)

This decision was market dominated and in-house technical expertise was built on these areas. To ensure availability of state-of-the-art application software products, HCL identified suppliers and entered into a reseller agreement with them.

IMPACT: Clients appreciated the technical expertise of HCL engineers and took advice of HCL for resolution of the problems. HCL was perceived more as a consultant than a reseller.

- Workstation-based CAD software was costly and resource intensive, apart from being complex in nature. Most of the less sophisticated users (a growing band) of CAD found it beyond their reach. An increased number of CAD softwares running on low-cost PC were also made available. Looking at the potential, a strategy addressing this market was worked out by Amit. This was a success as ever increasing number of small organizations got acquainted with the use of CAD.

- As usage of CAD/CAM software proliferated, the need for trained manpower was also felt. HCL made a strategy to address this. This consisted of:

    - Providing engineering colleges/institutes with low-cost, PC-based application software to be used by students for small design projects.
    - Organizing onsite as well as offsite training for client engineers on a regular basis.
    - Collaborating with application software suppliers for advanced training.
    - Getting in partnership with premier institutes for organizing training.

IMPACT: Increased sale of CAD/CAM products. Availability of trained engineers increased consequent customer benefits. Reduction of design cycle time of clients due to enhanced expertise level of engineers. Clients perceived HCL as a partner. This also helped in reduction of sales cycle.

- Around 1988, HCL started manufacturing high-performance engineering workstations under a technology transfer agreement with the OEM supplier. This was named as NX series of workstations. The name was coined by Amit. This facilitated order execution, as earlier workstations were imported and required compliance of statutory requirements which were time consuming. Amit also worked out a replacement strategy for these imported workstations with indigenous ones to address the issues related to maintenance.

IMPACT: This led to easy availability of workstations by cutting down lead time to deliver products. It enabled HCL to configure systems as per client needs. Product maintenance became much easier.

Impact on the Industry

- Client's expectation changed as instead of mere product clients started looking for a solution of their problem.
- Consultancy-based approach to sale of solutions became the norm. In fact, it enabled HCL to get some large value orders from corporate clients.
- HCL is the only vendor with manufacturing workstations in India.
- Presence in all segments of the industry, viz., training, supply of low-end, PC-based CAD to workstation-based CAD was a unique feature and an indication of full involvement.
- Growing skill in computer integrated manufacture (CIM). Clients were able to account for special manufacturing requirements in design phase and tie into material requirement planning systems. Clients gradually started moving up the value chain of CAD/CAM solutions to derive the maximum benefit.

Arjun Malhotra
Suvra Basu
Sushmita Sengupta
R.K. Gupta
Bobby Srinivasan
Kashi Samaddar
Ayush Nadimpalli

6

SOFT TURN TO SUCCESS

Leader's eye for detail, and thereby profiting by design and soft turn to success. AutoCAD was run on PCs and no one really looked at this business opportunity, which had a huge market potential in India. Amit identified and effectively exploited this opportunity to the hilt and stood for causing an eruption in PC–CAD usage in every segment and in every corner of India. Parallel to an aggressive engagement with corporate and government organizations for doing this, they also nurtured, in the background, a quiet operation for engineering colleges, AICTE, and World Bank–funded implementation agencies, to standardize their products as the de facto standard for technical education. It took painstaking work of years to achieve this, but it created bedrock of patronage for today's students/tomorrow's practicing engineers.

HOPE—The Soft Turn to Success (1988–2010)

Arjun Malhotra and Sushmita Sengupta
Suvra Basu
Director and Member of the Board of Axis Inc

When Amit and other five contemplated the formation of their own IT company, in 1988, little did they knew about the twists and turns, and reshaping that the company would go through in the next 20-odd-years.

Let's see how HOPE was formed. These HOPEful six (Amit Dutta Gupta, K.P.G. Nair, Dilip Phadnis, Saroop Chand, Sujit

Baksi, and C.S. Patankar) followed a few ground rules that they weren't going to enter an existing market and fight for market share. As being a small organization, it would be suicidal to battle established companies on their ground. Logically, therefore, they were left with the choice of identifying a new market niche or an existing one that was not being properly exploited, such as, AutoCAD and PC market.

When they were working in HCL, they came across a very good market research report from IDC, which had surveyed the home market. Looking at the overcrowded PC market at that time, they felt that the home market would be a good opportunity to address and to start with. Subsequently, they decided to branch out on their own and prepared a project report and submitted to TDICI (Technology Development and Information Company of India Ltd) in 1988. TDICI approved the project.

Well, as they geared up to come out of HCL, one severe blow that fell, almost dislocated them from not starting at all. It was the absurdly, untimely death—in his early 30s—of C.S. Patankar. As Amit would remember,

> "Patankar, undoubtedly the smartest and most competent of us, even before the company registration, he proposed the name Hindustan Office Products Limited, and then came the trauma of his fighting for life after a very serious brain aneurysm rupture. The supreme irony was that as life ebbed away on one side, new life was formed at the same time, as, on the last day, his wife gave birth to a daughter whom Patankar never saw."

In Patankar's fond and precious memory, they retained the company name as he had visualized it, although they never did office products at all. According to Amit, if they left the company name as is, there was a distinct possibility of people shortening it to HOP Ltd, which wouldn't have been elegant at all! So they added an E (Electronics? Enterprise? Take your pick, or give your own expansion) and made a logo "HOPE." As expected, this gained currency fast, and everyone forgot Hindustan Office Products.

So after a few years, they went back to the Registrar of Companies, and filed for HOPE Technologies Ltd, which went through without any demur.

One commendable thing about the promoters was that they didn't leave HCL en masse. They informed the HCL management in advance and then worked out a departure plan where they gave notices of 9–12 months, so that HCL didn't have to face any problem. Finally, they started leaving HCL one by one from August 1988 to January 1989. Interestingly, they still enjoy a very "warm" relationship with HCL.

HOPE started with an investment of ₹35 lakh, of which 45.5 percent came from TDICI. I do remember that Amit had borrowed some money from me. They were getting some equity from TDICI, and one of the conditions was that I convert my loan to equity which I did. So I still have some equity somewhere with Amit and his group in that company.

In the beginning, they concentrated with the portfolio of two portable computers—Dolphin and Palmtop, both from United Kingdom. The Dolphin system slated mainly for children, however couldn't take blow of PC prices being slashed from ₹22,000 to ₹10,000 by ET&T Corp. At this price, HOPE was not in a position to offer Dolphin systems, and hence stopped its production and distribution.

The Palmtop was still kicking. What exactly was the Palmtop? It weighed 350 g. Its dimensions were 165 mm × 85 mm × 47 mm. It fitted in a palm. It had the CMOS 6303 processor with a clock speed of 1 MHz. It used four AA-type pencil cells with external AC adapters. Its 32 KB ROM contained the operating system, utilities, and palmtop programming language. It could accommodate two built-in solid state drives and had a 16-pin slot on the top to accept the COMMS-LINK interface to give RS232C communications up to 9,600 bauds. It could even be attached to mainframe.

The market positioning of the Palmtop was a diary or a confidential data keeper, calculator, for job card, data capture, crime data collection, and scientific applications. HOPE made significant sale for this product with a heady clientele list to their credit, such as, Modi Xerox for field invoicing, HLL for salesman data capture, Mohan Meakins for depot invoicing, ITC for data capture, MTNL for meter reading, BSF for crime data collection, SAIL for maintenance operations. Others include DESU, ICICI, UCO Bank, IIT Delhi, L&T, Escorts, LIC, TISCO, Goodyear, and many more.

Foray into CAD/CAM

Amit felt that the business cannot grow on the Palmtop sales alone, and he sensed the opportunity of AutoCAD and PC market that was yet to be explored in India.

HOPE signed up with Autodesk Inc. as their distributor for SAARC countries with the objective of promoting their suite of CAD/CAM products through an indirect sales channel (that is, through value-added business partners [VABPs]) in 1993.

> *I got to know Amit da in the mid-80s when I was at Apollo Computer and he was involved with the CAD Division of HCL, HCL was our channel to India. At that time, I first met him at the Nehru Place office of HCL, he certainly left a very positive impression on me. Fast forward, I then many years later was running the Autodesk business for the SAARC region and reconnected with him. Although the financial state of HOPE was not the greatest, I felt that Amit da could be a game changer for Autodesk as we build a market in India. So we made the change and sure enough, Autodesk's rocket ship ride in India had begun. We worked very closely together and I did get to know him.*
>
> *He was the Renaissance man, he could eloquently speak about Tagore, Indian history, differential calculus, and on and on and on. He was there when my father died and through thick and thin. I remember him as a listener, thinker, and most importantly as a good friend. Take care Amit da and you are here in my heart forever.*
>
> Bobby Srinivasan
Ex-Head Autodesk, SAARC Region

In 1992–1993, Autodesk was also going through a transition in terms of their product roadmap and worldwide Go-To-Market strategy. Those who have been exposed to CAD/CAM would recall that in those days Autodesk was synonymous with AutoCAD—their flagship 2D drafting software, which enjoyed a very dominating world market share in the 2D drafting application space. Autodesk was able to achieve this dominant market position, in part, by developing easy-to-use, intelligent, and feature-rich software which helped create demand and on the supply side, ensuring availability of trained resources through their authorized training centers (ATCs). Added to this was their successful authorized developer network (ADN), which allowed independent software providers to develop and market various applications and tools catering to productivity and industry-specific needs by using AutoCAD's application programming interfaces (APIs).

As the CAD/CAM world started moving increasingly towards 3D-based solutions and usage in the product and process engineering domain, Autodesk too embarked accordingly on restructuring and refining their product strategy and road map by releasing newer versions of their products with enhanced features and 3D capabilities. AutoCAD users would recall that it started with AutoCAD Release 11 with AME (Advanced Modeling Extensions), then further to subsequent versions, Autodesk Mechanical Desktop was released as a complete mid-range modeling platform for 3D software for mechanical engineers (as was Architectural Desktop and Civil Engineering Desktop for architects and civil engineers).

During those days, the Indian CAD/CAM market was relatively in its infancy though fairly segmented with "high-end" softwares, which included CATIA, Unigraphics, IDEAS, PDS, PDMS amongst others, holding the fort in 3D mechanical and process engineering applications while Autodesk products (primarily AutoCAD) were confined mainly to the 2D drafting world.

The high-end softwares were traditionally strong in product design and development domain of automotive OEMs, aerospace, heavy machinery and process engineering industries, and the then existing market for AutoCAD was largely driven by drafting board replacement opportunities.

> As a partner for Autodesk, Amit da was at his best to take on the Goliath TUL. One could feel the genius in Amit everyday of this association. Somewhere, I think Autodesk will owe a salute to Amit for establishing them in India.
>
> R.K. Gupta
> President, Neilsoft; Ex-Country Manager, Autodesk India

It's against this backdrop that HOPE started its journey in the world of CAD/CAM solutions. Amit strongly believed that the timing was perfect and that the Indian CAD/CAM market was poised for a significant take-off. The Indian economy was also opening up considerably on the domestic, FDI, and export fronts, and there was a fairly bullish sentiment around.

Given a scenario where Amit as the master strategist, motivator in-charge, and marketing guru; Saroop (Chand) as the sales leader par excellence, brilliant thinker, and analyst; Dilip (Phadnis) as the expert on process and production, it was imperative for HOPE to quickly develop a detailed game plan with time lines and priorities. Amit led the initiative for the company positioning and differentiators, which was also equally important and it was decided that they would drive growth by providing value through relationships and position themselves as an industry (vertical)-aligned engineering software solutions provider with Autodesk products forming the core platform. Thereafter, all their strategies and plans were developed keeping this in perspective.

As they had an indirect sales model with Autodesk products, the first task was to establish their geographic footprint by appointing value-added resellers (VARs) across India. The cities and towns were carefully chosen based on various parameters, and the target VAR profile was debated, discussed at length, and strategy finalized. After couple of rounds of ads in selected media outlets, the senior executives were dispatched to different regions to identify, discuss, and sign up VARs initially in all major cities and then on to B class cities and industrial towns. Further, in order to ensure that VARs were seriously interested and committed to aggressively selling Autodesk products, the eligibility criterion included ability to stock and pay for a minimum number of AutoCAD licenses upfront, this was a task easier written than done! While Autodesk and AutoCAD were well known, HOPE was virtually unknown in the CAD/CAM world and there was a fair amount of apprehension from potential VARs to sign up.

In many such situations, Amit's persuasive skills, charm, track record, and pedigree came into play and coupled with dogged persistence and missionary zeal of the team, they were able to rapidly build a VAR network in all major cities initially and subsequently in selective B class cities and industrial towns, the initial advance payments also helped their cash flow! It would be worthwhile to mention here that they had selected a few startups as their VARs, such as, Wrench Solutions, Pinnacle InfoTech, amongst others, who today have grown and matured into successful business enterprises.

Simultaneously, there was lot of thought and internal debate going on with regard to organization restructuring and revamping to align and reflect the corporate objective of being an engineering software solutions provider. A bold and seemingly radical decision was taken that instead of being a product-driven organization, they would build a vertical (industry) solution-driven company with Autodesk products at the nucleus. From an investment and management perspective, it would have been easier to have taken the product route as the investments required (money, resources, and time) in building a company around industry-based solutions were very high. I would like to highlight to our readers here that while vertical/domain/industry-driven practice is pretty common these days, however, in early 1990s, it was a trailblazer of sorts among software companies in India. And among engineering software solutions in India, they were arguably the first to adopt and implement this structure! As Amit used to comment in jest, "We adopted the vertical structure even before Autodesk did!"

However, the logic and reasons behind adopting this structure were very clear. To be a dominant player in the engineering software solutions space, they had to increase their mindshare (and wallet spends) from customers, edge out competition by changing the bone of contention, provide higher value offerings built on expertise and competency. A product-driven structure would have severely constrained their scope and coverage!

Based on market potential and industry maturity levels, the verticals were defined which mainly included AEC (architecture, engineering, and construction), heavy engineering, plant and process, GIS and multimedia, and detailed plans and strategies for each vertical were worked out. In order to offer best of breed solution to their customers, they leveraged the Autodesk Developer Network and signed up with other software companies for specific industry solutions (for example, sheet metal applications, finite element analysis, mold flow analysis, NC programming, raster to vector conversion tools, etc.).

One of the other dilemmas they had was related to the profile of their sales and business development team: "Should they hire hard core salespeople, train them on CAD/CAM basics, and let them loose?" or "Do they hire Techies and convert them into sales and business development engineers?" The convention wisdom was to opt for the former as this was the model followed by all software marketing companies who had front line salespeople with little technical knowledge backed up by a strong technical support team. The other concern was: "Would techies have the thick skin and fire in the belly associated with hard core sales executives?"

This was an important decision not just for organizational structure and development, but for foundational purposes too as this could decide the fate of the company in the long run.

As their sales model was an indirect one, they realized that the hard core front line sales executives were not essential to close deals, rather they needed engineers who understood technology so that they could analyze customer pain points and requirements in depth, thereby generating increased demand for the product and solutions. And this was much better served by demonstrating competency and expertise rather than pure sales pitch. They figured out that existing and prospective customers would be more comfortable talking to engineers who could speak the same language and be on the same wavelength. Moreover, as their aspiration and objective was to grow into an industry-aligned engineering solutions provider, it was important that their customer facing teams have the technical ability and bandwidth to understand the industry solutions so as to apply them in real-life situations for their clients. Also, this would obviate the need to have a very large technical support team.

Therefore, despite the prevailing trends, they took the contrarian approach and instead of hiring hard core sales engineers, they decided to hire engineers from different industries, who were users of CAD/CAM, and turn them into business executives. They were clear about hiring the best and brightest available in the country. The selection process was very stringent, exhaustive, and included engineering aptitude tests. Their objective was to nourish a culture of empowerment, build a team focused on pursuit of excellence in their chosen field, and provide them a motivating environment to further develop their skills, flourish, and succeed.

However, they realized that it would be a challenging endeavor to find such resources given that technical engineers were very wary of anything to do with sales, and hence would be very hesitant to take up such roles, and that too in a company which did not have either brand name or track record in CAD/CAM community. Amit, nevertheless, was confident that once they sat down with the shortlisted prospective employees and explained their mission, and how it was an once-in-a-lifetime opportunity for them, they would be able get them on board. As Amit said, "The excitement of the journey, fulfillment, and promising future has to be communicated and realized by them." While AutoCAD name definitely helped in kindling their initial interest, however, as many of the team members later confided, it was the vision, plan, and conviction of Amit, Saroop, and the existing team that finally convinced them to join. Amit and/or Saroop attended all the final interviews before selections were finalized. Very soon, they had built up a formidable team of technologically savvy and experienced research engineers from companies, such as, Bajaj Auto, HAL, Thermax, Godrej, Kirloskar, Thapar Group, M.N. Dastur. Subsequently, as they kept growing and adding new industry solutions, the engagement model and recruitment strategy remained the same.

An interesting point to note: there were hardly any sales-related designations in the company—common designations were application executives and application managers. This was consciously done to reflect their corporate aspirations.

Every batch of inductees had to undergo a two-week intensive and structured orientation program where besides technical sessions, lot of emphasis was laid on problem solving and business case studies. Amit took the business sessions, and for people who had attended such sessions, they would know the extent of learning and knowledge that one came out with! As everyone who has worked with Amit knows, he was an exemplary teacher and his sessions were, simply put, enlightening! His sessions were a mix of deep analysis, logical thinking, and intellectual challenges interspersed with real-life business examples, stories, and generous doses of humor.

> *Amit da was probably, the best speaker, I have come across. Once, at Birla Auditorium in Kolkata, I took him for a presentation. A large group of approximately 500 Intellectuals were eagerly listening to him and almost after half an hour, I noticed the whole audience is tuned to him, if he shakes his head the audience does the same. What a great speaker!*
>
> Kashi Samaddar
> Ex-Country Manager, HOPE

He continued his teachings and mentoring at all formal and informal occasions; while on the way to customer meetings, during branch/regional get-togethers and quarterly/annual review sessions. This, coupled with Saroop's intensive review meetings, became the change agent for the techies and laid the foundation for a technically sound, business-savvy team eager to succeed!

Once the team was in place, they absolutely went to town in terms of sales and marketing efforts. All the VAR coverage areas were mapped and strong demand generation programs were implemented. From a large deals perspective and competition standpoint, it was also important for them to build strategic relationships with major computer hardware companies as they did with Wipro, HCL, and IBM. One of the successful customer loyalty cum demand generation program initiated was through industry-specific workshops and seminars, where prospective clients and existing customers were invited. They covered a whole range of topics and held sessions on productivity, tips, and tricks for better usage, heard their pain points, and exposed them to their solutions. This became a very powerful strategy to increase traction with prospects and customers so much, so that every week, there was a workshop being held by them in some town/city of India.

These were the some of the defining strategies, and it paid very rich dividends for HOPE in terms of revenue growth, market share, brand, and customer equity. It also created the biggest differentiator for them in the marketplace—none of their competitors could match the talent pool that they had, and this was reflected in the dominant market position that they were able to achieve. In a span of three years, they became the leading engineering software solution provider in India and the market leader in terms of total number of AutoCAD licenses installed and a customer base of more than 1,000, which was only possible under the leadership (Amit would modestly call it "stewardship") of Amit. It also became the inspiration and launching pad for venturing into engineering consulting and services initially in India, and thereafter globally. As Amit used to say, "So long as you are able to align customer interests and company objectives with your employee's aspirations, success is guaranteed for all the participating stakeholders."

> As a salesperson, it was natural that I met industry heads. The reception to us would change when we mentioned that we are from Sri Amit Dutta Gupta's company. That was the only way we knew about his greatness, because in all individual meetings that we had, he would take great care not to appear unreachable.
> I think that is a hallmark of a great leader—walking just a few steps ahead showing that he can be reached with a little effort. Each one irrespective of his experience would feel the same, meaning he could guide all levels of people with utmost ease.
>
> Ayush Nadimpalli
> CEO, Adroitec Engineering Solutions Pvt Ltd

By 1998–1999, HOPE was recognized as an organization that, along with its "virtual corporation" of 60 dedicated dealers all over India, stood for causing an eruption in PC-CAD usage in every segment and in every corner of India. The principal driver was the full range of products from Autodesk, embellished neatly with third party software configured with AutoCAD to give a vastly effective solution in vertical engineering spaces.

Parallel to an aggressive engagement with corporate and government organizations for doing this, they also nurtured, in the background, a quiet operation for engineering colleges, AICTE, and World Bank–funded implementation agencies, to standardize their products as the de facto standard for technical education.

It took painstaking work for three to four years to achieve this, but it created a bedrock of patronage for today's students/tomorrow's practicing engineers.

Adroitec Information Systems

With proliferation in both the commercial and the education segments, HOPE decided to go beyond the shores of India. With the aggressive thrust of Indian IT into global markets, why would they be left behind?

So, with the decision taken to fan out, a small services company was created. It established the flag firmly in the United States, Japan, Germany, and the United Kingdom. It was a new and heady experience for them, and they were fairly gung ho about global services business accelerating compared to product sales. Everything was falling into place. But unknown to them, a small dichotomy began to affect them negatively—it was the very brand name, "HOPE," that they were so proud of. Unlike Indian customers who could relate emotionally to their company name, the global mind, especially the Western mind, would tend to be literal about the whole thing. "HOPE? Isn't that the name of a charity or an NGO?"

Amit and his team got quite tired explaining the whole genesis of their brand name. So they finally decided to change the company name. Broadly, it would have to be punchy, intellectual, and connote a capability which customers should feel immediately. After a lot of cogitation, they selected "Adroitec" (from "adroit" or "skillful"). For satisfying the registrar of companies, for whom the name would have to be explicitly descriptive of the nature of business, they added "Information Systems." For the last few years, they have promoted this new brand name across all customer and market segments. Today, it is well established, and only old timers mention "HOPE" with nostalgia.

So that's Amit for you. Where will we get another person like him who was so intelligent and innovative, yet humble, full of humanity? A friend and colleague who had helped me think through some of my most difficult moments. Who had very often helped me look at the world in a different light, and had helped me keep my feet firmly on the ground. I was looking forward to spending my retired days continuing some of our discussions that "would change the world." I will miss having him around.

Amit and HOPE Team
Source: Purnima Dutta Gupta.

Amit and Autodesk: International Alliances
Source: Purnima Dutta Gupta.

Arjun Malhotra
Shiv Nadar
Ajai Chowdhry
Bikram Dasgupta
C.P. Gurnani
Sujit Baksi
Pradeep Gupta
Raj Sirohi
Rajeev Sawhney
Mohan Rao
Subroto Bagchi
Sumit Bhattacharya
R.P. Singh
R.K. Gupta
Pradeep Sen
Ravi Thumboochetty
Naren Ayyar
N.R. Panicker
Satyen H. Parikh
S.V. Sriram
Shravani Dang
Suvra Basu
Anup Kumar Ganguly
Ayush Nadimpalli
G.S. Sachdeva
Sushmita Sengupta
Amol Redij
Amit Dutta Gupta

07

7
AMIT—THE LEADER AND MENTOR

Arjun Malhotra and Sushmita Sengupta

Amit was a combination of what great people are made of—a pure heart combined with a great head and mind. He always treated everyone with dignity and believed in upholding the self-esteem and pride of his people and colleagues.

He enjoyed the mentoring process thoroughly and did it with a lot of passion. Anyone who wants to be respected and loved by one and all can draw inspiration from him. I have never seen Amit treat anyone with disrespect, and even in the most frustrating situations, he would at best make a joke out of it. Never did he lose his temper on any one. He could counsel anyone with patience. He had time for anyone, and it is this quality that made people approach him with their problems at work or even in personal life. He commanded respect of all. Amit had given himself the title of "uncle of the nation" as everyone went to him with their tales of woes and he was overloaded with this task. He made immense contribution in the retention of people, which was so necessary in the formative phase of HCL's growth.

Remembering Amit—The Leader and Mentor

In 1986 campaign, our regional managers were all like samurai, I went to see this once. The product launch was scheduled on Monday, the previous day when price list was announced, we went to various locations. So we all spread in multiple locations—Amit went to Calcutta, Arjun went somewhere, Ashok Jain went somewhere else. I said I'll go to Delhi office. On a Sunday at 11 o'clock, when these people had done most of these things, I went and sat right behind; I will give you the name of the person later, who was presenting the price list. After going through all the prices comparing with the tenders, they (sales guys) found that 9 out of 10 tenders we will lose. They (sales team) said, "Best way to handle this price list is to put it into the dustbin." No one knew that I was sitting behind. Regional Manager, Wing Commander Verma said, "So we all know that head office has come up with one more bunch of nonsense and we have to make this work." You know who was presenting the price list from marketing side? It was Neelam Dhawan; she is the head of HP India today. Amit mentored people like her, she was the product manager. Do you know who was the product manager of Unix products in Amit's team?—Vineet Nair (CEO, HCL Technologies Ltd). So we had some real leaders being mentored out here by Amit. Amit was the executive director and they all looked up to him with great respect. He was very patient and trained them all.

Shiv Nadar
Founder, HCL; Chairman, HCL Technologies
and Shiv Nadar Foundation

The treasury of knowledge can enlighten the erudite or the uneducated, no matter the subject. The ELOQUENT Conversationalist capable of engaging the old or young with equal engrossment for long hours at a stretch. I recall the early morning flight I missed, captivated by Amit's talk the whole night. The Understanding Boss when meetings wouldn't get extended beyond "Mental Menopause"— The Philosopher who could relevantly quote from Einstein, Gita, or the scriptures with equal flourish. The Mentor who held the hands of so many and guided them in their professional and personal lives. The Disciplinarian when "BR or UR" was the message for clearing outstandings. The Friend whose humility brought people far less gifted, attracted to, and then glued in his circle ....

Amit—The humorist with the gift of the gab. Can't forget Raman blushing when Amit as the marketing head, defined his position, when the field sales guys were screaming for deliveries. He likened himself to a "pig with 6 tits and 12 piglets nibbling at them."

Mohan Rao
Founder and Director, Spatik Consultants Pvt Ltd

There are moments in your life, when you come across people, experiences, situations, incidents, which create far-reaching impact on your self-development. I have been through some of these situations in life, which had a huge impact in my life so far. Normally your parents start the process. In my case, my mother has been a huge influence in my life. She was an exceptional woman.

Amit da and my relationship with him, both personal as well as professional, was yet another experience in my life which has had a lasting impact. I had first seen Amit da as a debater in RE college, Durgapur, when I was a school student and he was a final year engineering student. I was a keen debater myself and used to always go for debate competitions. I was spellbound to hear this good-looking, ever smiling person talking against the motion and tearing the opposition to pieces smilingly. I never knew then, that I would work with him one day.

Amit da played so many roles in my life. A boss, a mentor, an elder brother, a teacher, a leader—all rolled into one. When we started PCL and Amit da also got into his own, I remember those Sunday morning sessions we used to have in his house. I, Dadan (Dadan Bhai), and he used to sit for hot cups of tea, discussing anything and everything under the sun, including strategies. He always had huge respect for HCL, and so did we. We always felt (and still do) we owe a lot to HCL.

Bikram Dasgupta
Founder and Executive Chairman, Globsyn Group;
Co-Founder, PCL

It is difficult to articulate as the words suddenly blur and seem insufficient when one is asked to describe Amit Dutta Gupta. A man born with the perfect DNA of an inspirational leader and a great motivator, he has been a mentor and a guide for many who had the opportunity to work with him and for him. Amit da had that innate yearning to go beyond the horizon in his pursuit of knowledge, and this very unique identity led him to leave his footprints everywhere the man trotted.

To single down Amit da's forte is an excruciatingly difficult task, this human being has negated the phrase "jack of all, master of none." With positivity inculcated in his approach, he moved from the structured MNC life to an IT market in its infancy where with his thought leadership he created and executed valuable strategies with equivalent effectiveness. Amit da's stay at HCL is one of the exemplary instances, which highlight his pioneering role in the evolution of the IT sector.

A single round of discussion with Amit da would suffice to capture your mind; while on one hand he would intrigue you with his sheer in-depth knowledge about multifarious fields, on the other hand you would be left spellbound by the sheer humility that a man of his stature had imbibed in his very being.

Ajai Chowdhry
Co-Founder, HCL Group

Amit was a person with an open mind and out-of-the-box ideas. When I joined HCL, I had just retired as a wing commander from the Indian Air Force, and I already had Doctorate in Law to my credit. Thus, I could present myself in diverse persona, so he suggested I get business card made in three different styles. He advised that as part of my liaison duties I could meet government officials like in the Ministries, RBI, CCIE, Customs and other Governmental authorities as a retired wing commander; officials in the Department of Electronics, UGC, and university professors as a doctor, and for sundry visits it could be without titles. I effectuated his advice and the options worked really effectively and facilitated my functioning.

G.S. Sachdeva
Ex-HCL, Professor, JNU and NALSAR

Amit da's knowledge is legendary from mythology to western philosophy, to science, and the arts. His language skills and lucid articulation

> *of complex issues, simply explained, brought even the dullest things to life. I remember him explaining the complexities of management as Chanakya wrote about it—Rajniti and Anveekshikee or the art of thinking. Drawing insights from Chanakya, he often said that when opportunities are lost, obstacles definitely arise as well because "success and failure are common on all paths."*
>
> *Amit da was also called Dotty by many, a short from his last name Dutta Gupta. His sense of humor was great, and he was often heard saying that just like our colonial masters, the British, we too have the privilege of double-barreled surnames like Dutta Gupta!*
>
> Shravani Dang
Group Vice President, Avantha Group

Shiv Nadar
Founder, HCL; Chairman, HCL Technologies and Shiv Nadar Foundation

While parting ways with HCL and venturing out on his own, Amit told me that he was very clear that he won't compete with HCL in the marketplace and deal with products and services, only those were not in competition with HCL. He kept his promise throughout his life even in most difficult times in business, when any other person in his place would have given in, no matter whether it was in competition with HCL but that's Amit and his ethics for you, whereas there were others who parted ways with HCL with similar agreement and assurance, broke that at a later stage and became direct competition to HCL ... but not AMIT.

> Every business be built on good management principles and it depends on its leaders to define that. No matter how trying the times may be, a true leader always stands by solid management practice and business ethics. (Sushmita Sengupta and Amol Redij)

C.P. Gurnani
Managing Director and CEO, Tech Mahindra Ltd

When I joined HCL in 1986, as a territory manager, Amit da was the executive director of CAD/CAM Division. He took a chance and performed an example of good management at a very vulnerable part of my life. This spoke high of his personality.

I was working in the Computer Division along with my sales lead, Puneet Pushkarna. During this period, we were assigned a project that had to be delivered over the weekend. These were the direct instructions from the IAS officer in charge, responsible for the completion of the project. Since the product was in its nascent stage, I informed him that though the R&D team was on the job, I was apprehensive if we could deliver the same on time.

Meanwhile, a call from the then director general of NIC changed the situation, and we worked overnight to deliver the project. The then prime minister, late Rajiv Gandhi, was keen to see the product demo. Anish Suri of customer engineering and Rakesh Dodeja, Manager R&D, worked overnight. We were able to deliver this project on time and were even given kudos for the prompt delivery of the same. However, the IAS officer in charge felt offended and complained to Amit da to have me dismissed from HCL for agreeing to work when the director general called, and of not having followed the IAS officer's instructions. To his misfortune, Amit da turned the table and supported my stance. He turned around and told the IAS officer without any KNOWLEDGE of what had happened over the weekend—"... my job is to support CP, he is the man on the ground and in the bargain if I have to lose you as a FRIEND of HCL I would ...."

It did not matter to Amit da whether the problem was work related or personal, Amit da had a view. He had the guts to follow his ideas.

> Leaders always stand alongside their troops, physically or virtually, no matter what. The resulting effect on thought–through execution, not letting the leader down, not letting the organization down, and taking responsibility for one's own actions runs deep. (Sushmita Sengupta and Amol Redij)

Quite unlike now, back in the 1980s, owning a VIP briefcase was like a status symbol, a possession one valued and everybody was keen to acquire. In HCL, only employees at very senior level were awarded such briefcases. The quality of the briefcase depended upon the position of the person holding the office. In one of my conversations with Amit da, I just happened to mention that I would be thrilled to own the type of briefcase he had. He just smiled and gave a nice answer … I had youth and did not need jewelry to show what I am worth. At that point, I was not totally content with the explanation and was still desirous of the briefcase. However, as the months went by, I got over it.

I was pleasantly surprised to receive the same VIP briefcase when Amit da decided to part ways with HCL and start his own company. He had returned his VIP briefcase with instructions to have it delivered to me. He remembered our conversation and my flippant remark of "wishing to have one too!" He indeed had a heart, which was larger than life!

> To remember business-impacting issues is good leadership, to remember promises is better, but to remember trivia and convert them into acts of love and affection is extraordinary. (Sushmita Sengupta and Amol Redij)

Apart from having batted for me professionally, he stepped in for me at a time in my life when I was coming to terms with my father's illness, who I knew was terminally ill. Those were the days when medical insurance/reimbursement wasn't a thing we took for granted along with our salary packages and a medical emergency towards the end of the month meant a lot of scrimping. In that moment of dire need, Amit da stepped in and not only helped me carry out my duty towards the treatment of my father at Batra Hospital (that was the only big private hospital in 1988), but also helped financially ease the way for me and my family. He took care of all the medical expenses that had arisen during my father's illness.

These are things you never get to know about an individual until you find them in situations that fall right into the "above and beyond the call of duty" of one, and this man had risen to them many times over the years. These are just a few instances of Amit da's mettle that I had seen in my time with him.

Across the industry there are many others like me, who try to emulate his qualities now that we are in positions that are recognized as leaders. Of the many lives that have been changed by us serendipitously straying into his orbit, I consider myself lucky to be one amongst those! He gave me opportunities, respect, and freedom to excel.

He was not only a mentor for us, he had groomed us into the people we are today and every life that we touch through our actions at work and elsewhere is tinged with some aspect of our interaction with this worthy gentleman—Amit Dutta Gupta.

> Treating colleagues as family is very difficult these days. It almost gets frowned upon. The impact of advanced, developed-country ways of doing this makes it worse. Great ecosystems are formed by the examples such leaders set. (Sushmita Sengupta and Amol Redij)

Sujit Baksi
Chief Executive, Business Service Group, Tech Mahindra Ltd

When HCL was to reinvent itself with the launch of Busybee, we needed the brightest from B schools to join us to assist us in transformation. Could not think of anyone other than Amit da to go to schools and present the challenge and purpose behind the SMT scheme. He traveled by train in a sleeper class with an associate, irrespective of the position he held in the company. In those days of load shedding, when we started the PPT at IIMC, the lights went off. And Amit da who always presented without a script started his session by saying, "We are here to find some sparks in this darkness." One of those recruits of that batch today runs HCL Technologies (Vineet).

> What would a leader be ... without an eye for a detail and a spark that would ignite several minds at a time? In the times when an organization is undergoing a transformation, and when the brightest minds are waiting to be tapped, it is only the communication and convincing ability that works, and it worked rightly here. (Sushmita Sengupta and Amol Redij)

When we started HOPE, four out of five did not have the money to be put in as share capital. Amit da sold his shares in NIIT and funded the gap. The no self-publicity humility prevented him from reminding anyone of us even once in his lifetime.

> Perhaps, it will be impossible to find a great company that hasn't had effective leaders. A good example of leadership portrays an ability to elevate the confidence of the team without putting self-interest in front, but instead by focusing on the common objective of the association. (Sushmita Sengupta and Amol Redij)

S.V. Sriram
Senior Vice President, Tech Mahindra Ltd

The instance where you taught us and coined the phrase "UR or BR" was truly memorable. This was in March 1983, when the bills receivables were out of control and you had a one-day workshop (on Sunday) to drill it into us—the cost of money and how a 1L receivable adds to ₹80 in interest a day. As a true mentor, you did sight the change in me, in 1985, when I was down emotionally and was contemplating to quit HCL. You spotted the change in me in the meeting room and when we met in the wash room, you said in your most friendly style: "Tiger, something is bothering you and would like to discuss this, can you join me for a drink in the evening?" When we met in the evening you taught me how to convert a threat into an opportunity, asked me to stay back, fight and prove my detractors wrong. Your mentoring was so effective; I went on to win the first sales contest (1985–1986) as best sales manager. I owe that to you Amit da! You are considered guru and a great leader because you used to help your team or even people who used to be in your team without considering any hardship to yourself and with so much good will.

> A leader must be equipped with the skill to train and share knowledge, and it need not be about business every time or in the meeting rooms. Imparting knowledge can be done anywhere, as long as it is methodical, conclusive, and sound enough to change the mindset of a person. Teaching or learning in such manner is far more effective and long lasting. (Sushmita Sengupta and Amol Redij)

The instance which comes to my mind is in January 1986 when you were the head of CAD/CAM, and we were in the Computer Division under Ashok Jain. You were on a visit to Chennai on Monday and were leaving to Delhi on Tuesday evening. When I approached you about the problem I was facing in breaking into TVS Group and being dropped out of shortlist and requested whether you are available for a meeting with Gopal Srinivasan, which could possibly change the course in our tide, you readily agreed and stayed back on Tuesday, to leave on Wednesday. Before the meeting at 4:30 p.m. on Tuesday, you asked me to detail the case so minutely to the extent of drawing the TVS family tree, Gopal's habits (post the detailing you even bought a pack of classic cigarette, which was never your brand). Post the call, we were in the shortlist and you again came to Chennai with Mr Raman on Thursday evening (same week) to close the deal in HCL's favor. (Post this, HCL had 100 percent market share in TVS for quite some time.) That day I learnt detailing from you and several lessons on marketing and sales.

> Mentoring own people is one sure sign of a leader. However, doing so beyond your functionary (which seems an unlikely situation today), and standing by them in the times of need, on ground or off the line, makes you even a greater leader.
> (Sushmita Sengupta and Amol Redij)

R.P. Singh
Founder, Corporate Value Add, UK

I first met Amit da in August 1981, when he interviewed me for the position of an area sales manager in HCL. I used to work for DCM Data Products at that time. A close friend from DCM Data Products had already moved to HCL who referred me to Arjun and Amit da, and perhaps the decision to hire me had already been taken but the questions he asked me during the interview were precise and probing. In my later life, I did so much recruitment in HCL and the questioning technique used by Amit da always formed the backbone of my assessment of candidates I interviewed.

Amit da did a prelaunch sales training when HCL launched the Workhorse range of products. He was so thorough in his preparations, I was amazed. He had, as if, put Philip Kotler (bible for all Marketing MBA students) in actual practice.

Shravani Dang
Group Vice President, Avantha Group

My first meeting with Amit da was on a mild October morning in 1981. It was my very first job interview, so I was obviously nervous and self-conscious.

Amit, the perfect gentleman, rose and greeted me, which really made me feel very comfortable.

During the interview, he never asked the standard questions of those days; "Who is your father?" (As a father in the civil services during the license raj era was considered an asset to the organization.) or "So when do you plan to get married?" or "What will happen when you get pregnant and have children?" He focused on my capabilities, aptitude, and talent. Amit da was nonjudgmental and clear, he was able to get the best out of me. Today after multiple job interviews, I smile a secret smile whenever I am asked about my family background, my marital status, and children. Needless to say, I have never taken on those jobs even if they are with marquee organizations. Amit da taught me that I must be my own person.

I joined later that month as a trainee reporting to Amit da who was always patient, and ready to guide and explain. And yes, it was the right thing to do, what I learnt at HCL with Amit da is priceless and is certainly a key success factor in my career.

It's been many years since my first job interview, but every time I've been asked about a reference check or a reference, I have always gone back to Amit da—each and every job of mine has a written reference from him. These I truly value, for he always focused on my skills, aptitudes, and potential. I have learnt to evaluate people like this as everything else doesn't really matter in the big picture!

> Right set of people are needed to deliver effectively in an organization and one unwise decision can be destructive while hiring people. Right set of precise questions can give you an insight of the person's mindset and thought process and help you map that person to perfectly fit into the big picture of the organization. This approach also becomes a directive for others as the culture of recruiting right set of people. (Sushmita Sengupta and Amol Redij)

R.P. Singh
Founder, Corporate Value Add, UK

Amit's sense of humor. He headed CAD/CAM Division of HCL for some time. While sitting with him in his office during a general crib session (I was not part of CAD/CAM but had a great relationship with Amit da), some ex-professional colleague called Amit da and seemed to be asking how things were. Amit da went on a big crib session with him—"No sales, so Arjun screws me up; if somehow we get an order, deliveries do not take place in time and the customer screws me up; even if deliveries take place, the product doesn't work, and I get further screwed by the customer; finally the money doesn't come in and Shiv screws me up." After all this, the caller apparently asked him in a typical Punjabi way "Amit da, aur kya haal hai?" That brought about the best out of Amit da in chaste Hindi. "The arse is on fire, rest everything is fine."

> Losing your temper with an uproar is an easy way out. However, using the right tone of humor at an apt moment can ease things for you to a far greater extent and save you from any other cyclic cribs. The ability to laugh at yourself and not always at others is a grand virtue to possess. (Sushmita Sengupta and Amol Redij)

Subroto Bagchi
Chairman, MindTree, and best-selling author of business books

Every day the sales guys fanned out, sometimes vanishing for an entire week to return and fill-up expense claims, puff on borrowed cigarettes, and exchange war stories. Most were about crazy prospect meetings. I had my share.

One day, after an entire day of fruitless pursuit, I found myself cold calling at a small factory called MDH, somewhere in West Delhi. The factory was run by a mustached patriarch, who somehow reminded me of old people on virility medication. The man asked me to see him the next morning. Come next day, I dutifully reported, only to be told that *lalaji* was in *bhajan* and that I had to wait. "Where is the *bhajan*?" I enquired. Someone showed me to the shop floor where the smell of coriander and turmeric and rock salt, and a dozen other aroma assaulted the nostrils. There, sitting on the floor with all his workers, the *lala* was singing away his *bhajan*s in a trance-like state. It was, I was told in a whisper, his daily ritual and everyone was required to sing along. Respectfully and mindful of meeting my target, I removed my shoes, kept aside my briefcase, and joined the prayer. That evening, when I returned to office and joined the debriefing session at which everyone had to report the day's trials and tribulations, I talked about my tryst with MDH and how I joined the prospect on the shop floor, getting God on my side before getting the client's cheque. Amit da listened to the entire story and in his classic style summed it all up.

"Comrade Subroto Bagchi, you should know, in hell there is a special place for salespeople."

Arjun Malhotra
Co-Founder, HCL; Ex-Chairman of Headstrong's Board of Directors

There was the cycle manufacturer in Ludhiana who told Amit that his biggest problem was accounts payable. He had to keep his suppliers happy, else something small not delivered on time would stop his production line.

After doing a detailed system study (as was the norm then), we recommended he buy our two-floppy machine (HCL 8C Level 20). To Amit's surprise, the client wanted to know how many *chakka*s (floppies) were in the machine that Amit's team had sold to Vardhman. That was a three-floppy (Level 30) system.

Then, said the customer, "I want one with four *chakka*s!" And he was sold an HCL 8C Level 44. The trip back from Ludhiana to Delhi was fun, with Amit trying to explain to his sales trainee that this was not the norm and that this was not how top-of-the-line computers were sold!

R.K. Gupta
President, Neilsoft; Ex-Country Manager, Autodesk India

When Amit da almost fell off the chair ... Amit da was travelling with me to Ludhiana, and we called on the owner of a company to close the deal. The owner was a typical *Sardar*. Amit, in his normal professional and sophisticated way, was trying to suggest him to go in for a configuration which was called Level 2. Let it suffice to say that it consisted of two round storage devices. When Amit went on for five minutes, the owner just looked at him and announced in his typical way in Punjabi that he wanted the machine with three *chakka*s and that was final, and whether Amit had any problem with that? Amit da found it so bizarre and humorous that he almost fell off his chair. This incident stayed with him for life and he would often recount this.

> Amit was one of the pioneers in building the brand HCL for SME segment. Each sales call is different and not always follow the seven-step selling process while creating newer markets. Yet the sales team got order, perhaps by impressing the prospect's mindset. Amit would appreciate the accomplishment, however would also wittily communicate the approach adopted wasn't right for selling top-of-the-line computers. (Sushmita Sengupta and Amol Redij)

Subroto Bagchi
Chairman, MindTree, and best-selling author of business books

Amit da was the ultimate strategist and sense maker; his vast knowledge of history, literature, economics, and technology made him one of a kind. I have not met a better read man in my life. He could quote from Sartre and Marx as if he had them inside of him. His affection for people who he knew was so huge, they returned to him long after paths changed. That included me. When confronted with imminent departure from my failing first venture, Project 21, I reached out to him and he did not take a moment to understand my situation. He picked up the phone, spoke to Rajendra Pawar at NIIT, and got me the introduction. Though NIIT made me an offer subsequently, I chose to join Wipro instead and life took me elsewhere. But he gave me the introduction when I needed it; he had my safety net stretched below me when my venture failed.

> What would be a better enticement in life than having made people confide and find an anchor in you in times of crises? People saw a promise in Amit and an assurance that their worries won't be left unattended. (Sushmita Sengupta and Amol Redij)

Pradeep Sen
Independent Consultant; Ex-Managing Director, NCR Corp;
Ex-Senior Director, SAP India

Work with the Troops

Amit da was asked to help us with the preparation for a bid to ONGC, which was the biggest opportunity at that time. He led the entire proposal, making and benchmarking exercise, which went on for days and nights. The proposal became a reference material for the company. Amit da converted pages of data and technical material into a very well-written document. It read like a passionate story with sheer power of language. He was a master craftsman when it came to word-smithing. Benchmarking was a very elaborate exercise, and we were able to achieve performance numbers that step by step improved by magnitudes that were unimaginable. Throughout this period, Amit da stayed in the office or the R&D at nights, resting occasionally on a table. We followed him with endless cups of tea and cigarettes, all taking the exercise like a war mission. Valuable lessons were learnt at that time:

1. Took complete ownership of the engagement; though it was not his area of responsibility, it was important for the company—think company first and ownership.
2. Worked with every one as a member of a team with no hierarchies, no departments, no groups, but division of tasks—brought the people together as one team.
3. He played the roles of a motivator and caretaker. He talked to everyone regularly, told them to stop and rest so that they could remain alert and fresh, made sure they had food, refreshments, and he took detailed status of each person's work—his presence, therefore, spurred the

team to put relentless efforts, never satisfied because they believed they could continuously raise the bar. This is really the role of leaders when they get everyone to pull in the same direction and give everything they have got.

4. He always planned for resources, knowing that at night all shops remained closed and no services were available. I remember his famous quote: "No battle should be lost for want of a horse shoe nail." So true, big things get done because of collective attention while small and mundane activities slip through the cracks. Very important lesson. Also, a manager has to make available resources to his team.

> Responsibility of a leader is to keep team morale high at all times, while accomplishing the task with meticulous planning in terms of identifying skills, assigning tasks, managing resources, and breaking the barriers of hierarchy if need be. (Sushmita Sengupta and Amol Redij)

Planning, Presenting, Idea Development

Now I will take you to the time I spent in the CAD/CAM Division. Following reorganization, Amit da became my boss. It was still a new area, and I picked up many tricks from him that time that I use even now. Amit da had the unique quality of doing the blue sky vision bit and systematically breaking it down to the lowest detail very quickly. He used to say, "Look at the problem from 40,000 feet and then come down to the trenches" and he used an expression that remained implanted in our minds—"from the sublime, to the ridiculous"—leaders have to constantly straddle both extremes.

Those days software had to be imported against a license, and I still remember my meeting with Dr Seshagiri, at NIC, along with Amit da. We prepared the most well thought-out presentation for importing AutoCAD licenses, how it will change the way designing is done, how it will increase productivity, and consequently elevate the nation's status as a country with engineering capabilities. The process of preparation under Amit da's guidance was an enjoyable and enriching experience. Good news was Dr Seshagiri cleared our license application, but not without an agitated and scathing outburst—"how we all had scant respect for the country's foreign exchange reserves." We know that was a necessary posturing.

As a marketer, Amit da always promoted the idea about creating solution values. In those days when computers were sold like expensive boxes, he emphasized innovative use of this expensive resource that could give the customer far-reaching possibilities and gains. This is a lesson that is as valid today, as it was then. In an ever changing world of rapid commoditization, differentiation through innovative thinking is the only way to market any product or service.

> The ability to envision a possible outcome with a strong conviction makes an effective leader. This requires one to perceive an end-to-end holistic view along with the infinitesimal details and "out-of-the-box" approach—as it prepares you to foresee every step and keep a vigil. (Sushmita Sengupta and Amol Redij)

Sumit Bhattacharya
SVP and Head of Global Marketing at Sutherland Global Services

Amit ... the inspirational leader who made the extraordinary seem commonplace and could extract amazing insights from the seemingly mundane.

It is September 1984, Rajiv Gandhi has announced the liberalization of import policy that included computer kits. It meant that in a few months, IBM-compatible PCs will be available in India. HCL was caught with a huge inventory of Workhorse 3B systems (at that time India's best-selling PC) that had to be either sold almost instantly or the company faced virtual extinction.

The twist in the tale was not only that we had to sell the machines; but we also had to collect the 100 percent payment—*in advance*.

The HCL mantra was "Make It Happen"—and the man for the job was Amit.

Those days I was heading operations in Chennai and that's where I saw him in action for the first time. When he walked into the conference room, it was as if a long-lost and much loved elder brother had arrived. People crowded around him and talked in such a familiar way that it was hard to believe that most of them had never met him before!

The first few minutes of the meeting were littered with laughs and smiles ... then it got serious.

Amit gave a background that seamlessly wove a bewildering variety of subjects, ranging from the future of computers and globalization to the dire straits of Indian cricket and the wonders of total football and what a travesty it was that Holland didn't win the 1974 Football World Cup.

And then in a grim reaper voice he intoned, "Gentlemen, the situation is simple: either BR (Bills Receivable) is there or UR (You Are) is there ... so not only do you have to sell all the computers, you also have to collect all the money—in advance." ... slightly fractured English, but totally solid message. The reaction ranged from the confused to the confounded—Is he threatening us hissed a sales executive to his next-seat neighbor? ... Is he serious? ... How does he expect us to collect 100 percent in advance?

Once the sibilance and incredulous expressions had subsided into sullen silence, Amit looked around with seemingly secret amusement and said, "Hands up all those who think I am mad?" When there was no response he asked, "Hands up all those who want to murder me?" Every hand shot up and the room was wracked by laughter.

Over the next two hours, he role-played numerous sales scenarios where the sales team tried to take revenge by playing ridiculously bolshie buyers ... but every time after a few minutes, he would prove to everyone that it could be done ... you could persuade people to pay 100 percent—*in advance*.

Fast forward another 90 days—and the crisis is over. The inventory is sold and the cash is in the bank.

> **Crisis and Recovery Management**
>
> Many a times, most managers today set boastful targets without any vision or action plan. This is often followed by stinkers to poke and push, which create a feeling of insecurity and anxiety among the people. On the contrary, the mark of a true leader is not only to convey "what to do" but also show "how to do it," and eventually get it done in a hassle-free manner. In order to envision how to achieve the desired result, one should also possess exceptional competence to counter any crisis situation by backing it up with a solid recovery plan. And all this need not always be in an authoritarian tone, but can also be conveyed by connecting with people in a responsive and humorous level. (Sushmita Sengupta and Amol Redij)

Arjun Malhotra
Co-Founder, HCL; Ex-Chairman of Headstrong's
Board of Directors

I remember the days when I used to visit Calcutta to meet prospects and customers. We had the HCL office on the 17th floor of Chatterjee International Centre. Thanks to the frequent power cuts there, Amit Dutta Gupta and I would walk up and down those 17 floors two to three times every day.

I remember, on one of those visits the entry to the building was closed because of a "gherao." People inside could not come out and those outside could not go in. We needed a set of loaded floppies (8″ ones, in those days) to give a customer demonstration. Amit stopped all the traffic on Chowringhee, while I collected the floppies in bubble wrap that had been thrown out of the 17th floor window. Never to give up/leadership skill/hands-on in crisis.

> Story of a pioneer of the Indian IT industry (Arjun Malhotra) and a marketing genius (Amit Dutta Gupta) who together were pivotal in setting up the industry, not just an organization, along with others. They were the ones who led by example and had an intense desire to perform, irrespective of at what level. This is a classic case that exhibits the passion and determination of effective leaders to get hands-on and control things as the need be, instead of just delegating or procrastinating. (Sushmita Sengupta and Amol Redij)

When Amit was the head of marketing at HCL, he and Late Dadan Bhai (in the East) had a special working relationship. With Dadan's high-risk thinking and Amit da's practicality, we had many interesting stories. Lots of them are part of HCL folklore that fresh trainees were told.

Once, a day before Diwali, Amit left for Calcutta because Dadan wanted him there for a big presentation at Bhubaneswar the day after Diwali. Dadan said there was a lot to prepare, and so they would drive overnight by taxi. During that Diwali night, as they headed to Bhubaneswar, a detailed briefing followed. And Amit figured he had little or no role to play in the presentation. "So why am I here?" he asked. "Good English," Dadan said, "We need good English." Only good-natured Amit would have found that amusing, and he enjoyed telling me about it when he returned to Delhi.

> Amit usually remained unaware of his own worth and for what people looked up to him. Despite it being an auspicious Diwali day, Amit was there to help out Dadan Bhai who too considered work as a priority on that day. It is this attitude of considering work as worship made them great leaders, quite evident from the fact that Dadan Bhai later rose to become the founder and chairman of PCL. (Sushmita Sengupta and Amol Redij)

I worked very closely with Amit on the "Breaking the Common Computer Myths" campaign that catapulted HCL from being just another computer company to the leader of the pack. This was my first and only experience of primary marketing, where we created and addressed a virgin market of computers for First Time Users (FTUs)—people who had never thought they could afford or use a computer. That market segment really excited Amit da, and he did a fantastic job on that campaign. The first ad tag line was: "A computer is so simple, even a typist can operate it." This was immortalized in HCL by late S.N. Chaudhry's comment to a prospective customer at a road show: "Why a typist ... even you can operate it."

> Armed with extra-sensory perception and meticulous strategizing, Amit could visualize an opportunity and turn it into a success. His completely out-of-the-box thinking to tackle the computer industry like a consumer industry was an absolute game changer at that time. The industry remains indebted to Amit's gift of consumerism of computers. (Sushmita Sengupta and Amol Redij)

> **Amit on Dadan Bhai**
>
> *Even at the crematorium, seeing Dadan Bhai so still, I felt that any moment he would grin and give me his signature: "Guptaji, as usual, you've got it wrong!" The trouble with Dadan Bhai was that he was much larger than life, too far ahead of his time, and he had a heart which was much larger than his head.*
>
> *Standing there at the crematorium, I thought that in a different day and age, I would have given Dadan Bhai a different send off that of a Viking warrior that he was. I would have put him in full armor on his warship, taken it out to sea, and set it on fire, on a happy journey to Valhalla. Knowing Dadan Bhai, he's landed there all right, with horns filled with heady wine for his friends.*
>
> Amit Dutta Gupta

Suvra Basu
Director and Member of the Board of Axis Inc.

I started my professional career in 1991 with Amit da, having been recruited through a campus interview at IIT Kharagpur, and distinctly remember my first day at HOPE with him taking my first "class" on transaction automation, programming techniques interspersed with anecdotes on the evolution of Information Technology in India. Amit da was the CEO of HOPE, and I was just a marketing trainee taking my first steps in the corporate world. My final semester project completion dates in IIT clashed with the Orientation and Training Programme scheduled for the newly hired trainees at HOPE, and because of this I had to join late and missed out on the normal training sessions. Since the formal training program had been completed when I joined, it was Amit da who took the responsibility of providing training to us (there were two of us). The training period was rigorous, yet informal with plenty of real-life case studies but what struck me was his uncanny and seemingly effortless capability of decomposing complex issues and problems into a series of simple and elegant dependencies and relationships. One of his favorite quotes was General Suvorov's famous saying—"Train hard, fight easy," and in the first two weeks of training, he had inculcated a life-long practice in me.

My first assignment at HOPE was exciting with frenzy of action and ideas—we had introduced a product called Palmtop, which, in my view, was ahead of its time in India and involved high level of concept and application-based selling, an area which was Amit da's forte. While it was a tough and challenging task, to say the least, as we had to pursue prospects during the day and work on application programming during the evenings sometimes stretching late into the night, however, for a rookie like me, it was an invaluable experience being exposed to different industries and applications. For example, in the morning we would be pitching to a lipstick warehouse owner in Sadar Bazar, Old Delhi, and in the afternoon presenting to director, IT at Food Corporation of India for a VT 100-based food grain wagon tracking system. In all this, I still recall the review and planning discussions with Amit da where he would lead us to analyze business requirements and client expectations through questions, examples, and sometimes similes, a process which I follow even today in my reviews.

> It is very essential to ensure that the company's vision percolates down the line so that people are well aligned and deliver better. Amit achieved this through interactive training and knowledge sharing sessions packed with real case studies to make it more impactful. (Sushmita Sengupta and Amol Redij)

We had just started our operations in Bangalore, where I was posted to build and manage CAD business for South India. We had been trying to engage a major quasi-government organization into accepting Autodesk products as their CAD platform of choice for quite some time, but were unable to get through to the final decision maker. It was frustrating for me and our team, and in desperation, I called Amit da and requested him to visit Bangalore to help close the deal. He asked me to explain in detail the situation and having heard our brief, he said we could easily handle it ourselves and to keep pursuing it. "By the way, do you know the postman & the family Alsatian situation?" "NO." He went on to explain,

> "You see, when the Alsatian sees the postman coming to the gate and dropping stuff in a box or someone from the family coming up to the gate to receive, he does not usually bark as he sees him quite frequently. Yet if the postman decides to enter the gate and ring the bell to deliver an important package, the Alsatian starts barking and chasing him. That is because the Alsatian feels that the postman is welcome to the home, but only up to the gate and not beyond. So you see my friend, you just have to earn the trust beyond the gate with the potential customer and the situation would be different."

We went on to win the customer, but these words have stuck with me throughout the years and still guide me in my career.

During one of his visits to the United States, the CTO of one of our major clients had invited Amit da for dinner at his home, in upstate New York, and being the local representative, I tagged along. It was a rare honor being invited to a client's home in the United States, but we were understandably a bit nervous about the event. However, as I expected, within half-an-hour of exchanging pleasantries, I watched as Amit da regaled our hosts discussing the intricacies of British and US literature on one hand and the impact of US currency on US–India relations on the other. The next time I met the CTO, not only he was all in awe but also wanted to bounce ideas on his business issues with Amit da.

> Handling difficult customers can be frustrating at times. Effective leaders know how to easily align the mindset of their people to overcome demanding situations and make them view it from a different perspective, which gets the people back into action. (Sushmita Sengupta and Amol Redij)

In times of uncertainty and setbacks, he was the calming and reassuring face for all of us. I remember, in a span of three years, our Noida factory was burgled twice and during that period, I was posted in Kolkata and was also supporting our Jamshedpur operations. There was a sense of despondency and gloom amongst many of us as to the future of the company, and I was concerned too. Amit da was visiting Kolkata on a business trip, and I distinctly remember the reassuring yet determined phone call to me advising me not to worry and that all of us would ride the waves together. There were times when self-doubt would creep in, and it was the calm and motivating assurance from Amit da that would keep us going. It was not just words, but the commitment in his actions that made so many of us to carry on when the all one wanted to do was to give up! He believed in people and passionately nurtured them and worked hard to unleash their potential.

> Tidal hardships are a part of any business. While it certainly worries the leader, such situations scare employees the most. A leader has to then sensitively undertake two fronts of managing the crises, and also keep the morale of the employees high. (Sushmita Sengupta and Amol Redij)

When it was decided to open our US subsidiary in early 2001, I was given the responsibility to set up and manage the operations. On the day of departure, amidst the last minute hullabaloo, I went up to his office and asked him if he had any last minute advice for me as this was a major initiative and step forward for our company. With a hug and a firm handshake, he said, "I wish you the very best and in terms of advice, I can only share with you some of the principles which have helped and enriched my life and hope it would do the same to you too." I strive to follow them to this day.

- Do what you think is best for the company.
- Don't forget to have fun and be not afraid of making mistakes.
- Evaluate situations and people on their innate strengths and merit. Treat people as the most precious assets and nurture them. One advice I recall was Einstein's quote: "If you measure the performance of a fish on its ability to climb a tree, it will spend its whole life believing that it is stupid."

> Amit would occasionally impart such learning—very concise and of supreme importance. (Sushmita Sengupta and Amol Redij)

Anup Kumar Ganguly
Global Director, Customer Life Cycle Management, Emptoris, an IBM Company

There was once a problem with one of our projects and Amit da called me into his room to discuss about it. When I went there, he asked me to sit down and explain to him in detail about the problem. After I had explained to him the situation and also shared my frustration of not being able to find an appropriate solution, he asked me, "Anup, have you ever heard of the LAO principle?" I was completely caught off guard at that moment and had to sheepishly admit that indeed I didn't know about it. He then got up from his chair and went to the white board hanging in his room to explain to me about the principle. In order to explain, he drew a rough sketch of a bridge, then some mountains, followed by a forest, and ultimately a river. He then made two points/dots, one at the starting point of the bridge and the other after the river. He then asked me, "Assume that you are at this starting point before the bridge and you have to reach the point beyond the river as that's your destination. How will you go about doing that?" I was a little dumbfound and at a loss to comprehend where he was driving at, and I asked him the same. He then patiently went on and explained, "If you look at this drawing, you will find quite a few hurdles that need to be overcome in order for you to be able to reach your destination, but if you think of all those hurdles at one go then you may not even attempt to undertake the journey, isn't it?" I agreed. He then said, "Then why do you consider all of them at one go? Why not focus on the immediate one and think about the second one only after you have overcome the first hurdle?" His logic made absolute sense and I agreed with him. He then went on to say, "This is called the LAO principle (least achievable objective). When confronted with complex situations or problems, always use this principle and you will be able to get a solution more easily." That day I learnt a very valuable lesson from Amit da on how we can turn our problem situations into goals or objectives to be achieved, instead of getting bogged down by them. From then till now, I have used the LAO principle a countless number of times, both in my professional and personal life, and I must say that it has worked for me most of the times, barring a few where I myself was at fault for not having made the correct or most accurate assessment of a situation—addressing a problem in a methodical manner, using the LAO principle.

> Amit had a mind of a genius. He would approach a problem meticulously and arrive at a solution methodically. Another very prime characteristic about him was his zest to share his knowledge, and he did so at every opportunity he got and always primed his people with problem-solving methods.
> (Sushmita Sengupta and Amol Redij)

Amit da always had the zeal to try new things and gain new experience, and he did his best to enjoy them to the utmost. I remember one incident when he went on a visit to Japan. After coming back, I got a call from his cabin on my extension and he called me in his trademark style, "*Batsa, chole esho. Tomake kichu daikhabo* (Son, come down. I want to show you something)." When I went down, I found him in the office pantry waiting with a couple of other colleagues. Once he saw me come in, he explained to us that he had brought back some Japanese green tea with him and would teach us how to prepare and drink the tea. He then with a lot of meticulousness proceeded to prepare the tea, and while doing that he took us through each of the steps in detail to ensure we too learn the process. After he was done, he handed each of us a cup, while he took one for himself. Those of you who know about Japanese green tea and the way it is prepared will know it's quite different and requires somewhat of an elaborate process than the way we are usually familiar with in the Indian context, and the way Amit da went about explaining the entire process was in itself enlightening as well as enriching.

> Amit, though a very mature and sagacious man, had a child-like mind always full of curiosity and eagerness to learn. He would explore things, reason out things, and gather knowledge from everything around him. However, he never kept that learning to himself and would enrich everyone around him, unlike what some many would do to show their supremacy. (Sushmita Sengupta and Amol Redij)

Ayush Nadimpalli
CEO, Adroitec Engineering Solutions Pvt Ltd

There were those moments where Amit da would put on his headmaster hat. He would ask some mathematical questions, which of course none of us had the answers to. Some of the questions that he asked were: "Make a formula for the number of hexagons on a football .... Sales man's folly, golden ratio, and golden triangle. We would try and create an excuse and escape whenever we saw him getting into the mathematical mood."

> Amit had innate love and admiration towards mathematics and problem solving. He would devise problems and solve them. There were moments when he would present problems to his people and ask them to find solutions. Though it seemed to be a grilling exercise, in a way Amit was sharpening his own and his people's skills that would equip him and others to undertake any intricacy in all walks of life. (Sushmita Sengupta and Amol Redij)

As a leader, he had a great personal relation and I was one of the many touched by his fatherly affection. He would remember the names of my entire family not after I became a business head, but even when I was a sales executive. And the last time I met him, which was last month, he asked me the name of my new born and as always gave the compliment ... "Nice Name" and blessed saying, "May he become a worthy son!"

> Amit was highly respected as a leader for his quality of touching people's lives both on professional and personal fronts. With extremely balanced qualities of a dedicated professional and humane slant, Amit indeed was an illustrious example of a leader. (Sushmita Sengupta and Amol Redij)

Naren Ayyar
Senior IT Management position with HCL, IBM, DELL, and Apple

My thoughts go back to the HCL days in 1980–1981 when he had a cubicle on the 8th floor of Siddharth, Nehru Place. He was heading the marketing team, which included Doc (Dr A.K. Dey) and Neelam Dhawan (then Marwah). We used to come to Delhi for regular performance reviews. After a session with Shiv, the mind was numbed and jumping from the 8th floor was a serious option. One often met Amit da in the narrow corridor and got quickly pulled into his cabin. Over cups of lemon tea and topics that ranged from philosophies of Karl Marx and Bertrand Russell to Rabindra Sangeet by Pinaki Bondhopadhyaya and Baul songs of Bankura to Coca-Cola's marketing strategies, one regained a zest for life once again. He was an adored leader and motivator par excellence; nothing less can unwind one from a review with Shiv in a couple of hours. His contribution in building HCL is next only to that of Shiv and Arjun.

> Motivational exuberance is one aspect that always makes a person seamlessly transform into an operational leader. Amit possessed this incomparable trait along with excellent communication skills that made him easily connect with people. A virtuous leadership achieves such stature surpassing all barriers of age, hierarchy, and class. (Sushmita Sengupta and Amol Redij)

I never reported to him directly, yet I learnt most from watching him and listening to him. There were many fine English speakers in HCL management. But when Amit da spoke, the communication happened at a totally different level and everyone stopped to listen. I remember Dadan Bhai mentioning an incident at IIT Kharagpur when they were hosting an intercollegiate debate competition. Many participants with Doon/Sherwood schooling spoke with élan. Finally, a boy from NIT Durgapur rose to speak, when most in the audience were getting up to leave. With the first five sentences, he riveted them to their seats and walked away with the "Best Speaker" prize. His name was Amit Dutta Gupta.

> A true leader believes in convincingly getting the message across at the required appropriate level. What is essential for this is the power of knowledge and meticulous observation skills that help you to calibrate yourself to communicate accordingly. (Sushmita Sengupta and Amol Redij)

I had the privilege of being his neighbor for many years, residing in the flat just below his, in Kaveri Apartments, Alaknanda. On most weekends and festivals, such as Holi, HCL colleagues will drop in and we will gather around Amit da. He never went to a business school or had a formal management degree, but his grasp of strategy, economics, and finance was amazing—leave alone marketing, his forte. He would explain the pricing strategies of HCL with the economic theories of efficiencies of scale and scope. He would draw an MES graph on the back of a scrap of paper and explain how to create barriers for competition through your cost efficiencies and differentiation strategies, quoting fluently from Peter Drucker, Michael Porter, and other management gurus. And he combined his insights and wisdom with a rare sense of understated humor. His observation of various forms of HCL's "Jugaad" had most of us in splits. He would mimic a Punjabi SME customer for 8C (*ekku Chakke di gaddi*) and a Parsi builder in Mumbai who was sold the AMC before the machine.

> It may be a broad perception today that having a "premier-management-institute" tag helps a great deal in becoming a successful leader. While that aspect cannot be denied, opinion is not completely true. There were times when people did not attend such institutes, and yet became great business leaders. Amit is a realistic example of this. Quest for acquiring knowledge and process of continuous learning can still make you a great leader. (Sushmita Sengupta and Amol Redij)

N.R. Panicker
Chairman and Founder, Accel Ltd

Actually, I had very few interactions with Amit during my HCL days, in fact just one or two interactions while he was handling CCG (Customer Care Group), which made me an admirer of Amit.

When I was trying to launch my start-up company, Accel, after resigning from my job with HCL, I thought of taking Amit's inputs on my business idea. So during my visit to Delhi, I visited him at his residence, in Alakananda. I had a self-made project plan in a 10-page write-up. I gave it to him, and asked him to read and make comments. He went through the report in 10 minutes and told me not to think twice before starting the venture, and that my report was much better than what he could make and the contents of that report had shown that I knew all about what I wanted to do. This comment of his gave me tremendous confidence and motivation, and that was one of the turning points in my life. He was a real mentor and motivator. After five years of my entrepreneurial journey, I visited his office on one of my visits to Delhi. I told him that my startup had grown to a ₹10 crore company, and that my being an introvert and not able to make good sales pitch is one negative factor for my company's growth. Then he told me that it is not at all a weakness, but it is strength. As you visit your offices, make it a practice to visit one or two clients. Client is not looking for any sales pitch or "selling" from the top man. Just a visit and a few pleasantries will give the assurance that you are interested in their business. So don't bother about the weakness at all!! So I started practicing that after that meeting.

> People often perish when there is no vision. However, only having vision does not necessarily translate into success. The competence to see through a hypothetical situation and deem its output as a success or failure is what a true leader should possess. This is achieved by channeling the powers to quickly identify the dimension of several business variables, which gives a purposeful perspective to accomplish the desired objective. (Sushmita Sengupta and Amol Redij)

There was another memorable incident when Amit had visited my office in Chennai when I had suggested that, probably, HOPE can be merged with Accel. I was actually keen to have him alone from the top management team of Hope, though I didn't mention that to him. I got surprised when during the entire conversation, he was always advocating for the team and the partners in his business, and how it is important to keep their interest in the front and that it can only be with all of them together in the new merged entity. So the discussion could not be followed up further. But this incident showed his character, and the level of his integrity and commitment to the team.

> Life presents every sort of temptation to take the easy way out. In such cases, it is only your value system that safeguards you from giving into such lure. In business, especially when in the commanding position, it is easy to become an opportunist and think of personal growth. Would that make a good leader? Napoleon said, "A leader is a dealer in hope." How then can a leader deal for self when hopes of many are riding on him? (Sushmita Sengupta and Amol Redij)

Satyen H. Parikh
Founder, Team Talent & Empowerment Consultants, Business Coach and Mentor to Established and Start-up Companies in Information Technology

ADG was asked to move in to Mumbai and take control of an otherwise pretty volatile situation in terms of business and overall regional governance ... this was in 1982 (I joined in August 1982.) and ADG came to Mumbai somewhere around October 1982.

The four to five odd months which he spent stabilizing the regional office gave me and another very good friend and colleague (Sanjit Sengupta) enormous opportunity to work directly with him (though this was our first job and we were designated as installation coordinators). Seeing the energy, positive outlook, and personal affinity with which he was addressing the tricky situations gave me immense learning. He used to reminisce about his Coca-Cola days of pushing the cart and delivering ... anecdotes to us with the clear message that no work you do is menial, and the objective is to focus on doing it right—the first time.

> If you are the only one, would that make you a leader? It is the people who create the leader. Thus, it is prudent to understand the importance of people and have skills to resonate with your people. It is just not important for the leader to know the route, but should also walk the path and show the way.
> (Sushmita Sengupta and Amol Redij)

Pradeep Gupta
Chairman and Founder, Cyber Media Group

I joined HCL, and we were immediately put through an intensive training program. Towards the end of the program, there were classes on systems applications and technology and because I had such a background, I was asked to take a few classes. I found one senior person attending the classes who sat and absorbed like a student. That same evening, I came to realize that he was going to be my boss in Kolkata. He knew it all along but never asserted himself. He always knew what to do in what role.

> It may be a common scene in today's business world where some have a perception that "bosses know everything," and hence feel uncomfortable or inferior when confronted with apt knowledge from a subordinate. On the contrary, Amit was open to knowledge at all times. Continuous learning, no matter from where it comes, was a munificent trait of any successful leader, and Amit was a real-life example of that. (Sushmita Sengupta and Amol Redij)

There was this customer who would take the smallest of matters with the highest amongst the hierarchy. Once he wrote about his issues to Amit da and CCed the entire top brass of HCL on it. Amit da called his secretary and asked him to write to everybody that the letter need not be replied. The secretary had sent the letter to everybody marked on the CC, including the customer himself. I don't know whether it was a genuine mistake or Amit da actually gave incomplete instructions, but from that time onward, the customer stopped complaining to everybody.

> Disputes or issues are common things when they come to daily operations in business. However, not all need equal importance for resolutions. Practicing good management regimes enables one to ably sift between disruptions that need significant attention and issues those are petty. True leaders are not only able to easily identify such nuances, but also foresee the outcomes with confidence and direct their people accordingly. (Sushmita Sengupta and Amol Redij)

Once it rained cats and dogs and many other animals in Kolkata. The office was in Chowringhee and Amit da was staying in Jodhpur Park. But he decided to prove a point that you could reach the office whatever be the conditions. He and his Marketing Deputy S. Majumdar (Benu) waded through long stretches of flowing river on Kolkata streets to reach the office. Only four people landed in the office that day. I was one of them, as I had locked the office the previous night. Of course, I was much closer to Chowringhee. I was in Camac Street.

Anyways, four of us could not have done any work, and we decided to move to Jodhpur Park to play on bridge until the rain subsided. But we had no playing cards. On the way, we found one small little kiosk selling cigarettes, candies, etc., and voila; he had playing cards. We bought it, waded our way to Jodhpur Park and realized the cards had nude pictures on the inside. Amit da refused to play. We did manage to convince him in an hour's time that this was the only way that we could last the 48 hours of rain.

Amit da issued a verbal circular that I was not supposed to crack any jokes till 5:00 p.m. I guess it was because lot of us youngsters would waste time in bull sessions. But very often at 5:05 he would come and say, "Okay, so let's have some stories."

> While it is apt to be a disciplinarian when in the commander's position, striking a chord with the people using the right blend of humor is also equally important. Connecting with people in such manner makes them feel at ease, thereby increasing their confidence in the leadership, and hence boosting their productivity level.
> It is very essential to realize this aspect when performing a leader's role. (Sushmita Sengupta and Amol Redij)

We had a very important presentation to be made to a potential customer and Murphy's law kicked in few hours before the demonstration. A lot of stuff on the periphery was working, but the critical core was not. So we all got together to work out a script where we would show whatever was working and at the right cue simulate a power failure. Kolkata was amongst the first cities in India to be hit by power cuts, load shedding in the 1980s. Therefore, we did have a good excuse. Of course, whatever was working was shown in such a professional manner that the customer was convinced that the rest worked and we got the order.

> A leader is identified by the results, and not the attributes alone. Results may best be displayed by thinking of an apt resolution strategy and delivering it at the appropriate moment with zealous involvement. Taking up such an approach will instinctively make your people look up to you as a leader, wouldn't it? (Sushmita Sengupta and Amol Redij)

We had this very important software demo to be done at NSSO, Delhi, and Kolkata region had taken the task of developing the same. At night, my team and I gave final touches to the programs and left office. We were shocked when we arrived next morning. The building staff of Chatterjee International Centre had gone for an indefinite strike and were not letting any of the office people go in. Under the leadership of Amit da, we worked out a plan. One of our office peons used to stay in the office itself and, therefore, his movement in and out was allowed, but he used to be searched each time by the strikers. We finally asked him to tightly pack the floppies, put them loosely in a soft plastic bag, worked out torch signals and asked him to throw the bag from 11th floor of Chatterjee International to Chowringhee. The signals were most essential to ensure that the packet did not fall on anybody's head as Chowringhee is a busy street. We were successful and got the floppies all intact, which were then taken to Delhi for the NSSO demo.

> Leadership is grooming your people and growing up with them as well. It is essential to make them feel that you are one part of them. There should be no distinction, especially at the time of crises, when working to achieve a common objective. Harness your leadership skills by getting hands-on with the job. It will build up a confidence among your people and inspire them to emulate you. (Sushmita Sengupta and Amol Redij)

R.K. Gupta
President, Neilsoft; Ex-Country Manager, Autodesk India

Amit da could switch easily across different levels. He was as much at ease in discussions with an intellectual as with a rookie. It was so difficult to fathom the man who could in a pee break, during an intense/heated discussion, crack a semi non-veg joke and then get back to business. While he projected the image of a serious person, somewhere there was a child in him. How many of us would believe that he jumped off the table in a cramped cabin on the 5th floor, Siddharth, Nehru Place, to come out and then bunked the office with a couple of us to go for a movie!!

> Does a strict authoritarian make a good leader? Perhaps yes, but not always. Leader is someone whom people should follow voluntarily. And this is achievable by connecting with people in the right manner, not only at an intellectual level but also at emotional level. Inspiring leaders conduct formally and informally, as the situation demands, with their people and, thus, know how to hold the people together. (Sushmita Sengupta and Amol Redij)

If Amit da did not exist, it would have been almost necessary to invent him. An enigmatic guy, he was almost mythical. He was a walking encyclopedia. An atheist who knew all about religions and Gods. One who knew all about music, dance, drama, literature ... I recall the time when I wanted to lease out a particular house, here in Bangalore, but the landlord was a tough nut to crack. It was a coincidence that Amit da and I went to meet him (it was accidental as Amit and I were to go together for a meeting after that) and what luck. In no time, the discussion was on totally different subjects and of course the deal was closed. It did help matters that the landlord was also an intellectual Bengali.

> Today, seldom do we see professional relationships blossoming beyond the office premises. However, it wasn't so then, when the pioneers of India's computer industry were setting up their operations. Thus, in a way, the leaders touched, transformed, and enriched people's lives. (Sushmita Sengupta and Amol Redij)

Raj Sirohi,
Ex-President and CEO, HCL Technologies America Inc

Amit da was my first boss when I joined HCL on 1st September 1981. Amit da was then heading the very successful "marketing department" of HCL.

"VALUES" that I learnt from Amit da, and which helped me tremendously to remain sane when I came to crossroads in the corporate world, were—fairness, integrity, hard work, and discipline—in this order. Values that remained glued to me when times were tough—I went through my share.

Amit da had time—very patient and very eloquent. He had time for rookies like me who were new to the company, and he had time for seasoned sales managers who used to drop in to his office quite frequently. For 12 months, I sat outside his cabin and was a witness to the "mentoring" meeting that he had with a number of HCL managers. And not once—not once—even in post-HCL life when I met him, did he ever say anything negative about any one. He never sympathized with you about the difficult people you had to work with. A rare attribute.

It was the way Amit da trusted you that made the difference. There wasn't anything you couldn't talk to him about or share with him or laugh about. And it was not only me but it seemed to be everyone, from the no-nonsense accounts department of HCL to the very serious HCL R&D.

Amit da taught me about working in a corporate world—all the basics that haven't gone away even today after 30 years. The "get it done" attitude, the planning skills, ability to break down all actions into small activities, the humor, lots and lots of humor. He taught me how to run and not get tired. He gave the latitude and power to a rookie like me and made me feel confident.

I remember my first report that I gave him—his comments "you have submitted a diarrhea of information." In his feedback— with examples and stories—he was imaginative, innovative, and successful in getting his point across.

It was the best possible start to the working world for me with Amit da as my FIRST boss. He made me learn to be responsible, he made me good at my job, he taught me to work comfortably with really smart people, and have loads of fun doing it. And I owe so much to Amit da to give me those basics that helped me down the road.

While in HCL, America, when I got my first big promotion he had sent me a handwritten five pager which I very proudly shared with my father—as if it was a trophy. He had very eloquently, in his five pager, described how he was proud of me and made me feel that I fully deserved the promotion. I still treasure the note.

A few years back when my son was entering the corporate world, I silently wished him good luck for getting a boss like the "luck" I had with having Amit da as my first boss.

> There are examples of leaders who tell their team members what to do, then there are leaders who make their team members—eager to listen, eager to learn, and willing to try new things. This style of leadership especially comes from the leader's behavior in business situations, which are stressful and demanding. Amit never explained this; he demonstrated this with everyone he met—consistent behavior whether he was meeting the managing director or the regional manager or the office assistant.

Ravi Thumboochetty
Ex-CEO and Director, International Operations, HCL Infosystems

My first meeting with Amit in the mid-1980s, during my final interview with HCL, is still vivid in my mind. It was in Arjun's room, in Nehru Place, and there were a lot of people in the room of whom I can only remember Arjun, Dr Koreth, and this perfectly dressed person Amit. The interview was not too long, Arjun asked some questions on my background and Amit, with a smile explained to me, very articulately, HCL's vision, and if I wanted to be a part of this dream. Somehow, even at that time one never doubted Amit, and I joined HCL that day.

> Putting things across transparently helps people in making important decisions and makes them feel a part of it instantly. Amit had this innate quality of telling every detail with great conviction that would convince even a stranger. Adopting practices like these also give an understanding of the organization's work culture. (Sushmita Sengupta and Amol Redij)

My last meeting with him was at a dinner on 11th August 2006, the 30th anniversary of HCL, and it was my final day in HCL. Amit and I were together catching up with old times, and

Mr Nadar came and hugged both of us in one embrace and said, "Nobody ever leaves HCL," which is very true.

> Bonds established between the people who were a part of HCL's formative years were purely because of the strong leadership it had. HCL, under the headship of people with strong values, were able to institute a work culture which only strengthened the bonds between the people and which remained intact, despite of having parted ways from HCL. (Sushmita Sengupta and Amol Redij)

Rajeev Sawhney
Former President, HCL Europe and Global Public Services

In early 1981, I had the privilege of being under the tutelage of one of the finest professionals in a lifetime, which till date remains unmatched.

Many lessons, which I learnt from Amit da, are as much relevant in today's Google plex as they were in the early 1980s.

How the Bazooka Was Fired for Growth

Little did we know that we were creating the foundation for a $100 billion industry that would contribute to more than 5.5 percent of the GDP of India in times to come! Many of the early participants would become founders/chairmen/CEOs/presidents in a flourishing IT industry, whose seeds were being sown in the early 1980s by the likes of Amit da. It reminds me of the 2 mm rule in Golf. You hit the ball 2 mm away from the sweet spot and the ball goes out of bounds. If you are at the sweet spot, the ball goes to the center of the fairway at 300 yards! It is the initial action that determines the trajectory getting magnified along the course.

With the first three deals won in a "make or break" campaign, the seeds were sown to penetrate and radiate what was potentially a colossal market segment of SMEs in India. At first count, Amit da told us it was close to 40,000 suspects in Northern India alone! Before this, many marquee deals for programmable calculators had been won from leading institutions, such as, IIT Kharagpur, Garden Reach Shipbuilders & Engineers, Institute of Oceanography, and many others, but now with the first visual display unit-based 8-bit microcomputer with a floppy drive, a differentiated mini floppy drive, and a power fail auto restart facility to mitigate the poor power capacity and reliability of the country, the opportunity was immense. The challenge, however, was to create SCALE through REPEATABILITY, which still remains a mantra for the profitable software services companies that make up most of the Indian IT industry.

Seizing this challenge, Amit da, with his legendary communication skills, gave us a bazooka to go to war. I had just won three deals in the campaign. Armed with these three powerful collaterals of customer references and a compelling proposition that told the story, we were all set to storm the market. The story had the following tenets, which are fundamental to any business:

> Where do I earn my money the most? How do I augment it? (Aka Growth)
> Where do I spend my money the most? How do I reduce it? (Aka Cost reduction)
> Where is my money blocked? How do I release it? (Aka Cash Flow)
> Most successful business leaders never take their eyes off these questions.

Come to think of it, these very simple questions were relevant, are relevant, and will eternally be relevant till business is done! Amazing simplicity! Incredibly powerful questions! These will always be fundamental to the success and failure of business! Any industry, any size, anywhere in the world! What a lesson to learn when you are stepping into the world of business! Most successful business leaders never take their eyes off these questions.

Moving on, these visually appealing slides, supplemented with gripping powerful voice-over audios, were slickly woven into a persuasive story and packaged as an audio–visual projection system using the 35 mm slides and a portable projector, and a cassette tape player. Each office was equipped with several of these "sales kits," and the sales soldiers vied to get prioritized access to lug these to their prospect's office and establishments, and deliver their pitch with great aplomb and reassuring ceremony. This eliminated the need for the prospect to travel to our offices, served as a good substitute to glossies, created live entertainment with a value proposition, and sharpened the pitch of salespersons besides registering; they had made a valuable sales call by taking the AV system to the prospect. It was a means to qualify the pipeline for the sales management, considering this would inevitably happen when your "suspect" (aka potential prospect) was becoming a "warm prospect."

In living history of the IT industry, there never was and never has been a campaign as powerful and magnificent as this one! All stops were pulled off and now the "brightest young people with their minds on fire," equipped with the potent audio–visual sales kit, blitzed the streets of every major metro in India. The firepower was exponentially increased with the hiring of college students who could earn a stipend and lots of valuable experience. The leading daily newspapers carried full-page advertisements like screaming sirens. As the samba beats grew louder, all streets led to the glorious roadshows that were held in prestigious five-star hotels, mostly in the presidential suites, where "suspects" were persuaded to visit in enigmatic surroundings and see with their disbelieving eyes what magic the 8C/2 computer could do! At the press of a button, reams of computer stationary would print out ledgers and financial statements on ultra fast, heavy duty line printers. This was the pinnacle of the computerization story that every salesperson looked forward to and seeing their "suspects" turn "prospects," and now ready to sign up for the coveted computer that would eliminate their miseries of accounting and significantly enhance their business management.

Amit da, as the field marshall of the operation, had clearly visualized and communicated in his words, "the ridiculous to the sublime." The campaign briefing had the all-important messages of "*Why* are we doing what we are doing?" to the "How this campaign would unfold?" to the "duties and responsibilities" of every soldier in the field. His ability to create the "science of selling" from the "art of selling" led to breaking down the sales activity into meaningful stages of "need identification," "need crystallization" to "need justification," and finally "closure." "Some of these stages could simultaneously and concurrently occur," he explained. This was converted into a management information system through an innovative automated system called SPRING (sales progress reporting information generator). Undisciplined salespersons (the artists) found it painful, but the organized engineers (the scientists) found it an amazing tool to get meaningful information (analytics) from loads of the "Big Data" of those times. Every single sales call of every single salesperson across the country was captured in-depth and analyzed, using our homegrown automation. I am sure Salesforce.com would be put to shame if they knew that an advanced system, such as, SPRING was invented in the early 1980s.

The competition was quick to respond with a me-too offering, but they lacked the ferocious passion that Amit da's team was soaked with. Needless to say we struck with stunning alacrity. On the other hand, "spies" did intelligence gathering on the competitor's tactics reminding one of "The Art of War," by Sun Tzu, (one of Amit da's favorites and a must read book) and blow after blow admonished them to be the laggards. What the heightened action in the field did was to create a market that did not exist, and enlarge the pie for the green shoots to emerge and create what was going to be the Indian IT industry on steroids!

This "months-long" campaign was a landmark success, and it had created a momentum that was humungous to say the least.

The rest is history for those who have observed the Indian IT industry, but some essential learning from this was there.

But most of all, it was the beginning of the transformation of how India Inc. would embrace computerization and evolve into an IT superpower. It was the "golf swing at the sweet spot" that would create the trajectory of a $100 billion+ industry.

1. *The industrialization of the sales process.* This has always remained and will always remain a challenge in the business world. Businesses continually strive to optimize the sales process, and by now it has become an industry in itself. This campaign of the 1980s will remain for posterity a fine example of how a systematic analysis of a sales process can be defined and executed with military precision.
2. *Reduction in the cycle time* for a sale which climbed down from 40 to 50 calls to less than five sales calls, thereby cutting sales cost dramatically. Costs are always known to go up like rockets and come down like feathers. Clever ways to determine growth paired with reduced cycle time can indeed provide the competitive advantage, which results in sustainable profits and leadership in the market.
3. *Providing momentum for growth* through repeatability and achieve scale of gigantic proportions. It is evident that the science of selling in this case illustrates the mythic dimensions of growth that were achieved.

How Empowerment Can Strengthen an Organization

The campaign for India's first visual display unit-based microcomputer 8C/2 was in full glory. The phones wouldn't stop ringing, and the young salesmen led by their able team leaders were trooping in and out as though going thru revolving doors. In this entire melee, I forewarned my team leader that I was bringing a "prize catch" into the office. This was later going to be the very first customer for HCL in this high-stakes campaign that had the potential to make or break the company. I was extremely nervous about the risk I had taken, particularly when I had invested several painstaking hours into the prospect identifying his information needs, crystallizing these needs, and justifying to him, his father, and the rest of his clan, the benefits of computerization.

Any sales 101 will tell you that establishing a strong credibility was essential to influence the decision positively, and hence I had given elaborate details of our "Singapore Operations" with a fertile imagination. The prospect was terribly excited with the details of the hi-tech work done by us and that too being done on scale in a "foreign land." Bear in mind India was a closed economy in the early 1980s. For a moment I also believed in the figments of my imagination that we were a Fortune 500 company! At least that's the belief we had, that's the way we behaved, and that's the way we came across ... very confident.

Listening to this with a great deal of enthusiasm, our Mr Prospect wanted to embrace computerization with the best firm he had just discovered! The credentials of what was an unknown firm now appeared to be impeccable! And here I wanted to jump under a bus for having conceded to the prospect's desire to visit the HCL office, in Delhi's Nehru Place, and validate some of the claims and promises that had been discussed.

In the humble beginnings of Hindustan Computers Limited, the northern India headquarters' regional office was a modest flat in the "most modern" precincts of Nehru Place, in New Delhi, which later would decay into the shabbiest slum dwellings for offices. There were two office cubicles in the flat, which were earmarked for the regional manager, who at that time was Amit da and Benu da (the Deputy Regional Manager). The cubicles were infested with mosquitoes ("young sparrows" in the words of Amit da).

"Setting and managing expectations" of potential customers is an integral part of a salesperson's life. So there began my spiel about "the way business in Nehru Place had suddenly exploded and the infrastructure were having a hard time to cope up with the growth," in a way preparing him to walk into a dilapidated business complex. The food courts, the sophisticated description of hole-in-the-wall unhygienic food shops that would dispense rice and chickpeas/kidney beans cooked in contaminated water with a million flies in animated suspension hovering around the cooking area. Mr Prospect and I walked into the eight-storey building and there was no electricity. This meant the elevators weren't working! Now we had to walk up the flight of stairs to the 6th floor. Just as we walked in, my next dilemma was, "Where do I seat Mr Prospect?" In a tiny office that could barely seat 10 people, we were bursting at the seams anyway with more than twice that number.

Here was a qualified prospect that was ready to close our very first deal of the campaign, and here I was a nervous wreck realizing I had walked straight into a beehive of an office. Amit da spotted me walk in with Mr Prospect with sweat beads over our faces and panting for breath, having climbed the building. It didn't take him a second glance to understand my predicament. He walked out of his chair from the "regional manager's cubicle" and ushered in Mr Prospect, telling him politely, diplomatically, and gently that the discussions would be led by Mr Sawhney. He vacated his own office, and it appeared to the prospect that I, Mr Sawhney must be a fairly senior person in this company as I was going to conduct the meeting in a cubicle in a Nehru Place office. He hadn't realized that Amit da had discretely vacated his office with the intent of making me "feel empowered." In those days, given India's obsession for organizational hierarchy, having an office such as this one denoted the prestige and authority which was a necessary condition to conducting serious business.

After protracted discussions, Mr Prospect wanted to shake hands with the regional manager (with an ulterior motive of extracting some discount) but Amit da spoke to him with conviction that the final decision rested with Mr Sawhney (I could die if he only knew I was a sales trainee), and even though he was the super boss, he could only give the price and terms that Mr Sawhney would agree and finalize. After the prospect left, he took a debrief and inspired me with many encouraging words.

> Words of encouragement have the power to give people hope and courage, and believe me that this meeting with the prospect in our office and the way it was handled, and the encouragement I got was pivotal in accomplishing a very major win ... what would be the very first win for HCL's high-stake campaign.

Trivial that it may seem now, this was my first lesson in management that I learnt, and it has since been indelibly engraved in my mind! Here was empowerment in action!

First of all, it seemed like unseating God when he decided to vacate his own office. Given the custom of India and reverence for hierarchy, it was an act ahead of its times! There was no "hot desking" in those days, leave alone asking the top man to vacate his office for a trainee!

But the biggest lesson in empowerment was Amit da telling the prospect that the executive dealing with him was fully authorized to take all decisions! This did many things in one stroke:

1. It gave a clear message to the prospect as to who would be the person he should negotiate with, paving the way to advance the conversation.
2. It injected an industrial dose of energy in to me and provided an instant ignition to the change in my demeanor. I was suddenly hugely confident, took charge of

the situation, and drove the conversation to its logical conclusion.
3. It spread the message into the rank and file that we were an empowered lot and that enhanced the responsibility the team had to shoulder.

Hire the brightest young people and set their minds on fire! This experience just did that!

The Construction of a High-Performance Organization

"Train hard, you fight easy," said Amit da to me. He probably said that to every team member. He believed in it. Very soon we all believed in it. Today, when I reflect over the last 35 years, I can say with conviction that good training as also yearning for learning are hugely important in building a high-performance organization.

> A critical success factor for HCL having a sustained No 1 position in the industry for decades was the quality of talent that was hired and the training that was imparted to build a cadre of loyal, die hard, highly persuasive people with a high achievement need.

These were the essential ingredients to build a high-performance organization. With all the wisdom and experience I have gained over the years, I can bet that these tenets are as much applicable today and tomorrow as they were yesterday. The only challenge is that the war for talent has got a lot tougher. The people you want are rare and precious, and the ones you don't want are available in abundance. Having said that, it is an imperative to be absolutely stringent on the intake of new hires. No compromises at all! This is even more relevant when building a new organization or undertaking an organizational transformation, especially in the technology industries.

Today, large organizations prefer to outsource the training function or have a functional group called training/people development and various other names. The one distinction that I can make from my experience starting with Amit da's first sermon.

> "Train hard, fight easy"
>
> These words are self-explanatory. It is imperative to get your teams to intensely train so that they can deal with real life challenges with relative ease.

"Train hard, fight easy" was that he believed in the line managers taking full responsibility and ownership, and personally investing time and effort to groom youngsters. It is no coincidence that many successful industries have that as a normal way of working. My son, who works with a leading media channel in the United Kingdom, is currently "shadowing" a senior. That's the way the media industry builds up capability in their talent today. That was the way we were groomed in the 1980s. It's not only understanding the function that is important, but also equally how it works in the context of the specific organization's DNA. So even though times have changed and with the advent of internet today, one of the most effective way to groom talent still remains "shadowing" or the line managers taking personal interest in addition to class-room and others.

Given that pretty much, the early HCL was made up with nearly 100 percent engineers and they were addressing a commercial market place with mostly commercial solutions; it was amazing how the work force was trained with deep domain knowledge. Every single person in the field knew the industry's heat map, value chain, processes, pain points, and an equally good understanding of the application solutions that were being proposed to the customers. Even a standard proposal had been designed with exceptional knowledge, anticipating every single business challenge that was likely to be discussed by the potential buyer to anticipating the questions that were likely to come in the way of a sale.

Under Amit da's leadership, all his managers painstakingly led from the front and walked the talk, while newcomers shadowed them all the way through. They were encouraged to make a mistake, but could get slaughtered if they made the same mistake again! That was unpardonable and that was the learning. The interesting part was that because of the attributes of the hires, they were all fast learners and had a burning desire to learn and learn real fast.

The world knows today that the lights are shining on India for having created an IT industry and every major fortune 500 company finds it fashionable to tap the Indian talent, but the world owes this to the founding fathers of this industry and people such as Amit da with extraordinary courage, conviction, and talent that helped to create incredible India.

Khorkaai and Childhood

River

- Monsoon: In full spate, millions of muddy brown snakes writhing, slithering, wriggling forward in silent menace.
- Summer: Constricted, languid, thin. Pushed to a corner by bank-to-bank swathe of burning white sand, lush green kankri fields.
- Dark sal forests: Moist, brown and green, soft undergrowth, brown hares, the santhal hunter, and the trapped baby deer.
- The sand slopes—Exhilaration of jumping off, flying through air, slamming down on the slope, slide down into the cool, cool water.
- Baiting the sand insect in its conical trap.
- The gypsies every year. Tall, gaunt, big-boned men, statuesque women, the smithy, ferocious hounds (chase over kankri fields), hunting birds with the hawk.
- The distant railway bridge. Haunting whistle of Bombay Mail at mid-day.
- The river takes at least one life every year. The body of the young boy.

Apu—Santhal Village

> "Apu" is the protagonist of Satyajit Ray's *Pather Panchali*—perhaps, the finest piece of filmed folklore based on Bibhutibhushan Bandopadhyay's novel, *Apu Trilogy: Pather Panchali* (childhood of Apu), Aparajito (the unvanquished), and Apur Sansar (the world of Apu) and had won many national and international awards. Amit related himself significantly with this character. "Apu," a romantic, supremely idealistic intellectual Bengali whose passion for life enables him to rise above all limitations. The story is based on interminable courage of the human soul in the backdrop of an insightful social and political commentary on a profoundly changing culture.
> Amit was a middle-class boy who came from a small town, while Apu came from an underprivileged class and village of Bengal.

Close to our house was the Khorkaai river, and the deep sal forests starting on the other bank had not yet been desecrated on the altar of modernization, new town planning, and laying out of new industrial estates.

Many are the days I spent in the jungle, along with Santhal friends. The sal trees were the favorite haunt for the huge chameleons, which I used to hunt with my sling. Bothra, my Santhal friend, was much older to me—in his teens actually—but we were great friends. So many times on a Sunday, I would cross the bridge and cycle down to their village beyond the Adityapur town. The whole village of Santhals would greet me with smiles and give me exotic fruits in sal leaf containers.

Bothra would teach me how to make professional bows and arrows, with which you could even kill a tiger. There is another neat trick that I learnt from him. If you shoot a normal arrow at a bird sitting on the top of a large jungle tree, you might miss with the arrow getting stuck in a branch. So Bothra would cut out a small bamboo cover for the steel arrow tip. Now, you could stun the bird and make it fall. But even if you missed, the arrow would fall harmlessly to the ground.

We spent magic hours laying out simple traps on the jungle floor for catching rabbits and partridges. Having laid out the traps, we would hide patiently behind trees and bushes. Then there would be a scuffling sound and screeches, which meant that our trap had ensnared a rabbit or a bird. Quickly, Bothra would run to the trap, pull out the animal or bird, quickly wringing its neck and depositing it in a bag dangling from his waist. We would go back to his village, and I can never forget the rabbit and partridge stews with hot rice that his mother served.

But wherever you were—the forest, beyond the forest into neat Santhal villages, on the newly made concrete bridge—you finally fell back to the river. Silky smooth surface, the water rippling sinuously through the granite sentinels, the rocks, flocks of white herons skimming over the water or standing patiently on one leg near the shore. They were so deceptive to watch—eyes almost closed, one leg raised in a gesture of relaxation, standing still. And then the sudden downward stroke of the long bills, like chopsticks into the water and out again in a jiffy, a tiny silver fish thrashing in arcs of head and tail, trying desperately for the release that was never to be, as the heron stretched its wings, flapped them vigorously, and rose majestically to fly back to its nest and the eagerly awaiting fledglings.

As the summer heat kept going up ferociously, the river started drying up. Soon, the continuity of one water body was fragmented into disjointed pools of muddy water. I loved sloshing around in these pools because they contained tiny punti fish and even smaller shrimps. All it took was an old, discarded piece of cloth, heaps of patience, and hours of tracking the fish, gently putting the cloth under them, and then one yank, and you had four or five of the fish thrashing around on the sand. A quick transfer to an old Horlicks bottle kept ready with clean water, and you had your own little aquarium to run back with to show to the whole family. At that moment, even if one had few creature goods, it was a moment of triumph that no king had ever enjoyed.

No visit to the river was complete without my own inspection of the railway lines scrambling up the river bank slope till one was at the end of the railway bridge, with two broad-gauge lines coming in from the distant horizon, and seeming to meet there. The invariable electric line poles would hum their own pastorals, changing the pitch and frequency continuously. Then the deliciously heart-throbbing onslaught of a big mail train coming in, making me jump a safe distance away from the tracks. The heavy onrushing train would gallop past, with a swish of a great wind knocking about, accompanied by the steady beat of the wheels going over the points. Then one final burst of air, a hollow in my stomach, and the train was gone.

My friend, Bothra, once proposed that I should spend a full day with his family. It took a lot of persuasion for my parents to allow me to do this on a Sunday. At first, they were both very firm about not allowing me out of home for the better part of a day without anyone else accompanying me. That, surely, was a red rag to the bull, and I retorted emphatically that I was grown-up enough to take care of myself. Seeing my keenness about the expedition, they relented at last and I got up very early on that Sunday morning to keep my tryst with Bothra in his village.

It was a glorious autumn morning. The early morning breeze, coming off Khorkaai flowing by close to our house, had a sweet, earthy smell borrowed from the wet earth, green grass, and the varied flotsam brought down from the Chaibasa Hills. Mother had made a small packet of sweetmeats for Bothra and his family. I dangled the bundle from the handle bar of my cycle. Then I spent half an hour in lovingly getting my bicycle ready for a long trip, cleaning, greasing, oiling all joints. A final swab all over, and we were off!

The road to the Khorkaai Bridge was lined with large fruit trees, mainly mango, and also jackfruit, guava, and banyan trees. As I whizzed by the tree shadow darkened lane, the trees, blown about by the soft morning breeze, seemed to nod their heads and limbs with joy, wishing me Godspeed on my mission. To my joyous mind, all of nature seemed happy to celebrate my feelings of liberty, self-indulgence, the prospect of the day ahead turning out to be a beautiful holiday. Birds flew about, the fresh flowers on the trees nodded and swayed in their own dervish dance, and even the neighborhood stray dogs wagged their tails vigorously, even if they didn't know me at all. All in all, all of nature and its inhabitants joined together in a hosannah to the happiness and freedom felt by a young boy swishing away on a cycle towards his friend's home, fortunately a good distance away from the signs of a town.

Very soon, I had left the government colony in which we stayed and all its annexes built later, and was moving at a fast clip towards the Khorkaai Bridge. The bridge, although short, was sensibly rather wide, so that even two large buses could pass side by side. Normally it didn't have too much traffic, and that being a Sunday, traffic was more or less not there at all, with a car whizzing by occasionally, and other cyclists like me ambulating slowly.

From the bridge, the river looked much larger and full-bodied. Every time you looked down on the broad, slowly twisting sheets of water, for a precious moment, the water seemed still and when the trance was broken, the water started moving again, and you held back in your mind the languid image of a great, eternally restless mass being frozen forever for your careful scrutiny. But there were others too, who even if they didn't have your sensitivity, enjoyed the river in their own ways—the black, water buffalos wallowing in the shallow waters near the river banks, and the herons in precision flights like a squadron of fighter planes, whisking in full formation right under the bridge.

I took all of this in while I crossed the bridge. Within a few meters, the bright and sharp sunlight gave way to gloomy dark in the morning because I had entered the dark sal forest. The tall trees rose straight to a massive height, so that you had to crane your neck to look up at the canopy top. The whole jungle, which was at least a kilometer deep, was redolent with the musky odor of the jungle—a combination of the fresh smell of the tree branches and leaves, along with whiffs of decadence from the jungle floor.

The jungle was also full of its own orchestra of different kinds of sounds. The predominant one was that of the autumn breeze rippling through the trees. Different types of cicadas and frogs chipped in with their staccato croaks. Distant honking of car horns would periodically rise to a crescendo and then die down lingeringly to remind you that while your imagination wanted you to believe that you were in the middle of an Amazon jungle, in reality you were just cutting through a small forest in Jharkhand.

Very soon, the Adityapur forest was left behind and the road snaked ahead through rolling, dusty flatlands, villages, patchwork quilts of cultivated fields, and sharply etched cameos of neat little huts and trees, carved out of the horizon as it were. And to provide relief from this repetitive collage, huge, pitch dark boulders rose from the earth in majestic patterns.

I kept soaking this magnificent scenario mile after mile. Bothra had earlier mentioned to me that the way to identify his village would be to watch out for a small rivulet, go over it, and immediately turn left into the village. As a precaution, one could ask any passerby whether one had reached Murmu's village, Murmu being his father and village headman. That's exactly what I did, and in less than 10 minutes I was ringing my cycle bell in front of a largish cottage where Bothra lived.

By now, the word had spread around the village that a non-Santhal boy had come on a visiting, and was therefore the honored guest of the whole village. So I was promptly surrounded by about a dozen dogs and an equal number of tiny, naked children, whose dusky bodies shone like ebonite. From different doorways, shy women measured me up. The menfolk had no need for shyness, of course, and one by one came up to hold my two hands in theirs and gave me a dazzling smile of their pearly teeth.

Khorkaai and Childhood   187

After all this initial excitement, after the dust had settled a bit, Bothra took my hand and gave me a quick tour of the village—about 15 spotlessly clean huts with thatched roofs covered by green creepers and plastered with a combination of sticky mud and cow dung, the unique Indian building material that provides bonding strength, antiseptic cover, and a pleasant canvas on which diverse artistic motifs can be painted, as I found them in plenty all over the village.

In my honor, the village young men, numbering about a dozen, had planned for a hunting expedition in the nearby forest. So off we went and shortly crept inside the dark tunneling of the canopied trees. In less time than it takes to go down memory lane, we had captured about a dozen fat partridges and half a dozen rabbits with land traps, and shot down a young buck. This was the first time I had fired a real arrow with a real steel head, and it had found its mark!

We returned to the village in a triumphant procession and made a heap of our trophies in the middle of the village for everyone to see and wonder at. When this was done, Bothra's mother came up and shooed everyone away, tasking the young women to quickly skin the animals and take out the meat which had to be cooked for lunch as well as dinner.

Very soon, the entire village was filled with the aroma of freshly cooking exotic meat. Another group of people started stitching plates from big sal leaves. Bothra and I went off to the nearby river for a quick dip and bath. By the time we returned, the meal was ready. What a taste was there in the simple dishes eaten with relish along with thick rice, squatting on the ground in the shade of a big banyan tree.

I didn't realize how soon the time flew, until I looked up to see the sun sliding down in the skies. Murmu came across to me and said that to commemorate my visit, they had specially composed a joyous song and dance number, which was going to be played shortly.

Shortly, ten girls wearing clean white saris, the hems of which just touched the knees and served to cover the whole torso, came up, stood in a line facing the same direction and held each other's waists. They were giggling nervously, and constantly resetting the fiery red palaash flowers in their hair. Then a Santhal boy leapt into the arena, his upper body bare and glistening with his big drum, the maadole, swinging from his neck. He first delivered a crescendo on the drum and then settled down to a lilting, swaying rhythm, his eyes half-closed in ecstasy and a smile fixed on his lips.

The girls responded by catching up the beat, singing a song in thin soprano, and swaying together like one sinuous snake, swaying back and forth and sideways. I was mesmerized—the glowing, fading sun, the clean cottages, the svelte young people, the undulating music—all ingrained into my memory forever.

When I returned home in the evening, it was like flying over the road and the river like a man possessed.

The Gypsies

Every year, during summer, the gypsies used to camp next to the Khorkaai River. Their bullock-drawn carts had unusually large wheels.

The men were gaunt, dark, and swarthy. The women matched them and were statuesque. They had a whole pack of Rampur hounds to guard them and their fun-loving frolicking children.

Every morning, the men went out into the town to sell knives and scissors made by them in hearths with bellows. The women went out separately, selling richly colored scarves. But you had to keep an eye on them because they would steal things under your nose in a jiffy.

An enduring image is of their hunting common mynah ("shaalik" in Bengali) birds with hawks. First they would throw some grains on the ground and let birds descend on them. Then the hunter would go cautiously upwind of the feeding birds, the hawk hidden in the loose sleeve of his gown. At an appropriate moment, he would then hurl the hawk at the flock. The hawk would hesitate only for a moment, and then straight as an arrow, it would put its talons into the back of one hapless bird.

In summer, the river shrank into a small stream, exposing broad stretches of fine sand which was ideal for growing tubers, especially "kankri," which is a long, green vegetable, delicious to eat even raw.

We used to steal regularly from the lush kankri fields; the gypsies were pretty mad at us and kept waiting patiently to catch us.

One day, three of us were stealthily removing fresh kankris, when, with a big shout, a gypsy ran towards us, a javelin poised threateningly in his right hand. He had also set on us one of the ferocious Rampur hounds. We ran desperately for our lives to the edge of the sand bank and jumped straight into the water. Fortunately, neither the dog nor the gypsy followed us, and we scrambled up the opposite bank which was part of the city garbage dumps. I finally got home and received from Ma a big thrashing, which was richly due.

Quiet Love

Ma was always more a friend than a parent. In fact, with Baba always a bit distant, private, and remote, she was the one who took me through the awkward dealings of birds and bees when I started grappling with the clumsy excitements of adolescence. And she had a shy smile on her lips, eyes refusing to meet mine, who told me about what happened one summer evening.

Baba had started his career in the steel plant, and his boss used to fondly call him Ganesh—the elephant god—because Baba was short and well built. After his retirement, the boss, Rajen Babu, was residing close by and used to go for a walk past our house every evening. If Baba or Ma were around, he would raise his walking stick in salutation. Once in a while, he would come through the garden for a cup of tea.

That summer evening, after the Sunday siesta, Baba and Ma were sitting leaning against two pillars, a few feet away from each other. They were lost in watching the crazy colored sunsets that were always set off by the steel plant fumes. Lost in each other and the shared sunset, they didn't even notice Rajen Babu walk past and stop. Noticing their reverie, he just smiled and walked on.

But on his way back, seeing the bewitched couple still sitting on as before, Rajen Babu opened the gate and walked in. Now Baba and Ma came out of their trance and almost jumped up. But Rajen Babu extended both arms and said eagerly, "No, no, don't get up—Please stay sitting as before, completely suffused by the eloquence of your silent love. This is truly God's blessing, and I pray that it lasts forever!"

Obstinate Grandpa

From the time I remember, Ma would have drilled it into me at least a few thousand times that while my Grandpa's legendary obstinacy had diluted down somewhat in Baba, it had blossomed fully in me. She would reinforce this with anecdotal support, borrowed from legends recounted to her by my widow Grandma.

Apparently, Grandpa was very devoted to his mother, my father's Grandma, who had been widowed as a young girl with the infant Grandpa and had struggled a lot to bring him up in life. Every evening, Grandpa, on returning from court, would hand over his official shawl to his wife, go to his mother's separate widow's kitchen, snack up on his favorite tidbits, and then go to his own room with her permission. One evening, though, she, looking drawn and pale, said that she was not well, hadn't cooked anything, and asked him to go straight to his room. Something was amiss and raised his suspicion. He queried her closely, but she wouldn't come forth.

Finally, his wife gave him a whispered update. In the fetid, rivalry-ridden pond that rural village life is, a lot of jealousy had recently been aroused by the growing prosperity of Grandpa's family. This was getting manifested in many lurid forms. Now, in the watery deltaic region of East Bengal, each village had several ponds, one of which, by common consent, was used only for drawing water for drinking and cooking. Like everyone, Grandpa's mother would also draw her little pitcher full every day from that pond. That morning, the owner, watching her come, said with unhidden viciousness, "One hears your son's making a lot of money these days! Why do you still have to beg for water and not have your own pond?" The old lady turned right back, came home, doused the cooking fire, and awaited her son's return. Grandpa went through the story with a stone face. Then without uttering a word, he put on his shawl, grabbed a hurricane lantern, and walked off 10 miles in the night to the railway coolie camp on the banks of Padma, where the gang had to keep shifting the steamer station with the meandering river. The overseer was a friend and without any ado, Grandpa told him, "I want 100 coolies right now to come home with me and dig a pond before sunrise." The coolies on hearing the background, dropped their dinners, said that they would not charge a paisa, and marched back. The first, muddy pail of water was drawn from the newly dug pond just as the first sunrays hit the treetops. The grand old lady cooked her boiled rice and gave the first few morsels to her hungry son.

Of Persistent Monkeys and Slippery Poles

Causality is a funny thing—it's absolutely unpredictable, contrary to popular belief, as to where a causal chain can lead to.

When my father was three-year-old, his mother was bitten by a rabid fox. Treatment would have been a fair challenge even in a big city. It was certainly not the best in a small Bengal village. So she was quite ill and took a long time to get back to health. So to hasten the process, her father took her off for a year to Shillong, considered those days to be quite a health resort. This left my father, a restless child, in the care of his old grandmother. Very soon Baba was getting out of hand, and finally the old lady persuaded her son, that's my grandfather, to put the brat in school at the age of three.

In those days, this was a travesty of decent childhood practices, because you went to school at a proper, mature age of about six or seven! Being forced, therefore, to start school at four, my father developed a lifetime hatred for the formal school process. So when he himself became a father and begot me, he announced that I would bypass the formal school process altogether, study at home to become a complete man and would appear for matriculation exams in one shot to get into college. This was a wonderful arrangement for me, and I had a wonderful, wild time when my mother put her foot down and forced me to go to school. But that's another story.

In the meanwhile, I had a fantastic, chequer work quilt of education, which mainly comprised banned adult books read on the sly and traditional fairy tales. To this was added Dadu, my mother's father, who was a maths freak, a station master—posted in a nearby town. Every weekend he would drop in and straightaway start with Jadavbabu's *Patiganit*—the final and definitive junior school maths book. We would tear together through chapters, and this left in me a lifelong love for—and at the cost of immodesty—a certain amount of proficiency in maths.

Many are the fond memories of the different, exciting forms of problems I learned to tackle, but the pride of place certainly goes to the problem of the monkey who was trying to climb an oiled, slippery pole, jumping so much with every heave, but also slipping a bit every time. So how many heaves would he take to get to the top? The maths of it, as it went, was simple stuff, but the whole indelible cameo—glistening bamboo pole, persistent and determined monkey with gleaming eyes, Dadu's eyes gleaming even more as he egged me over the finishing line—a crescendo of mathematical music!

And it all started with one mad fox biting one young village woman more than 80 years ago.

The Station Master

Mother was the only child of her parents. Of them, grandmother, Dida, lived very long and even took care of my sister's son when he was a toddler, but grandfather, Dadu, unfortunately passed away when I was not even eight-year-old. I wish he had lived a lot longer because he was certainly one person who influenced me a lot about developing intense passions about different things, persistence in achieving goals, and a never-say-die outlook at all times, however tough the situation might be.

Dadu served the Indian Railways all his adult life. He was a diligent and hard worker, whose simple ethos was "work is worship." So he rose through the ranks, and at the time of his unfortunate death at a relatively young age, he was the station master of Adra, a small town otherwise, but a very important railway junction and workshop. Dadu was the boss of it all, and whenever, during summer holidays, we visited there, we got special treatment from everyone around because we were the "Masterjee's" family.

Being a railway man, Dadu needed no tickets to ride in any train. He was also eligible for a family pass. So once when I was very small and hadn't started going to school, a grand religious tour was decided on, with the team comprising Dadu, Dida,

Boro-ma/widow of my father's late eldest brother. She was staying with the next brother, who was a bachelor and myself. We took off on a summer morning and started visiting Deoghar, then Gaya, Benares, Haridwar, Lachman Jhula, and back. The part I liked in this whirlwind tour was pressing my nose against the glass windows in the rail compartment and see wonderful country whisk by. The part that I didn't like, and which has probably left a lifelong aversion in me, was the mandatory visit to the main temples—dank, dark, overcrowded, with slippery floors, shark-like guides, and an overall stench of rotting flowers, milk, and stale condiments. But one experience wiped all that away. Dadu and I, both like two small kids, crossed the Lachman Jhula bridge with the clear Ganga rushing far, far below. What heady joy, what romantic overtures from the hills and forests all around!

The other memory is of Dadu encouraging me, while holding my hand, to take a dip in the fast-moving Ganga canal cutting through Haridwar. Non-vegetarian food being banned in the whole town, huge-sized sole fish grew unfettered in the waters. All you had to do was to drop into the water small pellets of a paste of water and flour used for making rotis. Immediately a dozen fish would attack that small morsel, and the water would foam and agitate from the movement of the fish. And if you were standing in the water, as I invariably did, the greedy and fearless fish would actually touch you as they swam fast. Or they would come towards you anyway in the fond hope of getting food. Amidst all this, our famous Dadu—grandson duo would be screaming and jumping up and down in sheer ecstasy.

I think the infatuation that I have with maths can clearly be attributed to the innumerable maths problems which I did together with Dadu. My sister wasn't born then. Dadu, requiring no tickets, would drop in from Adra every weekend. After a cursory "How are you doing?" to my parents, he would straightaway sit with me on the floor, and pull out the famous maths book for children—"Jadavbabur Paatiganit," which was a compendium of difficult mathematic problems which most of Bengali boys had to go through mandatorily in their childhood.

My father wanted me to have good foundational inputs before getting into formal classes. So Dadu's maths lessons being the only educational input, I would bring to it a totally and fiercely focused attention. To cap this was Dadu's unique brand of teaching, which I can only describe as a pulling and stretching up towards success, rather than the teacher pushing me towards the goal. If I got stuck somewhere, Dadu would give me a few hints, scowl hard at me, and make me stretch, stretch, stretch my mind into and around the problem until I got the solution. Dadu would break out into a celebratory yell, and I would join in lustily. Our joint conquest of a particularly tricky or tough concept won over by my successfully doing each of the exercise sums would usually be celebrated by a small prize from Dadu and over-indulgence in some usually forbidden sweets.

Till date, the most commonplace artifacts and human activities arouse in me the challenge to promptly turn it into a mathematical proposition, and I get no rest until I have solved it. An office paper coffee cup, the geometry of a football, why communication antennas have to be parabolic, how do you get an EMI interest rate—every one of these was turned into a problem and solved, in an ode to the great Dadu who triggered it all off so long ago.

Going back to Adra, I'll never forget one memorable summer when my new-born sister was hardly a few months old, and we went off to Adra to Dadu's place to give my mother some well-earned rest, not as you would assume from her new baby duties, but more from the constant pranks and mischief from me.

Bang opposite our house in the colony was one of the outer cabins of Adra Station. Dadu, in his rounds, would visit this each morning. Sometimes he'd start his day there. I was told repeatedly, on the pain of a severe beating, not to touch anything in the cabin. The only exception was a bank of old-style signal levers, some of which had gone dead, and therefore allowed to me for playing with.

As one might know, the active levers were very hard to pull and lock, putting a distant signal down, but could be released to spring back by just pulling a clutch handle, unlocking the lever, and letting the whole lever fall back with a bang.

And that's exactly what I did one morning, when the Bombay Mail was expected any moment. I went to the bank of levers on tip-toe, fiddled with the depressed lever, and "bang," it went off, putting the downed signal up again.

Dadu, busy with his Morse message trans/receiver, realized all this only when the furious driver of the Bombay Mail, who had dutifully stopped, though totally perplexed, at the signal because it showed "no passage," hooted the skies down. Dadu, kind of woke up with a jerk, quickly sensed that a major accident was in the offing shortly and tried very hard to pull the lever back. But it was too tough for his thin, wiry frame, and soon he gave up, bolted down the steps of the cabin, and started yelling for the railway laborers of his team.

Finally, one of the stout laborers arrived and quickly downed the lever and signal, and let the train pass. Dadu would definitely have lost his job that day if it came out. Luckily it didn't, but once we got home, I got a royal thrashing from Dida and Ma.

But it goes to the eternal credit of that loving man that despite all this, his love for me didn't reduce by even one notch, and my enduring sorrow lies in the fact that he passed away after only a few months. Age wise, he could easily have been around through my school life. But that was not to be, and I still weep silently for my maths guru and one of the few men who opened all the windows for me.

Timetable Mania

One of Baba's legendary qualities was his ability to sit in front of absolutely obnoxious people for hours with a fixed Mona Lisa smile on his face, and an occasional, gentle understanding nod, listening to whatever rubbish was thrown at him.

This obviously encouraged the other person to believe that Baba was hugely enjoying his company. So doubly encouraged, he would go on and on, while Baba suffered in mute agony.

But with one person, only one, even Baba's resolute iron will broke, and he started taking evasive action. This was a man called Jha, whose single obsession in life was to deeply analyze and memorize railway timetables. This was the only subject he liked to talk about, so it is not surprising that he was not the life or soul of any social gathering, nor did he have too many friends.

I don't know where he and Baba had met, but Jha, having discovered Baba's pliant nature, quickly latched on to him and started frequenting our house almost every Sunday evening. The sessions started lengthening with the whole house echoing Jha's monotonous gibberish about routes, junctions, gauges, and connecting trains. Finally, even Baba's rock-like patience broke, and I saw him do something for the first and last time in his life. Around 4:00 p.m. on a Sunday, I was playing in the front garden. Baba was relaxing with a book in the drawing room. The curtains having gone for washing, you could see right into the drawing room even from a great distance. Suddenly I spied Jha coming along about half a kilometer away, across the open ground in front of our house.

"Jha kaku coming!" I yelled. My father, instead of getting up from the chair, when Jha would have definitely seen him, dropped like a stone to the floor and started crawling out of the room like a crab to the back verandah, and then into the store room at the back.

While I was staring goggle-eyed at this spectacle, Jha had reached our house. Ma smiled at him. "So where's Lalu Babu?" asked Jha, "I have some great news for him about a new connection to Gaya." With a straight face, Ma said that Baba was not at home, and she didn't know when he would return.

This charade was repeated a few Sundays. Finally Jha got the message, and dropped out of our lives. And Baba could stop his crab crawling with great relief.

To Jalpaiguri Every Year

Annual summer pilgrimage with Dida to Jalpaiguri and Moinaguri. Sealdah to Monihari Ghat—train—packed like sardines-hot, fetid, stink of urine, but who cares? Morning, train stops on white sand near Monihari Ghat. Gather luggage and run for steamer. Can't afford anything more than lowest class in cavernous, claustrophobic belly of steamer. After eons, the great wheels start chugging—slow drift out over the Ganga—a little bit of fresh air at last. Slowly the steamer approaches Sakrikali Ghat—pulse starts beating faster, get ready for mad scramble with crowd. Tiny body almost faints for lack of air—cling on desperately to Dida's hand, move unseeing over narrow gang plank. Suddenly break free and run like mad towards train on siding. Defying all laws of science, entire trainload of people from metre-gauge Monihari side get packed into thin, shorter narrow gauge train on Sakrikali side! Train speeds up. Wondrous new terrain of North Bengal—green little patchwork quilt plots of land, ponds covered with hyacinth, and wonder of wonders, wooden huts on stilts ! Soon, Siliguri (land of lots of "guris"—Jalpaiguri, Moinaguri, Dhupguri—what's a guri? Dida, tired, sleepy, snaps back, asking me to shut up) station. Quickly change to even smaller train. Race on, almost wishing it to fly—Jalpaiguri at last. Cycle rickshaw, narrow crowded streets, turn into lane—Mamabari! Every year, first shy glance at a small cabin in front of the house—I was supposed to have been born there.

One year, by weird coincidence, the governor of West Bengal goes with us to her summer capital, Darjeeling, and returns also the same night to Calcutta that we do. On the outward journey, memorably, entire trainload of people prevented by menacing police from getting down at Monihari Ghat, until she gets into jeep, drives to special steamer, and special steamer—more like a snowy swan—gets across to mid-Ganga. First taste of the power and privileges of the powers that be!

On return leg, even more impressed. At Sealdah Station, walking fast along the hot platform, sudden gust of cool, cool air from a compartment. Next moment, two huge albino Alsatian dogs jump out with their handlers, leaving large tin trays filled with ice. Not as good as AC compartment, but how can the governor's beloved darlings travel in hot compartments like ordinary humans? They are highly pedigreed after all.

Values

After all these years, the one thing that I remember most fondly about my school was the untiring commitment of those good fathers towards building in us a solid foundation of good, strong, and enduring value systems.

To them, school was not just a medium for transferring doses of learning and knowledge to us. It was, rather, a meeting place of intellects for constant interaction and pondering on basic issues of strength of character, courage, eternal curiosity about life all around us, social responsibilities, and healthy competitiveness.

There were several instruments and mechanisms that the fathers created to achieve this daunting task. First, the whole school's student population was divided and allotted to four "houses," or micro-societies, namely, Jaguar, Cheetah, Leopard, and Lion.

I was a proud member of the Jaguars. All activities were programmed around this house structure; so beyond the usual competition between different classes or standards, there was this underlying competition between houses, predominantly in physical activities, such as, daily half-hour marching practice, quarterly marching squad formation, and uniforms' dressage competition. The whole thing culminated in the annual sports day where the where the creme-de-la-creme of school athleticus (Latin word meaning sporty) competed till the last breath for winning the house awards. Till date, through college education, doing different jobs, and in situations of friendly to outrightly hostile professional environments, one has not forgotten those rules of the game which kept us on our toes, but didn't stress us and stretched us without strain, and continuously gain joy from the game well played, whether won or not.

The other great institution was the medley of societies and clubs that were available and where becoming a member of at least three clubs was mandatory. Each club had a senior teacher or father as the mentor/moderator. I don't remember the exact number of clubs, but it would have been at least 20: Debating, Dramatics, Classical Music, Maths Club, Geography, Photography, Botany, Museum Society, Hindi Club—the works, from which the difficulty was not selection, but the agony of which to miss out on. I was a member of the Debating Society, the Drama Club, and the Physics Society. We met at least once a week after classes and spent time on readings, special lectures, experiments, and practical lessons. This was a great means for building scientific curiosity among us, added to seeking intellectual and aesthetic joy from different sources and gaining professional insights to different vocations.

The school inculcated the right values even through small devices. Throughout the year, different teams were formed with three to five members from the class, and for a week, it was their job to clean the classroom after school got over. The school supplied brooms, swabbing clothes, glass cleaning fluid, etc.

Then there would be a sudden inspection tour of all classrooms by the principal, and the winning class would be allowed to put on display the prize pendant on the class notice board for a full week. I recall now, how, just for that puny little piece of cloth, we gave our best to make the class shine.

Well, actually this exercise had far less to do with teaching us social hygiene, as it had to do with humility, imbuing the value of the dignity of labor, team work, and once again, healthy competitiveness.

I wonder if today's schools do any of this. Of course, times have changed drastically. Today, thanks to communication and media methods and diversity, and certainly Internet, there is a virtual explosion in the amount of information that children have access to. The methods of our schools would look archaic but somewhere, aren't our school children becoming isolated, not from information, but from each other?

Make-Believe

If you are a small boy, in a small town in the 1950s, with small formal modes of whiling away your time beyond routine services, and economically you don't have the wherewithal to possess lots of toys and gadgets to mount your imagination, you have to fall back on make-believe with almost everything around you. What else do you do otherwise to keep the voracious reading and bright colored and eventful imaging that is going around you and inside you all the time? You run the danger, of course, of the make-believe component soon overtaking the "reality" level, but what of it? Rather that than starvation of make-believe would be the unwanted, downward spiraling alternative.

As regards items needed to mentally move it over from the "real" world to the one of make-believe, the world is your oyster! Anything around you, anything at all can serve the purpose.

For all the small possessions that I had—a tiny, much abused spinning top, a dozen of assorted marbles, small metal pieces, and parts from all kinds of machinery and gadgets, and cut-outs of different kinds of articles and information from old newspapers and magazines—for all this, I had an old omnibus flat box in which wool had been bought sometime.

That hard cardboard box could take on any shape, size, function, and idiosyncrasies as the situation demanded. Here it was, a humble box, being pushed by me from room to room, when suddenly one looked up and there was half a squadron of fighter bombers flying in low, intentions absolutely clear about our mainstay in this theater, the intrepid aircraft carrier, complete with its own escort of destroyers and submarines.

In less time that would take to even start thinking on what to do, action had already been taken. The wool box was now the carrier on a slightly choppy sea. Alarm sirens, hoots from all the ships, and the sound of a ship's bows cutting fast through the water, and the planes revving up on deck, were now all being "simulated" by me. Quickly, the top of the cardboard box would be reconfigured in the mind. Up would come a smooth flight deck with tight heavy duty springs across for arresting the speeds of returning planes. The end of the deck would hang over the ship's bows and slightly turned up like the nose of an unhappy and cantankerous lady. This was actually to give better thrust to the planes as they quickly revved up and clawed their ways into the blue sky, headed straightaway for the visiting enemy.

Behind the main deck would be all the systems of a modern ship, complete with three huge masts in a row, missile and cannon turrets revving wildly round and round, and firing from time to time.

Everything above happened, as I said, in real quick time, and for the next half an hour, the little boy and his cardboard box—rather the carrier ship—had immense fun and excitement. Outside, life went on normally—crows cawing, siblings playing in their own world, Ma's quick feet going from room to room on the daily chores, but when to return to that reality, and how, was my choice in a world of which I was the uncrowned king.

That cardboard box and its eclectic contents had a lot of creative potential. But that did not limit the possibilities of fantasy plays, with even simpler, common, day-to-day mundane material. Our house bedecked with all kinds of trees, produced round the year all kinds of leaves that fell from them—small and large, thin and pulpy, smooth and rough textured. It is unbelievable as to what those leaves could be turned into in fantasy tales—the fully stretched out banks of sails in a huge pirate ship, the baffles and covers in an Arabian king's harem, and even a serried rank of soldiers marching out of the gates of a desert fort in the French Foreign Legion. All it needed was sufficient time—of which we had a plenty in our small town—a ferocious attachment to the idea of the "story," lots of imagination to create impossible transformations, and the anticipation of sheer joy in creating those magic moments stolen from reality. And I had all of those traits and beyond.

Quite often, your intervention in adding a few well thought out, but not drastic changes on otherwise natural objects resulted in amazing potentials of new fantasies. A well-sucked seed of mango, further sun dried became a light, hairy, and dry piece of wood. Near one edge, you punctured two holes near the end of the seed, turned it over, and punched two more holes on the other side. Towards the other end, with a black pen, you drew two large dots on two sides. Now you inserted four burnt match sticks into the four holes, and hey presto! You had, magically, a slim, well-built pig running for dear life!

Or take the humble walnut, of which there was never a shortage, thanks to people going on pilgrimages all the time, and distributing walnuts as the most popular *prasad* (a devotional offering to a god) from the trip. You carefully cracked the walnut by putting pressure on the joint seam running around the walnut, taking care not to crack the shell. Then you took one half of the shell, and cleaned out the inner wood with the help of a small pen-knife and some sand paper. It was already beginning to look like a fat, sleek river boat. One matchstick or toothpick upright, piercing a small piece of drawing paper in an arch and this stuck upright, and your "boat" had a sail too.

For years, on the wire fence that divided our house from our neighbors', white ants created a huge mound of light brown mud turned into hard, baked earth by the sun. The mound, with a little imagination, looked like an ancient fortress city on a hill with ranks of strong structures going up in step from the wide bottom to the sharp peak. You couldn't see the ants at all, they were all hiding inside.

Since white ants were considered to be one of the most hated insects by everyone because of the way they destroyed wood without your getting even a hint till all was over from inside, considering them as "enemies" was very much fair game. And such a huge edifice of theirs was obviously very fair game of a challenge to knock down their capital and all the building structures supporting it. The structure almost invited you to knock it down.

Which I did. Our colony, like many other places on the Chotanagpur Plateau, was very rocky, and any piece of land was littered with small to fist-sized rocks which could be thrown around. I was quite adept in using them, and my aim was true. So I would gather a few of them, and then approach the white ant citadel, and start lobbing what, by now, had become cannon balls and mortars. Swish, bang, went these one after another, and the walls would start breaking down, exposing labyrinths of passages inside the now broken and shattered walls. The white ants would scurry for dear life in all directions and their peaceful, calm lives would get suitably disturbed, and I could imagine white flags going up.

The good part of this fantasy—the reality game was that white ants would quickly rebuild their broken homes, and invariably with some new design, so resuming the "battles" soon would be a lot of fun.

With so many trees in the house, it was quite expected to continuously come up against every possible shape of small branches and twigs. A discarded shaving blade, a small piece of sandpaper, and lots of imagination, and you can extract, from these twigs, fantastic items which can be used in endless story sessions.

My favorite always was Colt 0.45 magnum revolvers, complete with holsters and belts, which could be strung around tiny plastic dolls for unleashing everything from OK Corrall to a real bloodbath in Jesse James attacks on trains.

The other set of implements, of course, was sets of all kinds and shapes of swords and daggers. I'll always fondly remember a six inch dagger that I carved out of an ordinary piece of bamboo—perfectly symmetrical, double-edged, and heavy hilted. It would have done King Saladin proud. Or the collected trophy of double-handled knight's sword, short dagger, shield, spear, and mace, all cut out from the thin aluminum sheet or foil that was used for sealing a new pack of good tea. I selected a small piece of plywood, polished it up, and carved and cut it into the shape of a bigger shield on which I mounted the smaller weapons with strings holding them tight. Finally, I put the whole assortment on the wall.

My father quickly realized that I was fascinated by all kinds of weapons and making miniatures of any interesting object. So, to my intense delight, he gave me a gift set of a small but very sharp handsaw for cutting wood, one hammer and nails, a set of screwdrivers, one pliers, and accurate steel scales for measurements. It was like a clarion call to my already—overheated brain, and over the next few months, I was prolific in churning out a whole set of new miniatures and objects—a doll's house for my sister, a tiny Swiss cottage, a squadron of different types of planes, ranging from sleek fighters to fat bombers, and three sailing ships from the middle ages.

Naturally, my value rose sharply in the neighborhood stock market of small children. Oh! the fun and ecstasy of distributing exquisite little miniatures among the children and gladly delivering on new objects that they indented. To tell the truth, even now, at this juncture in life where I am far removed from those carefree days of childhood, the prospect of turning a small object into a miniature gets my blood running faster and an amazing excitement about the possibility of creating a fresh make-believe piece of art. But it happens rarely that I actually produce it. Even then, the make-believe about make-believe is superb.

6½ Anna Bazaar

"Middle Class"—such a lovely term to cover up continuous want, small heartbreaks, greedy yearnings, but finally all overcome by getting delighted by smallest of rewards, cocooned in lots of love.

Eagerly looked forward to first Saturday of every month, after pay day—Baba, Ma, and little boy go to Bistupur Bazaar in the evening. First stop, five toy shops in a row—every toy for 6½ annas. Allowed to buy one. The delight, the joy, the launching of whole fantasies, and adventures around each toy. Will remember, till end of eternity, the chicken that lay three white eggs every time you loaded it and squeezed, and the two jerky, drunken boxers who could be set to endless rictus with plunger hidden under boxing ring.

Ritual concludes with visit to Maharaja or Gouranga Sweet Shop—royal feast—just that once a month—of one kalakand, one roshogolla, and one singara. They don't make kalakand like that any more ! Close by, Afghan restaurant for Kabuliwalahs—never ceased to be fascinated by their tall, warrior structures, rampant headgear, strange, guttural dialect, and horror stories of moneylending and ruthlessness. (So which "Kabuliwalah" inspired Tagore to write of such a gentle human?) Right after 6½ anna bazar, delicious, forbidden smells wafting all over, but father's stern

"No, it's unclean" every time. But once, only once, the insistence of the little boy, with doe-eyed supportive (a little greedy, shy smile also?) glance from Ma, tilts the balance.

Three of us pig out on Afghan paratha and red-hot mutton. Can the wealth of a Croesus bring back that night?

Starting in Delhi after College

When I came out of engineering college, the job situation was really bad, and the Maoist Naxalite movement had already started. I had one standing job offer—that in Durgapur Steel Plant—but I didn't want to remain cooped up in a tiny, little place, such as, Durgapur for the rest of my life. So I started looking out and applying everywhere. I was extremely fortunate in getting through, after several rounds of tests, into the prized Senior Management Trainee (SMT) program at DCM Delhi.

With a lot of trepidation in my heart, I reached Delhi by Kalka Mail and made a beeline for Kalibari—the favored destination of every wandering Bengali. You could stay in the guest house for a maximum of three days, after which I was worried about where to stay, have my food, get my clothes washed, etc. Fortunately, my college friend, Metallurgy topper Sudhanghsu stayed in Karol Bagh, and when I put my plight before his father, that benevolent gentlemen took me straight to the Bhowmik residence in 8A block, and in 10 minutes, the Paying Guest deal was struck.

The DCM office was close by—in Jhandewalan in fact, and I could get there quite easily every day for one of the most exciting management training programs that one could think of.

Thus started my life in Delhi, where I have practically spent the best days of my life.

Soon, as I made new friends, life became a rich smorgasbord (buffet) of plays, classical music concerts, movies, and classic Bengali *adda* (social meet between friends).

Festivities

Fairs and Festivals

Twice a year, at Ambagan grounds, vandeville fairs—vertigo inducing Ferris wheels, twirling and galloping horses on merry-go-rounds, the magic mirror halls, the calf with five legs and two heads, but thrill of thrills—"Well of Death"—giant latticed sphere stuck half into ground, with two motorbikes chasing each other at full speed.

Once a year, at Sakchi grounds, the breathtaking visit to the circus, preceded by nights of their giant searchlights criss-crossing the night sky. Two items etched forever in memory—the human cannon shell fired into the net and the high-wire trapeze artists, effortlessly leaving their swinging rods and reaching out for the safe, grasping hands of their partners. Much more than skill, such complete trust, such camaraderie.

Durga Puja—intense rivalry and one-upmanship on how many "thakurs" you had seen, but deep down, all that was really blasé year after year. What provided breathtaking thrills were the rows of tiny shops—toy stores, book shops, and a Solomon's riches crammed into one store—the famous Krishnanagar clay models, miniatures, and imitation fruits, lizards, cockroaches, and spiders. With total *puja* spending allowance of ₹2 zealously garnered from elders, oh! the heart-wrenching choices—the gecko with the cockroach in its mouth or the percussion cap pistol newly sweeping the market. Thanks to regular dosages of western movies seen every Saturday at school, the pistol wins, but forever in the mind, the cockroach tries feebly to escape the gecko's deathly grip.

Durga Puja—Small Town, Small Boy

> The ceremonial worship of the mother goddess is one of the most important festivals of Bengalis. Apart from being a religious festival for the Hindus, it is also an occasion for reunion and rejuvenation, and a celebration of traditional culture and customs. Celebrating the triumphant victory of Devi Durga over the devil of devils, Mahishasur, the people of Bengal engross themselves in the jubilant aura of Durga Puja during the autumnal season. Saptami, Ashtami, Navami, and Vijaya Dashami are the four main days of the festival when the idol of the goddess is worshipped.

Throughout my childhood, one of the most exciting events every year was the Durga Puja celebrations.

For the uninitiated, Durga or "Ma Durga," more precisely, is the divine motherly or feminine force—the "yang" part, as it were, of the oriental depiction. Her birth was through the confluence of all the gods contributing their respective powers and favorite weapons at a time of acute crisis. They had been just thrown out of Heaven by the *asuras*, or demonic forces, and were too weak against the *asura* chief—Mahishasur (Buffalo Asur, literally) and his magical skills.

Fed up with lost battle after lost battle, the gods appealed to the chief gods—Brahma, Vishnu, and Shiva to help out. Unfortunately, they too declined, confirming that individually they were no match against Mahishasur. But, they advised, if all gods got together, their collective force could create a supremely powerful entity who could take on Mahishasur.

The gods heeded good advice and together created the female force, Durga (she who helps overcome "durgati" or crises). The force emanated from each of them and coalesced to form the Mother. The gods then worshiped her, both in fear and with joy. She had 10 arms, and each god gave her their favorite and most powerful weapon, like the *vajra* or thunder from Indra. And the lion came and became her carrier. Then she set out for battle. The three worlds shook and shivered from the impact of battle in which the *asura* constantly changed his form magically. Finally, when he took the form of a huge buffalo, Durga cut off his head. From inside, appeared the *asur*. Instantly, Durga pierced his chest with a trident and slayed him.

Great was the rejoicing in all the firmament, and the gods returned to Heaven and celebrated the victory for days. Since then, this is the occasion to celebrate the victory of good over evil.

Mahalaya

> Mahalaya is an auspicious occasion observed seven days before Durga Puja, which heralds the advent of Durga, the goddess of supreme power. It's a kind of invocation or invitation to the mother goddess to descend on earth. Since the early 1930s, Mahalaya has come to associate itself with an early morning radio program called "Mahishasura Mardini" or "The Annihilation of the Demon." This program has almost become synonymous with Mahalaya. For nearly six decades now, the whole of Bengal rises up in the chilly predawn hours, 4:00 a.m. to be precise, of the Mahalaya day to tune in to the "Mahishasura Mardini" broadcast.

Durga was united with her eternal consort, Lord Shiva, and from that union was born Ganesh, the God of fulfillment; Lakshmi, the Goddess of wealth; Saraswati, the Goddess of all knowledge; and Kartik, the God of warfare. So when one worships the image of Durga, it is the collective group statuettes of Durga riding the lion and slaying Mahishasur at her feet, the four children, and Lord Shiva reclining on top. All these statues are put under one arched stand or back drop.

While the female force is worshipped by many names across India, it is only in Bengal and two/three other eastern states that Ma Durga is worshipped every year during autumn on the 7th to 9th of the new moon phase—Saptami, Ashtami, and Navami. The whole larger than life-sized statue ensemble is placed on a special stage in a park or household garden on the 6th, Shashthi evening, and the statue maker and chief priest together instill life in the images, thus bringing all the gods to life, and as participants in the ceremonies rather than as distant gods.

The kick off would happen with a radio program unique to All-India Radio Calcutta station. Seven days before the *puja* or formal worship started, there was a program called "Mahalaya" or the "great abode" or great tale. The best reciters and singers of Bengal got together at 4:00 a.m. and for about two hours, recited about the origin and deeds of Ma Durga, interspersed with beautiful devotional and celebratory songs. In an age when there was no TV, the radio was the main—actually only—device for programmed entertainment. So on Mahalaya morning, at 4:00 a.m., the entire neighborhood would burst alive with the radio going full blast in every house.

Then came three days of fun, total relaxation of time schedules of daily life, wearing new clothes, and catching up with all friends and relatives. As a small 10-year-old boy, I would get special pocket money not only from my parents, but also from uncles and relatives visiting us from Calcutta. For three days, one hopped with friends from *pandal* to *pandal* (decorated place of worship), and a great thing was made out of how many *pandal*s you had "scored"!

The main distractions at the *pandal*s were all kinds of eating joints, toy stores, book stores, and variety shops selling all kinds of stuff—from kitchen knives to coconut fiber ropes to the famous true to scale dolls of animals, insects, and fruits from Krishnanagar.

Throughout the day, different types of worship were done as prescribed, with two drummers belting out different beats on huge drums. The whole place would be thronging with thousands of people visiting the *pandal*, taking in the finer points of statue work and decorations. Incidentally, this would be an issue of ferocious competition between organizers of different *puja*s and in many towns, even formal prizes were awarded for the best stalls.

The nights were dedicated to entertainment programs by local amateurs and professionals hired out mainly from Calcutta. The quality of these programs was also a matter of ferocious comparison and competition. When I was very small, all we had was plays enacted in the classical *jatra* format. This was the most ubiquitous format in every corner of India before the advent of the stage and screen. In *jatra*, a slightly raised earthen platform, in the shape roughly of a square, was the open stage with the audience sitting all around, and one path formally connecting the dais with the green room. An orchestra of flutes, clarinets, harmoniums, and drums sat at one edge of the stage to keep playing appropriate music.

In this format, magnificent stories were unfolded—mainly mythological and middle-age romances of wicked kings, magicians, young royal lovers, patriotic soldiers, etc., in an epic format. To liven all this up and also to compensate for the stark lack of any props, two theatrical instruments were important. First, the narrator, who, as in musical morality plays, would appear from time to time and sing out on appropriate set of comments on what had happened so far, what was about to happen, and the morals to be drawn for one's own sake. He would also raise tantalizing questions on whether Right would finally win over Evil or not.

The other instrument was the group dance of "sakhis"—literally girlfriends, excepting that they were all men, hastily shaved up and suitably attired in fetching feminine attire. There was the thinnest of logical connection between them and the main storyline, but that didn't matter at all. They came, they sang, and romped over the stage, and the orchestral musicians went berserk and freaked out because these were the few moments when they got their spot in the limelight. And, of course, the audience loved it and lapped it up.

Looking back, today I wonder at the genius of those *jatra* players. In today's theater, there is the safety of being boxed in on three sides, the provision for melting away into the side screens, any amount of stage props, lighting, and modern gimmicks. The actors, indubitably, handle much more serious subjects, but their *jatra* counterparts were heroes in comparison, and had to create the illusion of a full stage in front of the encircling audience through the sheer power of great acting. No wonder then, despite all the popularity of the stage, *jatra* as a form has still not died and gets played even today—at least in rural Bengal, since urban areas have killed this format long back.

With time, the Durga Puja theme has been much "modernized," not necessarily, I believe for the better. In fact, many of the changes have been outrageous. The first outrage has been with the *protima*—statue set of the divine family. Initial experiments were with a weird list of materials beyond the clay with which the *protima* is traditionally made. Wood, copra, nails, matchsticks—anything and everything was passé. Then came "thematic" *protima*s and lighting. Ma Durga's face was deliberately transformed to that of a popular film star, the Kargil War meant batteries of Bofors guns firing together through lighting. And on and on—ad nauseam. The rivalry between *puja* societies has remained but now no longer with devotion as the measuring criterion, but one upmanship of gimmicks. The shops have also changed with time—three fourth being eating joints and the rest a rag-tag medley of electronics stores, music shops, etc.

So for three days, a hectic schedule of shuttling from *puja pandal* to *pandal*, eating every kind of junk assiduously avoided under duress for the rest of the year and yearned for, buying toys and small statuettes, going home in the late afternoon only to do a quick change of clothes, and off again to a *pandal* promising a hit *jatra* play preceded by the local talent breaking into song and dance. For some strange reason that I still haven't figured out, this whole entertainment package was called a "function." It had very little to do with any functionality—pure entertainment being the only objective.

Anyway, for three nights, one attended the best "functions," creating mental compendia to score over other friends in the neighborhood. Today, something like 50 years on from that magical childhood, where has all the innocence, thrill, and devotion gone? Today, you have to get into a *pandal* in a long queue because of the population explosion, and then through a metal detector frame and a cursory body search, checking of mobile phone, etc. by a security man. This is the part that I feel is the most dispiriting today, and successfully chokes and kills whatever romantic notions with which you wanted to visit the *pandal* anyway.

There is also a drastic change in the devotees: pure pleasure seekers ratio in favor of the latter. This is not to say that there are no devotees packing the space in front of the statues, but somehow the focus is more on having fun, and not really communicating with Ma Durga. It's all so skin deep, so formatted. Somewhere in that crowd, I hope, there is a small boy from a small town who is yearning for the missing freedom of 50 years back.

Lakshmi Puja

> Lakshmi Puja is another Bengali festival that is celebrated in every household. Goddess Lakshmi, the Goddess of wealth is worshipped just after Durga Puja. Lakshmi is one of the daughters of Durga who symbolizes wealth, peace, and prosperity.

Ma always dedicated to Lakshmi Puja every Thursday. Guess when life does not give you riches, devotion increases proportionately! Small oil lamp lit with love, family sits around. Ma, our

Lakshmi, reads out the Panchali—miraculous tales of the goddess' boons to the devoted—set to verse and read out in a sing-song tone with slight to-and-fro swaying of the body in synch.

Then, once a year, the grand annual Lakshmi Puja on the full-moon night, five days after the end of Durga Puja. All kinds of delicacies cooked throughout the day. The most thrilling part is Ma drawing incredible, circular decorative floral motifs on the verandah outside and just before you enter the *puja* room. And leading inwards from outside to the *puja* room, a series of figure of eight footsteps with five cute little toe marks on top—left foot, right foot, inviting Ma Lakshmi to follow those footsteps of yearning and pleas, come right in, and reside forever in our home—wealth forever. Oh! poor woman forever struggling with want, but still with hope lingering in one corner of the mind—she will come, she will come, we will have comforts beyond dreams—someday, someday, someday.

Saraswati Puja Celebrations

Saraswati Puja is one such festival that almost all the Bengali homes celebrate. On this day, the Goddess of knowledge and fine arts is worshipped with great fervor. The Bengali community considers knowledge and fine arts as an integral part of its life. People of all age participate in Saraswati Puja with unparallel intensity. The Goddess of knowledge and fine arts is clad in white sari with a "Beena" in her left hand.

The Hindu pantheon is supposed to contain 330 million gods and goddesses. That's too mind boggling a prospect for any normal mortal, so we have learnt to make convenient subsets of our own, depending on our favorites, inclinations, and needs. But a few gods and goddesses stand apart, and hold portfolios important enough to be in everyone's personal pantheon.

Goddess Saraswati is one such divine entity. She is the Goddess for all studies and fine arts, specifically music. Once a year, in January, there is a specific day earmarked for *puja* (worship) to Saraswati. It is a day that essentially belongs to school- and college-going children, and in our tiny colony of bungalows and flats, she had a special welcome every year.

There was a strange ritual associated with the worship of Saraswati. Since she was the Goddess of studies, one would expect that on her *puja* day, there would be a lot of fervent studying and use of all implements of knowledge seeking—books, notebooks, pens and pencils, and so on. In reality though, the ritualistic rule that you must not touch any of these things—no studying, in effect. This was a rule that was most eagerly followed by all children. What you did, however, was to place one of your favorite books at the feet of the clay idol of the Goddess, with fervent prayers that she grant you the boon of scholastic excellence. After all, what were gods and goddesses for, if, like you, they also didn't work hard at their end of the bargain?

Since it was a day specifically for the benefit of children, the day was celebrated with several extracurricular events. In any case, though the major support from Ma Saraswati was academic, she was also the goddess of fine arts, which definition could, with a little imagination and creativity, be stretched to all children-related activities, including athletics.

This is what was done in our colony. Throughout the morning and afternoon, all kinds of field events—short runs, long runs, high jump, etc., were organized with the accent being on making as many children as possible to participate. I enthusiastically took part in as many of these as I could, but unfortunately I was a tail ender. This is because throughout my early childhood, I had suffered from all kinds of diseases, and as a result, I was sickly and weak physically, although mentally I was as keen and alert as the best of them. But that didn't save me from the ridicule that I had to face every year from other children.

One year I said to myself that enough was enough, and I was going to do something about this, but quietly, and without anyone's knowledge. Now, the most prestigious contest was the longest run of 800 m. I decided that I would go hell for leather for it, although at that time even a slow 200 m run would completely exhaust me.

In front of our house there was a government high school, which had a huge playground used for football, cricket, and athletics. Throughout December and well into January till Saraswati Puja day, I started getting up very early in the morning, just when the sun rose and started going to the field and running for a short distance. In order to pace myself properly and not to tire out early, I kept the initial runs for 100 m only, gradually increasing it at my own pace to the targeted 800 m. In the initial days, I would start gasping for breath early on and feel my legs getting cramped. But slowly, yet surely, I started getting my first breath, and then my second breath, until I could relax and actually start enjoying the run.

Thus, over about a month and a half, I had quietly, without anyone getting a clue, mastered the 800 meters and was fully ready for the battle. Then came the big day and all the children of our colony had gathered together on the sports field. Event after event went past and I didn't move an inch, while in the previous years, I used to idiotically participate in almost every event, fail miserably, and become the laughing stock. This year everybody started laughing at me, assuming that I had chickened out.

Finally, the 800 m run was announced and about a dozen boys got together at the starting line. I walked over slowly and joined the queue. A big round of derisive guffaws greeted me when people saw me trying for the toughest race only. The main competitor was Bunu, who was a Santhal tribal, built like a stone statue of the gods and superbly athletic. With his stamina and natural talents, he would generally win any event hands down and everyone acknowledged that.

The race starter got us lined up. A smart shot in the air and we were off. Now the 800 m meant four rounds, of 200 m each, round the track. Everyone ran the first 2½ rounds in a slow shuffle, kind of measuring out each other, run a bit faster for 1½ rounds, and let loose a burst of speed in the last round. This year was no different excepting that I deliberately ran last, showing as though I was getting tired. A few derisive catcalls greeted me from the spectators, but I grit my teeth and kept my cool.

We had finished 2½ rounds. Now the tempo would go up slowly. But I changed that with my strategy, immediately streaking out at full speed. The participants were so stunned that they kept looking at me open-mouthed, disbelieving what they saw. Before they could make up their minds on what to do, I was ahead of them excepting for Bunu, who, natural athlete that he was, had instinctively started speeding up. So the last ½ round, or 100 m, was really a neck-to-neck tie between us, and imagine my delight when, at the finishing line, I just nosed ahead to win the 800 m! Thunderous applause broke out, and I can still hear it, not just because I won but mainly because I proved to myself that even if you start as a loser, there is little that you can't achieve with determination.

After a well-deserved siesta in the afternoon, I got up to get ready for the eagerly awaited Recitation Competition, which was a specialty of our colony. All enthusiasts were grouped by age into tiny tots, junior school, senior school, and adults. We, siblings, covered "children" completely, my younger brother in tiny tots, my sister in juniors, and I in seniors. One fixed poem was allocated to each group, and all competitors rendered the same poem to ensure fair play.

My father was a brilliant recitationist/orator, well known all over the town for his capabilities. People used to come from faraway places to learn from my father. He was an excellent coach. His unique capability lay in the fact that he never read out poetry in a particular manner or style, waiting for the student to imitate him like a mindless recording machine. He made you read the lines again and again, asking the student to explain the meaning of each word, until you suddenly knew how to recite a particular line perfectly, because by then you knew the true meaning, the very soul, of the poem, and unless you were totally insensitive, you matched your recitation with the poem—exactly as merited.

So it was hardly surprising that we three siblings carried away all recitation trophies in every competition anywhere in town. My father, of course, was one of the three judges on every Saraswati Puja day in our colony. He agreed only against a clear integrity issue being accepted by the organizers—my father would not judge the performance of any of us three siblings.

For me, that evening was the last time I would appear in the colony event because I was finishing school that year and would have to go out of town for college studies. Coincidentally, my brother was appearing for the first time. One by one, we three got up on stage and gave it our best rendering. Finally, after a tense 10 minute wait, the results were announced, and, as expected, we siblings had swept off the first prize in each corresponding group.

By then, since it was dinner time, everyone broke off and went home for meals. But the Saraswati Puja celebrations were not over yet, and the grand finale was the rendering of a part of a Tagore opera. The part that a colony girl and I played was for "Karna–Kunti Samvad." It is a highly emotive play, performed in blank verse.

It is one of the most poignant and gripping creations by Tagore. In the epic Mahabharata war, Kunti, the mother of the Pandavas, is mortally scared that Karna, the chief enemy warrior, had taken a vow to kill her son Arjun, also reckoned as Karna's only match as a warrior. Unknown to Karna, however, is the fact that he is actually Kunti's son also, although illegitimate, born to Kunti before her marriage, elder to all the five Pandavas.

Kunti reveals this secret on the eve of the battle to Karna, cleverly trying to weaken his resolve. She succeeds, but not before

Karna curses her for giving birth to him and then abandoning him. But at the same time, he assures her unequivocally that at the end of the battle next day, Arjun would definitely live. In fact, he gives his blessings to his brother Arjun.

That was the highlight of one Saraswati Puja program that I would cherish my whole life.

INTERESTS

Literary Sweethearts

My father had been forced, owing to circumstances that he couldn't control, to start going to school at the age of three, in an era, and in a village where you didn't even think "school" until you reached the ripe age of seven.

This left a lifelong scar on my father's psyche and an intense revulsion towards the formal school process. So when he begot me, he announced to the world at large that I would bypass the entire school education scene, sit as a private candidate for matriculation, and thence on to college.

This was an excellent arrangement, as far as I was concerned, since it freed me completely from any regimen and empowered me to continue my innovations on every kind of prank possible and unchecked hours of play on the Khorkaai sand banks and fruit trees in the neighborhood.

But more lastingly, it opened the floodgates of reading literature—first Bengali and then English, during the long afternoons when a tired Ma had her siesta, and I was banned from moving out of the house. Taking advantage of Ma's sleep, I also went through all the "for adults" books of my parents. Most of the characters etched indelible marks on me, but the pride of place must go to a number of characters of heroines, of whom two I'll always cherish as sweethearts first to a small, goggle-eyed boy, and then constant, imagined objects of love from teenage till date. One was Aparna, Apu's wife from Bibhutibhushan's Aparajito, and the other was Swati, the urbane, sensitive sophisticate from Buddhadev Bose's *Tithi dore*.

Bibhutibhusan enjoyed and continued to enjoy the status of a god in our house. Some of his books, such as, *Pather Panchali*, *Aparajito*, and *Aranyak*, must have been read more than a dozen times. Such a huge canvass of the simplest, most materially denied people from all walks of life! And of them, forever will burn in my heart, the character of Aparna.

The coming together of Apu and Aparna was ordained to happen through a seriocomic set of events in which Apu had gone to Aparna's house only as a friend of her brother to attend her wedding. Theirs is a well-to-do family and the marriage has been fixed with the son of a neighboring landlord. Unfortunately, it has been hidden from the girl's side that the boy is epileptic. The stress of the wedding rites and the day's heat conspire to reveal all, and seeing this, the bride's side refuses to proceed. But the girl, according to ancient rules, must be married before daybreak, or else remain a spinster forever. So Apu is persuaded to do the needful, despite being very destitute financially.

Aparna, though village bound all her life, was a perfect foil for the highly romantic Apu. On their wedding night, the calm and simple, beautiful teenager actually takes the lead in their first pillow talk, and Apu is delightfully stunned into admonishing himself for having had wrong notions about "romance."

The newly weds returned to Calcutta and Aparna was abruptly thrown against the sordid reality of Apu's poverty, and the imperative to adjust herself to one dirty little room next to a railway yard, and hence loud noise, dust, and smoke all the time. The girl who was the darling of the family, living in a spacious old building and with every material comfort possible in rural Bengal, almost gave up. But then, Apu's helplessness, his deep love for her, and crucially, his tremendous dependence on her for the smallest of things, made her rally around bravely, and her calmness and delightful smile hid from Apu her true inner feelings.

Then Apu, too, could get over his guilt, which had built up right from the wedding day, about giving Aparna a rough time. And his love for Aparna grew deeper, compared to and beyond the superficial ecstasy that he had found in her beauty. And Apu spent with her most of the little free time that he could manage. Her calmness, sweet sense of humor, the joy of seeing her put on a special ornamental dot between her eyebrows because he loved it so—all combined to take Apu to new levels of love that he could never have dreamt about.

And then Apu went overboard and excitedly proposed to Aparna a visit to Apu's mud cottage in the villages, quite different from city facilities. Aparna immediately agreed and the young couple took off. They reached their home a little after dusk and borrowed a small lamp from a neighbor. Aparna was hard pressed to hold back her tears and extreme depression at seeing the roof almost missing, the walls mostly crumbling, and the whole unkempt place covered with weeds.

Yet she fought back and by the middle of the next day, she had got the place down to reasonable control and serviceworthy. While she cooked their lunch, she felt a warm glow of blessings from Heaven from all of Apu's ancestors, especially his mother, who was the last person to cook in that hearth.

After a week, Apu and Aparna returned to Calcutta. Shortly after that, Apu had to send Aparna home for delivering her first baby. Apu felt a strange kind of excitement at this prospect. After the due date, he waited eagerly for some news. It came in the form of his friend, Pranab, with whom he had gone to attend Pranab's cousin Aparna's, wedding. Pranab appeared heart broken, and, in a few disjointed words, informed Apu about Aparna's death during childbirth.

Strangely, instead of breaking down, Apu was in a much more normal mode than Pranab, urging him and persuading him to provide more and more details. It was as if a great hollow had been formed right in his soul, never to be refilled again. While reading about this, I felt exactly like Apu and my heart yearned for the calm, slightly withdrawn, yet also slightly amused, visage of Aparna, now never to be seen again. She will remain in my mind and heart as the epitome of womanhood, the ideal life time companion who would not only love, but also inspire, guide, and share, drinking together to the dregs of the wine of life.

The other literary sweetheart was Swati, the enigmatic heroine of Buddhadev Bose's landmark book, "Tithidore." Swati was the youngest of the five daughters in a middle class, but socially well-established, Calcutta family. Her mother died while bringing Swati into the world, but her loving father more than made up for it.

The story unfolds at a point of time where the first four sisters have been married off. Both the parents of Swati having been very handsome people, all the sisters were extremely beautiful. Swati herself had just finished high school and joined college. She was at a delectable point in her life, transforming from the magical teens to young adulthood. She had also started falling in love with one of the younger professors—Satyen. The two of them made a wonderful couple—young, inexperienced, naïve, tentative, and yet reaching out to each other like the tendrils of a pair of young creepers on the vine.

Through the book, Swati gradually discovers the joy of her womanhood, and the inevitable, attendant spell that she casts over several men. The most obnoxious of them is the neo-modern Harin, who is the leader of a group of supposedly emancipated young bucks, whom, however, Swati effortlessly exposes as being shallow and people who mindlessly imitate the worst aspects of Western deportment. This ability of the very young Swati is what endeared her most to me.

The denouement comes with the death of Tagore, when Satyen hurries to her home and picks her up for joining the long queue of people accompanying the body to the crematorium. Nothing is said between them—it is not even necessary. The passing away of someone, who's even more than a family, binds both of them, and removes the final barriers, if any, that might have existed. Swati finally blossoms out fully.

The last part is about the actual wedding night. The author portrays it brilliantly as a collage of phrases and half completed sentences, where, for over five pages, one enjoys the myriad sounds, scenes, odors, and touch that paints a glorious, uninhibited hosanna to the worship of youth.

It is an unforgettable experience in pure romance.

On Writing and Acting

From my very infant days, I have been greatly intrigued by the science and art of writing. Of the strange magic by which a group of words is made to communicate whole stories, a picture, thoughts, feelings—to be captured forever in a unique lattice of profound meaning. By the same token, I was equally intrigued by bringing those written words alive on stages to audiences captured spellbound in front of narrators of timeless creation.

Writing began classically, as it happens for any Bengali boy. It started with "Haate Khori," a quasi-religious ceremony on the auspicious day of the *puja*, or worship, of Goddess Saraswati, the patron Goddess of all education and learning. Small children, who had so far had no exposure to the alphabet, lined up at the *puja pandal* with small slates and chalk (khori) pieces. A priest first invoked some special mantras, conveying the aspiring students' desires to the Mother Goddess. Then he wrote out a few of the alphabets on the slate, made the boy hold the chalk, and while holding his hand, guided it over the alphabets to initiate the lifetime habit of retracing what were essentially pictures into meaningful text. My initiation rites happened with such electric movements and chanting of the deep, sonorous Vedic ritualistic mantras.

The English and Hindi texts, of course, were picked up in school, along with the Bengali learnt at home. Mr D'Souza and Mr Pandey, respectively, were responsible for these initiations.

The true majesty of the written English language was unfolded before us by Father Power, who taught the language with Teutonic military discipline. First, he got each of us to invest in ten visiting card sized blank cards each. On each of them, on one side was written a new word, and on the reverse, a sentence using the word to expound its meaning properly. You were supposed to keep referring to these cards until you had mastered all the 10 new words. At that point, you transferred them to a visual word bank on a drawing sheet sized paper and replaced them with a fresh set of 10 new words. And, thus, was your linguistic skill supposed to increase by leaps and bounds. Subject, of course, to a constant and vigilant check that the new words were being used in your daily and weekly assignments.

Father Power also focused on things like similes and metaphors in his own inimitable style. For about a month, all we would do would be to practice writing metaphors and nothing else. He was highly appreciative of Barun, referring to a tiger's teeth as "carpenter's nails." As he was, in a create pictures with words phase, with my writing that the lord of the jungle sauntered through the tall grass.

The next thing Father Power did was to make us write book criticisms. He first taught us the elements of literary criticism. Then he announced that we would have to read one small book each over the weekends and write its criticism for submission on Monday. During the summer and winter holidays, we were expected to read a full scale novel and write its critique. And every time I have done so, I have discovered new shades and depths which have really been reflective of the maturing of my perceptions of life.

The logical progression, I believe, is from converting pictures into words, to converting those words into sound or speech.

Another way, probably, at measuring the issue, is to believe that initially, in all civilizations across the world, there was only the spoken word. Converting that into picture forms, that is, words came much later with articulation of specific picture forms into specific sounds or the "spoken" words.

This led naturally, and causally, to the whole art of acting, first without any words, and then with words and a definite script. To understand this, we need to throw back quite a few millennia to primitive man. He had progressed from the gatherer to the hunter and thence to the farmer, each stage denoted by the early, mid, and late phases. Survival, which was the key objective of life, depended acutely on procreation of the tribe and the ability to wrest from nature sufficient food to live another day. So it was essential that each generation learn the ropes from the previous one on how to garner food, especially food that was hunted.

So we imagine the primitive man's evening, the tribe gathered around the primal fire. Suppose their primary food is deer, either caught by hand in pit traps, or hunted down by spear, or bow and arrow. The young novitiates of the tribe need to understand the concept of "deer" without the benefit of pictures—later redressed by cave paintings—or the spoken word. So the senior hunters get up, and two of them mimic the deer and the hunter. The "deer" puts his hands to his head, denoting antlers, jerks his head from side to side, as a startled deer would, bends his body and legs and minces along, imitating the jump and run of a deer. All the while, he puts his nose in the air and sniffs around, as a deer would to place the scent of the big enemy—man. In the meanwhile, the "hunter" first demonstrates how you need to be upwind from the deer so that your scent does not carry through. For doing this, he pussyfoots round in a circle till the deer, initially startled, becomes complacent and settles down.

Then the "hunter" gets down on all fours and starts crawling towards the "deer," slowly inching forward towards the target. And then, the grand denouement of the plunging spear. The wounded animal writhes in pain. The hunter twists the spear in further. Then in a flash, the throat is severed and the hunt is over.

Now the second act of the "play" has to be rolled out. The triumphant march back to the tribal caves. The skinning and quartering of the deer, the roasting over the roaring fire, and finally the grand feast ending in couples sauntering away in the darkness to fulfill the first key imperative, procreation. This whole cameo—from spotting of the deer to the finale of tribal progression—was "acted" out in front of the novitiates and trainees, so that they got a holistic sense of life. And thus was theater born.

Naturally, over time, long before written scripts came into being, several embellishments happened naturally. It progressed rapidly from the primitive format down the ages. First came the use of over-sized masks to remove the inconvenience of observing facial expressions from long distances. Blank masks, forerunners of the theater of alienation, deliberately froze on one particular emotion or expression, removing the subjectivism of individual interpretation.

The masked actors were clubbed together to form the chorus which commented on the main stream of events in the play from time to time, drawing moral ethical lessons, highlighting weaknesses in the principal characters, and generally debating the various prospects of how events might shape up in future. This was an extremely important instrument for the playwright to provide an understream of commentary along with the main matter of the play.

For a long time, there was no concept of back, front, or side screens boxing in the play area. It was all in the open. The Greeks first introduced the concept of simple backdrops—side screens being a much later innovation. This has led to an interesting legend. In India, just before a play starts, we feel the front screen quivering in eager anticipation or "Yavanika kampamaan," literally, the screen, or "yavanika" is trembling, or "kampamaan." Now, the Greeks have been always referred to as "yavans" in our history. So this is direct evidence of the concept of screens being derived from Greek practice.

Screens immediately added new dimensions to the plays. In their absence, the writer had to put long, wordy text in the mouths of the actors for elaborate descriptions of palaces, gardens, battlefields, oceans, etc., which was for the benefit of the audience to imagine the ambience and get into the mood as it were. This, of course, was a tremendous wastage. With appropriately painted scenes, the story could be told much more shortly.

Another important instrument was the breaking up of one monolithic structure into three or five acts, they in turn being further divided into three to four scenes each, depending on the length of the play. One-act plays, of course, were broken up into short scenes only which were contiguous on one setting and props, so that there was no drop-scene punctuated delineation of the total matter.

Naatyakaal

The start point of my association with *Naatyakaal* ("era of plays") was Mihir, who was my first friend in Karol Bagh. He turned up at my paying guest home on a Sunday morning and easily struck up a friendship. He was an affable, warm-hearted, and helpful person, who very soon introduced me to the whole group which was involved in writing, producing, and performing agit—prop plays with a distinct Left bias.

When I met the group—Shyamal, Bachchu, Prodeep, Benu, Krishna, Sebabroto, Sidhu, Piyal, Soumitro, Dilip, Vito, Hem, and many more over the years—I was struck by the keenness and dedication with which everyone attacked each aspect of creating a play—selection of topic, research, creation of a specific dialogue committee for that play, set design, costumes, etc.

In 1970s, the group created many plays and performed them right up to Calcutta at various forums—play competitions, Puja festival, sponsored visits, and also a Hindi translation of the very popular play on the all-pervasive impact of advertising.

Over the years, the plays became popular elsewhere, and through the magazine of the same name, they reached smaller towns in northern and eastern India and were enthusiastically performed by local amateur groups.

Probably the most memorable play, from my perspective, was "Auho Bignyapan" ("Oh! Advertisement") in which, like in the play "Natok" (play), I was involved throughout the play in every aspect. Of particular importance was the technology of the eye-camera, that I got introduced in a scene done memorably by Vito at center stage. The main theme for that scene was "Advertise, or perish!" The introduction, with Sebabroto as the narrator, expanded on the onslaught of advertising, with the back stage half-lit, a giant net with a collage of ads hanging from the ceiling. We stood in front of the net in a row and shouted out some of the most popular ad lines of the day.

Soumitra Chatterjee's wife also ran an amateur theater group. We got in touch with them, and they sponsored two shows at CLT Calcutta in 1975. We performed Chalchitra and Auho! Bignyapan, and the audience was spell bound. It included Nirmalya Acharya, Editor of Soumitra's magazine *Ekh khon*, and the legendary Bijon Bhattacharya, whose house we visited the next day at Bhawanipur. He was delighted with our performance and gave us his whole-hearted blessings.

Somewhere along the way, we started a magazine of the same name. The cover background color, predominantly green, changed with each issue, with the name written in a beautiful font. Content wise, the main contribution came from members of the group with occasional outside content from poets and essayists. The magazine had a limited close circulation among theater enthusiasts in Delhi, Calcutta, and among small amateur theater groups across India. The content was mainly political with a slight Left bias, since in the 1970s, all over the world, Left orientation was sweeping across youth forums and colleges/universities. Parallely, more plays started getting created, and in the 1970s, as many as 12 plays got produced. All of them were not necessarily enacted, and we were quite content to produce on stage as many as five plays.

One perennial problem for amateur theater groups like ours was the shortage of actors and actresses. We had to carefully orchestrate the content to suit our manpower, and sometimes also assign multiple roles to the same person with quick change of costumes during the play.

Over the years, interesting and amusing incidents happened all the time during our productions of different plays. Some of them related to the venue, some to our own pranks, and some yet to the vagaries of forgetting one's lines during the play!

My wife, Purnima, my life partner, had always been intrigued by the phenomenon called Natyakaal and the influence it had on my adult life.

Entertainment—Then and Now

Somewhere in the last 1960s, Arthur Clarke had said that the sum total of man's scientific prowess in 1900–1960 far exceeded that from the time man was a semi-monkey to 1900! Every facet of life got impacted by a breath-taking launch of device after device from new technologies, but I think no area has been shaken up as much as entertainment—content, creation, and means of delivery.

Some of the technologies that played a pivotal role are the invention of transistors, television, telephones, automobiles, satellite communication, air travel, solid state devices for storing huge amounts of program software, computers reduced to laptops and PDAs, and, of course, Internet and mobile telephony.

I remember my childhood, up to high school, as one in which we had no telephone at home, and the only "technology" to see, apart from an old bicycle, was a large 6E radio in a huge wooden cabinet because you actually had valves and no transistors. There were also just three or four medium wave channels, including Aakash Vani or All India Radio and a few international channels, such as, BBC or VOA that you could get on shortwave.

Program content was also restricted to a few categories only—songs, a few talks on different subjects, children's special programs, and for me, the most gripping was the radio plays. Much later in life, while being involved in theater, I could fully realize how difficult it had been for those radio plays to communicate with the audience only through voice, with everything else to be imagined. Hats off to those brilliant script writers! How effortlessly they conveyed every human condition—passion, romance, heroism, duplicity, and every human milieu—villages, middle-age castles, modern drawing rooms. You name it, and there was a radio play somewhere that had captured the period, the place, and the mood.

There was only one program over which there was a regular stiffness in the house which was the weekly Binaca Geetmala, compered by the incomparable Amin Sayani. Father felt that the program, based on Hindi film songs, was not quite "Kulturny"! The rest of us differed politely and went ahead for that magic hour every Wednesday evening. But after that conversations would remain visibly strained for a while!

We were small boys in a small town where technology, other than radios, bicycles, an occasional car, and the ubiquitous sewing machine were totally absent. So we had to improvise our entertainment ourselves at low costs and low exertion. Sure, we didn't have today's gadgets, but that didn't prevent our daily routines not being totally packed with some program or the other throughout the year.

Many of these games needed nothing more than what Mother Nature had provided. A very popular game was Kabaddi, ideally played on the sands of Khorkaai. Our own variation on that was called Kharia-banda, a collage of two armies colliding skillfully on city edges, and swift reaction and reflexes to avoid getting caught. Then there were games where we made our own devices—stick and rugby ball in miniature, the famous *gulli-danda*, popular all over India. Then tops to spin, with the mother block of wood from sesame trees, to be carved into shape by a carpenter in the market and big nail inserted. Custom built Y-shaped slings for hunting big chameleons and stealing fruits from trees, ideally made from the springy guava tree. The straight, hard, and malleable sesame tree branches, duly peeled and scraped, provided marvelous cricket wickets. Marbles, constantly jangling in every boy's pockets, were put to use in innumerable games, some to test your ballistic abilities and others to test how best you could sling a marble from your middle finger while squatting. And last but not the least, the kite season, in which kites and string holding wooden drums, and spindles of course, had to be bought from the market but jealously guarded formula based "maja," a mixture of sticky materials and ground glass, was applied to the whole length of the string to get ready for kite fight in summer. Of course, the list would be grossly inadequate if one missed out on football, which was the mainstay for the bulk of the year.

In short, we didn't have ready-to-serve toys, or television, or CD-ROMs, but we had lots of imagination and the willingness to continuously innovate and have endless fun with so little provided to us by society of that era. Today, when I look at small children, sure, they are very smart, informed, and clever about manipulating life, but I bet 90 percent of them have been denied one of the greatest pleasures a small boy can have—climbing trees right to the top!

UNFORGETTABLE PEOPLE

Father Power

Father Power—mentor and kindler of eternal love for literature—his austere, usually stern face breaking into smile at my 32-page book review of Jean Christophe: "is not quite the right age for reading such a heavy book. Read it again later." Have faithfully followed guru's dictum—read the book after every 10 years, delighted anew every time with new understanding, new tastes, flavors, and new joys!

Father Power was 6½ feet tall, so I always had to look up a lot to him. Father Kirsch, on the other hand, was at an eye-to-eye matter of fact level. Gurus, savants, both, of the oldest schools of mind openers, knowledge givers, and explainers of the larger sense of life.

They taught English and Physics respectively—two of the most exciting subjects of limitless possibilities. Most intriguingly, Fr Power managed to teach English with a lot of the organic and mathematical discipline of Physics, and Fr Kirsch taught Physics with the romance of English!

Well, to be actually very honest, Fr Power's methodology and style came a lot closer to that of a Marines Sergeant Major than of a Physicist, and in the last 45 years, one has not come across even the mention of another teacher who followed these methods.

One did not know the term then, but Fr Power was definitely from the Method school. All matter, existing or to be created, first had to be diced and sliced into smallest measurable entities. Each would then have to be assimilated completely, stored away, and then, at an appropriate time would have to be strung together with other small modules to create a masterpiece.

Which is why, for more than one month, all we did was metaphors till we started having metaphor nightmares. Which is why, before we kicked off on "Romeo and Juliet," we had to listen to readings by the Old Vic Theater Company for more than a week, just to get the cadence of a Shakespearean playright. Fr Power also made us create a scale model of Shakespeare's old theater, just so that we would be transported four centuries back precisely into the passion, ecstasy, and pathos of Romeo and Juliet. It was also thrilling to understand what the implications were of not having any front screens at all. Later on, one could relate it to our own all-open-stage rural *jatra* format. One could also immediately sense the power of communication between the artists and the unalienated audience, not artificially differentiated from each other by screens. Of course, Fr Power did not say any of this to us. He did not have to. He got the scale model done, grunted once in satisfaction, raised one eyebrow, and asked one single, "Got it?" It was hardly surprising that this single-minded devotion to precision would translate to each and every play produced by senior classes in our school—the producer, director, stage, props, and costume director, all being rolled into—who else? Fr Power. Officially he was the Moderator of our Drama Society but de facto, he was the central force around whom all of us were tempered into steel, creating plays which rightly became cause célèbre not just of the school, but also of the whole town.

But to me, personally, he will always remain the guru of extempore speaking and debating. He was the dreaded and equally beloved moderator of the Debating Society. Looking back, one sees how his entire technique in honing our skills was always inductive, and not instructive. After every session of a debate, when a topic was "thrown open to the floor," Fr Power would rise with his detailed notes on each debator's performance. He was as ruthless in decimating you on a point of illogic, plain bad delivery, or even minor-debating protocol, as he was fulsome in his praise for even a small point made well. When I represented our school in the Inter Jesuit School Extempore Speech Competition and brought home the gold medal from Darjeeling, everyone in the team and back in the school broke out into celebrations. Fr Power did not say a word. He maintained a stony silence all the way back and waited for the next session of the Debating Society. He just said one line with reference to my victory, "It's good for the School to have won the medal, but frankly I thought we had no chance because it was a bad performance." Having delivered this devastating piece, he reached into his pocket, pulled out the famous notes, and proceeded to enlighten everyone on why my performance had been bad.

Every month, we also had to write a book review and a special effort was required for the summer holidays. Normally, a review was considered fairly adequate if it ran to 8–10 pages. That summer, I came across the unputdownable "Jean Christophe" by Romain Rolland. My mind and soul were put on fire. I wrote a 32-page review, a record for the school. Fr Power read it with his scalpel poised as usual, but for once, he couldn't find anything—not even a word—amiss. Another school record actually! All he did was his famous grunt and three teeth shown in what could be taken for a smile, and a "Very good!" A third record in a row. And then he signed off with "But 15 is too young to read this book. You should read it again when you grow up." I have tried to follow the guru's advice, since reading the book once every 10 years and discovering new tastes, aromas, and the very elixir of life in its joyous fountain spring every time.

Father Kirsch

Fr Kirsch—brilliant young scientist from Manhattan Project—turned to life of atonement after Hiroshima. Planted life-time romance of Physics, and fused it with faith metaphysics and not physics.

Along with Fr Power, the one other person who lit a fire inside my head, was Father Kirsch who taught Physics to senior classes. Which is probably why there has remained a lifetime love in me—through school, college, and later life—for Physics. Physics, right from Newtonian simplicity to today's abstractions.

In fact, quite often I have wondered why I like two subjects—Physics and Literature, which could not be more different from each other. It is probably that beyond a certain point both subjects become almost metaphysical in their appeal.

Anyway, when Fr Kirsch started teaching Physics to us in Standard IX, I jerked up in my seat for the first time, amazed at the sheer vastness of knowledge, panache, and style that an otherwise non-descript short person could bring into the class room. He almost turned the drab equations into lyrics, and the 45-minute session seemed to be over in a jiffy.

I at once set about trying to find out more about Fr Kirsch. But as we all know, part of the Jesuit Fathers' sacred vows at the time of ordainment was that they would never talk about their pre-priesthood common man's life. So it was pretty useless confronting Fr Kirsch with direct questions. In any case, his demeanor was also one that didn't quite encourage casual conversation.

This called for serious detective work! Finally, the good natured and jovial Fr Covely, as usual, was snookered into revealing all. Fr Kirsch, he said, had actually been a brilliant young physicist on the Manhattan Project, the one that made the bombs later dropped on Hiroshima and Nagasaki! After the bombings, like many others on the project, he was besieged by a terrible sense of guilt. After wracking himself in agony for days, he finally decided on penance, left his career even before it had started properly and joined the Church. And what a way he had selected for his atonement—not preaching, doing missionary work, running health homes for the old and the destitute but teaching Physics, the one thing in which he had impeccable capability.

Apart from class lectures, he spent his entire soul on the Physics laboratory, arguably one of the best in the country for that grade of class. No wonder that it was so good. As a member of the Physics Club, I once came to school on a holiday afternoon with other students to help Fr Kirsch unpack some US Navy surplus equipment that he had secured, with his formidable contacts, as a gift. I'll never forget heaps of oscilloscopes and a number of Geiger counters lying around like junk over which we walked! With stuff like that, it was no surprise that our annual Physics Exhibition, open to all, was one of the best shows in our sleepy little town.

I was fortunate in quickly becoming his favorite student who started getting full marks in the weekly tests—a very, very rare phenomenon in the entire history of our school! Later, just as I got unexpected honor from Fr Power who asked me one day to be his stand-in for a whole class period, Fr Kirsch also allowed me the role of the main exhibitor in the school Physics Exhibition!

No wonder he was heartbroken when, after Senior Cambridge, I didn't go for Physics Honors, but rather opted for Mechanical Engineering. Subliminally, I guess, I opted for that branch of engineering that had the richest field of Applied Physics.

The Potpourri

I spent five of the most happy years of my life at my engineering college, and it was exciting purely because of the collection of different characters—1,200 of them actually—and the unique characteristics that each had.

The first three years you had to share your hostel room with two other chaps. My roommates in first year were Ganga and Tulsi! I'll never forget Ganga for one tremendous capability that he had. He was a very short person, and his favorite position for studies was to sit on the edge of his bed and dangle his feet down from the knees. Because of his shortness, his feet would be just off the floor. Then he would sit erect and draw the study table as close as possible. So there we were, three students at work, say on a summer evening, when Ganga, who had been busy with solving a math problem on a notebook in front of him, would suddenly put the pen down, stretch, yawn, announce that he was feeling sleepy, and flop right back to hit the bed. His legs would still be hanging down and his body would be at right angles. He would fall asleep instantly and lie supine for exactly five minutes deep in his sleep. Then, suddenly, he would wake up, get to his previous vertical position from the torso, not say a word, pick up the pen, and start working on the next line that the sum required. Today, they talk of "power naps." I had the good fortune of having a power napper as a roommate, but of course, I didn't know the term then! It was a simple thing, but quite weird and uncanny to watch and get used to—stretch, drop pen, lie back, sleep instantly, get straight up from sleep and start working again without a word. A well-oiled machine, no wasted moves or distractions. Work-sleep-work in one fluid motion.

Tulsi was also a very cool person, but unlike Ganga, who spoke about five words in a day, Tulsi was very friendly but was also a very serious person and quite religious in his own way. He was what in those days was described as a "good boy," who never used bad words!

So one day it had to happen, when the unflappable Tulsi went berserk. Someone at the breakfast table mentioned that a human milk bank was being started in Cairo! Promptly, someone else added that Tulsi had actually applied there for the position of head milkman! Tulsi's face was a sight for sore eyes. He was very fair, with a golden tinge to his skin. Now it went tomato red, and he kept sputtering with rage and couldn't say a word.

Another interesting batchmate with whom I picked up a friendship almost immediately was Shyamal Da. He was interesting because there seemed to be several different persons inside contained in a common external persona.

To start with, he was extremely fastidious and prim about everything he did. He was particularly sensitive about the engineering drawing sheets which he jealously guarded and which he wouldn't share with anyone excepting me because he considered only me to be almost as good as him in drawing! This common love for creating neat, precise drawings of mechanical objects is what catalyzed our lifetime friendship.

We also shared a common yearning and fascination for good semi-classical songs and Rabindra Sangeet, the special creation of Tagore. Both of us liked the same artists and songs, excepting one about whom we had near-violent disagreement. And that was Hemanta Mukherjee, who, I thought, practically recited his songs without sufficient tunes and got away purely because of the dark, rich timbre of his voice. Shyamal, on the other hand, worshipped Hemanta, so over a period of time we learnt to keep our discussions off Hemanta because we valued our friendship a lot more than whether Hemanta could sing to save his soul or not!

One possible reason for Shyamal to accept me as practically the only true friend in our hostel was that both of us were tiny esthetes in our own ways. I mainly go through classic books and Shyamal through lots of good music. In fact it ran through his family, mainly from his father, the well-known Santosh Kumar De, Chief Publicity Officer of HMV Company. Way before I met Shyamal, I was exposed to the famous HMV ad, in magazines, about a happy home having an HMV gramophone record player in one convenient corner.

Shyamal carried his constant preoccupation with cleanliness to the point of a fetish. So he developed and continuously demonstrated a set of quaint practices to battle with the "uncleanliness" that was universal and rampant in a boys' hostel. This, of course, didn't go down well with the scruffy inmates who developed a counter stock of pranks for pulling Shyamal's legs whenever possible. It was all in good natured fun, although it looked a bit rough at times.

Anyway, this uneasy balancing of the act went on for a while, with I (as usual in many of the college and hostel strife situations) playing umpire, judge, jury, and gentle persuader. But one day, all hell broke loose.

We used to have time slots of one hour each scheduled every afternoon. Sometimes, if there were two periods off and only one to attend, we would pile on to the professor taking the odd lecture, and beg him to cancel it so that we could get the whole afternoon off to be spent fruitfully on a movie, deep sleep, or a deeper game of cards. If granted, the good news would be quickly flashed around the hostels for the benefit of all concerned. After that it was considered a major breach of honor to try and sneakily attend the class.

Which is what Shyamal did, despite repeated requests from many classmates to desist. He went off to call the young lecturer to take the class. The lecturer hated this more than us because he too would have been looking for an unexpected bonus leave and instead of that, would have to feel like a fool lecturing an empty hall with one zealous student sitting there.

When it was known that Shyamal had indulged in this betrayal, it was decided in the hostel to hand-out exemplary punishment to him. It was winter, so his bed mattress, cover, pillow, blanket, and all, were neatly folded up, dumped in one of the community bathrooms, square below the shower which was turned on full blast and everyone disappearing as far away as possible.

Shyamal came back from the lecture and library after a couple of hours. First his fair face turned through most of the colors in the spectrum. Then for 10 minutes non-stop, he let fly a stream of invectives that I can hardly repeat here.

Till my dying day, I'll pray for just one rerun of that scene before I meet my master up there!

College life would have become utterly dull and boring if all you had to do was to attend classes, do assignments, prepare for exams, and so on, and nauseam. Thank God, that peppered into all this was the continuous contribution of humor from a few really interesting people.

Ghentu Da (Ghentu + "Da," elder brother, an honorific and term of affection), two years our senior. That batch will always remain notorious in our college history, comprising, as it did, some of the most mischievous boys you could come across. And leading the pack of the usually quiet but silently mischievous was Ghentuda. Incidentally, this is the other thing that the college did. Once you had a sobriquet or pet name attached to you and it became popular, nobody would remember your proper, formal name, and the name given by batchmates became your real identity. Till this day, I don't know what Ghentu Da's real name was.

Then in one year we were in that delicious stage in autumn when the whole of nature was singing in joy of the forthcoming Durga Puja and the brief autumn vacations thereof. Our seniors decided to emulate the village *jatra*, theater and stage one. Very quickly, the whole college got totally engrossed with the hilarious idea and everyone tried to break into the eagerly guarded secret of the rehearsals, different roles, storyline, etc.

Ghentu Da had clearly ruled out playing any large role but to everyone's amazement, he agreed with alacrity to play the chief sokhi (palace mate girls of the Princess) and lead the other sokhis in the periodic dances throughout the play.

What a memorable night it was when Ghentu Da, and four other boys, all dressed as young girls, burst onto the stage and cavorted flirtatiously with sundry, visiting princess and other characters in the play. Everyone broke into peals of laughter. The most moved people was the small group of musical instrument players (clarinets, flutes, harmoniums, and others) who are an integral part of any *jatra*, and who had been professionally hired by the organizers for total verisimilitude. They were simply knocked over at Ghentu Da's "professional" dance girl act.

With the Puja holidays coming up, and with the prospect of many *jatra* shows planned, the musicians requested Ghentu Da to tour with them for about a week and make some decent money on the side as a dance girl! At first, Ghentu Da and all of us thought it to be a massive joke. But the men were dead serious and then began pleading in earnest. After a lot of good-natured chaffing, they finally gave up but not before an encore solo performance by Ghentu Da, with the whole ensemble of musicians and we joining in.

One year after we returned to college after the summer holidays, this is the story one heard about Ghentu Da's latest contribution. Apparently, he had gone to a wine store and asked for a bottle of whisky. "Sorry sir, we've run out of whisky. Anything else?" "Rum?" "That too sir, sorry." "Brandy?" "Unfortunately not available too." "So what do you have, my good man?" "Only beer, sir." "Good, then for myself and my friends, give us a thousand bottles of beer! Otherwise how do we get drunk, dammit?"

My last interaction with Ghentu Da was weird. I was selling computers in Kolkata and had gone visiting a large manufacturing company on Taratolla Road. Inside, the department people took me to the shop floor. As we were going around, I saw Ghentu Da going off at a distance. Before I could stop myself, I yelled out "Ghentu Da." He stopped, saw me, and rushed back. He stood very near to me, raised his short frame, and whispered "Please don't call me 'Ghentu' here, I am respected here as a shift foreman." "Well, that's all I know about your name." So he took me aside and gave me a visiting card saying, "Palash Chatterjee." It took six years to dig Palaash out from Ghentu!!

The New Tryst

I am counseled by reliable friends that today's literary style demands your launching the tale without any preambles or ados. So here goes: Shravan Kumar, my chauffer for 20 odd years, has switched to Christianity from Hinduism in mid-December 2009.

At this point, the gentle reader might interpose, perhaps with some irritation and query as to what is so earthshaking in the above statement. After all, a number of people change their religion every day. Or most people are tagged with one religious label or the other, and cheerfully go through life without actually practicing any religion with anything more than skin deep application. So why start the story with the religious inclinations of one Shravan Kumar?

True, true, excepting that underlying Shravan's religious camp switching there lays a sad chronicle of the struggles and preoccupations of a young man, desperately trying to eke out a near-decent existence in a big, faceless city, uprooted from the comfort of familiarity in a remote Bihar village.

Shravan's village is typical of the vicissitudes of a small village in Mithila, buffeted by mighty rivers whose annual flooding wreaks havoc with agriculture, roads and rail systems, and public health, forcing thousands of youngsters, such as Shravan, to run to cities and try to scratch out an existence.

Thus began Shravan's life in Delhi as a teenager about 25 years back, of which 20 have been spent in my service alone. Over the years, I have seen Shravan get married, create his own little dwelling in the outskirts, raise a family of two sons and a daughter, and procure a few basic goodies like TV, air cooler, etc.

The great thing about Shravan is that despite this relative upward mobility, he hasn't severed his moorings with his village and takes his summer leave almost every year to visit his village for a month or so with his family.

And it is here that Shravan's "religious" beliefs come into play.

Like every other god-fearing villager, he goes through the motions of every significant ritual, feast, or special worship days of all major Hindu gods. Recently I queried him as to why he did this, with what returns in mind. I was amazed to learn that his major preoccupation all these years had been a particularly malevolent spirit which just wouldn't let his family go, despite many offerings for his appeasement and many supplications to all major gods to step in and do something about it—to no particular effect.

Apparently, collective village diagnostics concluded that this evil spirit was at the roots of a long litany of mishaps in Shravan's family—acute colic in a newborn nephew, untimely death of his father, his eldest brother's wayward and profligate habits, fights, and lawsuits with neighbors over useless, small plots of land, and now, in the fall of 2009, his brother's absolutely untimely death, in a matter of hours, from vomiting blood without any obvious causes. This finally broke Shravan's back, in so far as the futility of Hindu religion was concerned. After all these years of spending so much time, effort, and money, if the spirit continued to rampage through his daily life, what was the earthly use then of hanging on?

In more than one way, Shravan was at the end of his tether, desperately seeking recourse from somewhere, anywhere. It is at that time and in this frame of mind that he met a friend of his close friend who had recently started regularly visiting the Church every Sunday, and through "Yesu," had gained a lot of peace and happiness. Shravan's mind was made up instantly, and he, with family, started visiting a Church, close to his house, every Sunday. He also procured a Hindi translation of the Bible, a tiny crucifix to hang around his neck and Jesus-on-the-cross statuettes to put up in his house.

Since that time, as per Shravan, the evil spirit has been successfully contained, and there are no fresh calamities to contend with. I, of course, am highly skeptical about the "spirit" theory, but what I have really liked is the fact that Shravan and his wife have started following the simple, but robust commandments in the Bible. For instance, a "love thy neighbor" conviction has enabled both of them to take a very charitable view now of a rather painful neighbor with whom daily fights over trivia was taken for granted. Now Shravan and wife have stopped bothering about him, and consequently the neighbor also is slowly becoming tepid, since there is no more pleasure in the daily fights! Shravan is also convinced that very shortly that neighbor will also come around full circle and find solace in Yesu.

As Shravan described all this to me, I realized that in all these years, he had never spoken to me at such length or with so much of radiant passion. I asked him the obvious question. If he was so happy with Yesu, wouldn't he contemplate conversion from Hinduism to Christianity? Amazingly, he replied, "Where's the need to do that?" "I am with good Hindu rituals and Pujas also." Was this a villager's shrewd opportunism, or had Shravan really crossed the restrictive border lines of this religion and that? Was he truly liberated from the narrow confines of bigotry, and was I witnessing a pan-social phenomenon? Well, while we sort this out, let peace on earth completely imbue Shravan and family.

Herman Schlenker

While working for the Coca-Cola Company, I used to visit the Cuttack Plant, but used to stay at Bhubaneshwar because Cuttack didn't have proper hotels.

One Sunday, a new guest joined us at the guest house. He was a German—Herman Schlenker—who had a strange profession, that of shooting films for different anthropological societies.

One day, he got a telegram from Germany, contracting him to shoot a fight between a cobra and a mongoose. Since he had no clue about how to achieve this, he requested for my help which I readily agreed to.

Herman was one of the most dedicated professionals I have ever met. He was keen, enthusiastic, and thorough about every job that he did. He had travelled all over the world—from the Amazon jungles to the Burmese hills. He used top-of-the-line professional equipment, including Hasselblad cameras for stills.

For our joint cobra–mongoose mission, we set out early next Sunday morning in a hired taxi. We found out about a village of snake charmers and proceeded at a good pace. En route Herman got enchanted by the sight of peasant women busy with the rice crop and insisted on stopping for some innovative photography.

Finally, we arrived at the village of snake charmers. The moment they saw a foreigner, they surrounded us, eager to make a lot of quick money. They released about a dozen snakes around us, and I was scared stiff. Through me, Herman explained that we were not interested in the usual snake dance, but wanted to shoot a cobra–mongoose fight. The snake charmers' faces fell, and they said that at best they could organize a snake attacking a rat. Herman said a rat wouldn't do, and he requested me to accompany him into the jungles in search of the real thing. I refused politely but firmly. Yet Herman persisted until I relented. So on our way back, the two of us took off from the highway into the adjoining woods, which were lush and green with densely packed trees and heavy undergrowth of shrubs and ferns. As we turned a bend in a small trail going through the woods, we actually saw what we were seeking—a snake and cobra circling each other, and rushing in every few seconds, the snake trying to sink its fangs into the mongoose and the mongoose trying to bite into the cobra's neck and tearing its head off. After an epic struggle, the mongoose won, and Herman, his camera whirring busily throughout, had got his desired film all intact and classy.

LOVE FOR NATURE

Trees

All sorts of trees had family member like memories and loving associations throughout childhood. Our old style British colony houses were full of trees—mainly fruit trees, but other sorts also. Looking back, most of childhood seems to have been spent clambering up and down trees like a squirrel.

The sal trees of Adityapur jungle just across the river—tall, straight, densely packed, brown trees with big green foliage, forest bottom dark even during summer daylight, carpets of moss, and rotting leaves making a delightful spring cushion to walk barefoot on. Continuous susurration of twigs and leaves in the wind, echoed by mysterious slithers and scrambles of all kinds of creepy crawlies, including snakes, on the forest floor. Occasional whisked flash of mud-brown rabbits, and once, only glorious once a bewitching little baby deer—as surprised and intrigued by us. Then, one vigorous shake of the tail, a golden flash, and the magic moment gone forever. The tall, stately near white sisam trees, with small green leaves, planted in nearly every house. Wonderfully stepped branches for excelling in the gentle art of tree climbing. Ramrod straight, springily supple branches an inexhaustible source of poor children's cricket stumps, and material for the great *gulli-danda* games—natural breeding for cricketing genius.

And in every house in the colony, filling the still summer afternoons with a feast of aromas, fruit trees of every type—five types of mangoes, jackfruits, blackberries, wild berries, wood fruits, custard apples, and bananas—an almost Latin riot of tropical excess!

What this surfeit of trees did for our play gang were several interesting outcomes. For one, for tree climbing skills, we could have put even a bunch of Terai monkeys to shame. Secondly, there was a whole series of games of skill, innovated by us, all relating to running up trees, shimmying down, breaking, and chucking branches—ad infinitum. But the greatest joy of joys was stealing ripe fruits from all neighborhood homes, including one's own! There was actually no need to steal, we were the collective family of the whole neighborhood, but not in vain had the scriptures ordained that "stolen fruits are always sweeter."

And today, living in this urban ghetto of steel, concrete, and asphalt, I suddenly realize with a shock that the majority of city kids have barely seen trees on roadsides, but probably the majority of them would not have ever climbed a tree or wouldn't be able to do it if their lives depended on it.

Mountains

The sum of my great love for mountains lies in the fact that it is only in the mountains that your head might be in the midst of woolly clouds, but your feet are still planted firmly on the ground. Probably it is this very paradox and coexistence of opposites—something wispy, ephemeral, formed but insubstantial and granite hard, prosaic rocky foundation—that makes up for the eternal mystique of mountains that people have been drawn to down the ages.

My first exposure to mountains, beyond the poky little green hills framing our sleepy little town, was during a school sponsored visit to Darjeeling, when I was 15. We were hosted by St. Pauls' and about a dozen of us were put up in a beautiful log dormitory, close to the stone walls of the main school. The first day was spent in long-walks all over Darjeeling. The entire northern skyline was the Himalayan range, but unfortunately, the fitful October clouds masked the snowy peaks, except for occasional and brief glimpses.

So we were quite morose and grumpy till the early dinner, after which, tired as we were from the train journey and continuous walking throughout the day, it didn't take too long for "lights out" and quick slumber.

Somewhere in the middle of the night, I woke up with a start and sat up under the thick blanket. We were sleeping in two long columns across the room, and a wash of brilliant moonlight fell through large glass windows over the dozen-odd beds. Right opposite me was one such window, and what had woken me up was the sound of a twig of wood roses gently knocking against the window with a light breeze.

I walked across to the window and pressed my nose against the cold glass. For a moment I was taken aback by a stunning sight. All the clouds had disappeared, and the full moon light had lit up the craggy earth, the dark forests, and the land sloping down, down into a valley before it rose to the ramparts of mountains.

And there, right across the horizon was the magnificence of the Kanchenjunga (literally, "golden thighs of the goddess") range, huge, majestic, foreboding in its icy silence. The moonlight turned it into a massive silver block, running from one end of the horizon to the other.

Throughout later life, I have seen other mountains—snow clad or covered with woods, or bare blue rock, but never could I compare their beauty with that of the moonlit Kanchenjunga on that magic night, a completely silent night, washed, and engulfed in a stream of silver.

The next time a mountain enthralled me, I was working in Delhi. Owing to the Holi holidays coming up over a weekend, everyone got four days of holidays at a stretch. My friends and I took this rare opportunity to get out of Delhi's sweltering heat, and we decided to make a quick dash to Ranikhet and Nainital in the hills. One of our group was posted at that time in Haldwani at the foothills. So it was great fun spending a day with him before taking off to the hills.

We went to Nainital first. Everyone hired horses to go to the top of China peak, but we had to be different, and trekked up the whole distance, wheezing all the way up over hours. But once we got to the top, the wearying it out was really worth it. There, far away, from horizon to horizon was a glistening range of the Himalayas—abode of the gods—the ice caps glistening and twinkling in the blazing sunlight.

Of course, to every joyous tale, there has to be a pathetic interlude. On the return journey, Shyamal insisted on hiring a pony. He got on board with a great flourish, and then found, to his utter dismay, that the pony insisted on walking along the edge of the winding road which was precipitous, rather than the insides next to the hill. Poor chap! He had to practically close his eyes out of fear all the way down to the Nainital mall.

From Nainital to Ranikhet, though, there was no problem. The bus wound all the way to the sleepy little town, and we got a lovely little hotel which gave a full view of the same range. However, no one excepting me seemed to be interested in relieving endless card games with treks, which is to me what going to the hills is all about. So I took off on my own, and very soon, found a small hill with a fantastic gouge on its side, ringed by sweet smelling pine trees.

So there I lay down for hours, inclined in the grass padding, the faint, sweet pine fragrance washing over me in a light breeze, and in front of me, the same peaks I had seen at Nainital, but here much bigger and much closer—Trishul, Nanda Devi, Nanda Ghumti, on and on, peak after peak. Glorious sunlight, wafting fragrance, craggy and glimmering mountain tops—and no hustle bustle of ugly cities, and the continuous pressure of survival.

Years flitted by. Work complexities and responsibilities grew, and so did my family. Marriage to Purnima, one son, Anirudh, after a few years, and another, Pablo, after seven years. Trooping off to the mountains and trekking away, with wife Purnima (sharing a common love for mountains), and quiet but highly mischievous sons.

Every year, we would hire a car and set off for the hills. The agency from which we hired the car insisted on giving us a driver called Vishal (huge!), who barely touched the 5 feet mark! He was a hill man himself and belonged to the select breed of "mountain drivers," cool, skilled, absolutely focused on the snaking road, and unflappable. But once, even his iron nerves cracked. My mother-in-law was visiting us, a trip somewhere near was on the cards, but for some inscrutable reason, she, my wife, and I kept on deferring the trip till almost the end of summer (end June), and we were finally pushed into feverish preparations because the monsoons would hit the hills anytime then.

The decision on the destination was shortlisted and finalized to our dear old Ranikhet again, and one fine morning, we set off practically at midnight so as to be able to reach Ranikhet the same evening. The journey to Haldwani, in the foothills, was free from any events excepting halts at roadside eateries for breakfast and lunch in Haldwani, at the foothills.

Post lunch we set off for Ranikhet, targeting to reach it little before the sunset. For miles, the only sounds were the snaking car tires' friction with the winding road and the susurration of winds blowing through the pine trees.

We shortly crossed a road turning to the left towards Nainital and carried on along the road to Ranikhet. There was a light drizzle from the clouds that came up from the foothills into the mountains. Everything around was moist and slick with green wet patches of lichens and moss. And it was getting perceptibly cold, so that we had to stop and take out light woolens from the bags. Wearing them gave us two joys—one against the cold, and the second in contemplation of our wretched friends in Delhi, getting roasted in the June heat.

We started off again, soaking in the beautiful views of the mountains—green, yellow, and blue with moist blocks of black granite, supporting every kind of creeper, and the distant white capped sentries of the North. Suddenly, without any warning, a huge block of earth, rocks, and surface vegetation broke off from the mountain on our left, crashed down on the road, and most of it rolled down further along the mountain. The avalanche was barely 5 meters away. Vishal braked hard. A little less luck and we would have been bang in the middle of it, our car crushed beyond recognition.

Vishal, the otherwise phlegmatic cool person, was shivering like a leaf in the breeze. My family was too shocked to even utter a cry of terror. After a few minutes, with a shaky voice I asked Vishal, "What happens now?" Vishal, by now back to his unflappable self, said "You're the boss, and I'll follow whatever you choose out of two possibilities. The first is still proceeding to Ranikhet. First the road maintenance truck will come and clear up the road. This'll take about two hours. Then, another three hours to Ranikhet. Problem is, you've chosen the landslide season to come here. So there is a good possibility that we'll get holed up in Ranikhet for seven to ten days because of more landslides. The second alternative is, we forget Ranikhet, go back a little, and spend three days in Nainital." A quick backseat conference happened, and understandably, disappointments apart, wisdom prevailed towards staying alive and spending the planned three days in Nainital, than trying to enjoy the more beautiful Ranikhet at the cost of our necks. So that's what happened. We backed away, swung into Nainital, and spent three glorious days at a cute little hotel bang opposite the *taal* (lake), and in exhaustive sight-seeing in and around Nainital.

Many moons have waxed and waned since then. The wide-eyed teenager gulping in the beauty of Kanchenjunga washed by moonlight, now has a young teenaged and a younger son himself. Times have drastically changed, so have contexts, and the scope and scale of living for each of us. Which is why, apart from viewing the mountains from treks and hotel windows, or windows of cars snaking along hill roads, there are also magical moments of seeing them alongside or just below from the windows of a passing plane, adding new magic to the already known.

That's how I'll always remember the early morning Delhi–Guwahati flight that brings you right up to the proud, aloof, pristine Everest, and holds the view for a good quarter hour. Through that time, it scornfully ignores the "oohs" and "aahs" of the passengers, gently twinkling in the morning sunlight.

Or the sweeping over a permanently ice-covered set of peaks, along with dark forests, as you plunge into the Srinagar airport. The mountains are barely a few hundred feet below and that's all you get as you break cloud cover. So to put it mildly, you need a very deft pilot who won't crash you in. Coming into the Kathmandu airport is even hairier because here you have to descend from the clouds and come right into a very narrow and long valley, along which you taxi in and then quickly plonk down on the runway.

But all this is like a cakewalk compared to the Delhi–Leh flight which takes you to Ladakh, the land of bleak beauty and threatening ravines and chasms which only the sturdy of heart can handle. As you take off from Delhi, in less than half an hour, you are over the Himalayan mountains, range after range like perfectly disciplined soldiers filed in perfect ranks behind each other. The combination of ice-caps of summer, green hills, cleft valleys, and white, frothy rivulets, is a heady wine and you keep staring down transfixed by the sight.

A little while later it's time to descend, and to your horror, the plane dives into a ravine with sheer rock walls on both sides. It goes on, the left side chisels down to the ground, but the right is still there and curving in! So you sweep around a total 180°, and quickly put your nose down on the runway from the opposite side.

Glory hallelujah !!

Hills

I have always been excited by hills and mountains, right from tiny hillocks that can be easily climbed, to distant ramparts of ice-clad Himalayan ranges. These hills and mountains have come again and again in my life, each with its unique character imparting its own unique thrill.

My first recollection of hills was in our own town. Being on the Chotanagpur Plateau, it was hedged on two sides by tiny ranges of green hills. Dimna "mountains" were to the North and Dalma to the East. Dimna also housed a lake, which was the principal source of the town's water supply. So with hill climbing, boating on the lake, and small walk trails, Dimna was a hot favorite for picnics.

Both Dimna and Dalma had their own distinct animal life. Dimna had more of wild bears and packs of wild killer dogs, while Dalma hosted a small but very active herd of elephants. I remember once while going to school, seeing a dead bear, shot and trussed up near the school. It had feasted on wild mahua, got drunk, and shuffled down to the town in search of food. The resident of one of the adjacent bungalows had seen this in the middle of the night and shot the bear—quite lovable when normal—but dangerous if drunk—to prevent any further mischief.

The Dalma wild elephants were not to be left far behind. At that time, the Telco unit was just starting. While the factory was being laid out, the township was also being constructed. Large tracts of farmland were being acquired, razed even in large land cut and fill operations, and mass housing being constructed on top. This enraged the elephants a lot because they were habituated to come down from the hills onto to the crop fields and take their taxes, as it were, in ripe wheat plant. Being thwarted by the mass housing plans, they expressed their ire in smashing down the newly constructed houses in their herd strength. This caused a big setback in the total plans for Telco, until the government sanctioned hunters to herd up the rogue elephants and drive them eastwards to the remote jungles.

The influence of Dimna and Dalma on a young, impressionable mind is easily imagined. It left me with a lifetime fascination for the wild hills, their towering trees and jungle tracks, and the way clouds nestled on their shoulders during monsoons, obscuring their flanks in wispy mystery, soon to melt and cascade in torrential rains.

My next encounter with hills was the routine journey from Jamshedpur to Patna in my Coca-Cola sales days, crossing over from the Chotanagpur Plateau to the vast Gangetic Plains in the matter of a day's car journey. It was broken up into distinct runs—first Jamshedpur to Ranchi with a lunch break. Then Ranchi to the Ramgarh jungles, growing denser as one moved past Hazaribagh. Then on to the Koderma Ghat or slope descending to the Gangetic Plain, and the final run to Patna by-passing Jhumri Tilayya and the Tillayya Dam.

Each of these runs had its own characteristic flavor. Jamshedpur to Ranchi was on the national highway NH-32, snaking over the plateau flatlands and crop fields for undisturbed miles. Thanks to the usual road construction corruption, the road was always in disrepair. Hasty repair work was done every year just before the monsoons. So as soon as the rains stopped, new potholes appeared all over, paving the path for everyone making money again next year. Anyway, trundling along, a quick stop at Bundu for refreshments and the ever amazing sight of people spilling out of shared cabs. It was astounding to see the number of people and children squeezed into one cab—up to twelve people at a time, including two in the dicky on the Bhagalpur—Jamshedpur run.

Ranchi was a quaint little town in those days, and not the ugly claustrophobic eyesore that it is today. The pride of place went to the three-storied Firayalal's store—the precursor of all Indian malls that are now the standard part of any urban center's skyline. Ranchi itself was on an elevation, good enough to have some old tea gardens just as you were about to enter the town. In fact, Ranchi was considered a poor man's hill station in Jamshedpur!

From Ranchi, on to the jungles of Ramgarh and Hazaribagh. First one went past the deserted prisoner of war Ramgarh camps from the 1971 Indo-Pak War. It thrilled one to feel a patriotic surge of pride for the motherland when one considered the momentous victory over a long-fought enemy. Although the camps were empty, it was easy to visualize how the hillocks and jungles would have wrung repeatedly with our soldiers giving voice to victory cries!

The other unforgettable part of the Hazaribagh forests was the flaming red palaash forests. For miles, thick stands of palaash trees grew along both sides with crimson flowers bursting all over. Running through that stretch, one felt purged and purified and elated with a romantic aftertaste left behind.

From Hazaribagh, the road snaked upwards towards the Tillayya Dam. The road snaked along the river bank, which coming close to the dam, widened out into a vast, glistening stretch of water. It glowed in the slanting afternoon sun. The road descended past the dam and was bifurcated into two branches—one gliding down towards the plains and the other snaking up towards the Kodarma Ghati.

We took the second road and went up to the top of the Ghati through thick forests. The road then started its long descent from the Ghat peaks towards the huge Gangetic Plain and on to Patna, which we would reach late into the night.

A memorable journey through hills, forests, and glades on a rain-soaked monsoon day, indelibly etched into the mind.

Clouds

Toy train from Darjeeling, glorious sunshine, somber, crystalline ramparts of Himalayas, tiny green hills at their feet. Batasia loop—train twists in—deep gorge runs down into hills. Far below, dozen fat, white clouds graze around hills. Suddenly, tiny rainbow arcs across a valley. The whole scene bursts into joyous hosanna to the abode of gods.

Summer afternoon flight Dakota Calcutta to Jamshedpur. Inane, imbecile businessman nattering away about cotton price. Plane droning into bright western sun. Below, green patchwork quilt of Bengal plains surges into the brown hills and granite walls of Chotanagpur Plateau. Unexpectedly, plane slowly banks to right. And, right ahead, across half the sky, boiling, dirty, grey mass of thunder clouds advancing rapidly. One small, impatient piece in the vanguard stops over tiny brown hill, lashes it with rain falling in large slants of a child's sketch. Bolt of lightning falls on tree. Bursts into flame, and instantly doused. Angry cloud still continues its lashing. Thin wisp of smoke rises in mute supplication.

Srinagar: Roadside tea shop ahead of Dal Lake on autumn afternoon nearing sunset. Clear, clean sky, mountains at the other end reflected in glassy water, gently rippling. Small, extremely busy looking white cloud moves in from nowhere, screeches to halt right over the sharp triangular peak of the tallest mountain. Slowly, very slowly, shrinks to oblivion—and out emerges a pristine white snow cap on the peak. Sinking sun sets it on fire. Lake shadow keeps undulating, now with a red and gold tip. Tired, after a hard day's work breaks into warm infectious smile—"all weariness gone, boss! What a sight!"

Nainital: Sitting on hotel verandah just opposite the middle of lake. Dark and brooding, ringed on three sides by dark hills, where lights are coming on like fireflies against the dying daylight.

On the left side, which is open to road coming up from foothills, silently, ghostlike, cloud rises, and enters town. Pauses over bus stand—tired, tattered, in shreds. Unerringly moves to lake, descending slowly, till it just touches the lake surface. Then slowly melts away all weariness of its 1,000-mile journey from Bay of

Bengal into lake's bosom. On the opposite hill, church bell sings an apt requiem.

Kharagpur Pond

Kharagpur house of Dadu—at the cusp of town and village—was mud and brick house, tiny, miniature pond in front. Refugees from Borisal, which is more water than land, yearning to replicate what they had lost forever.

Five weirdly twisted date palm trees, like dervishes in a row. Every late evening in winter, just as sun goes down, laborer hops up each tree, slashes cuts just below the leaves, and quickly suspends a small earthern pot below the cut. Throughout the night, delectable date-flavored juice drips into the pot. Early morning, all pots hauled down before the sun can heat and ferment the juice into toddy, and the winter chilled juice poured into large pot for preparing the famous *patali gur* (jaggery) cakes. But first, I, the pampered guest of honor, get to drink at least three glasses. Ah! Nectar from the gods!

Pond water, sluggish, slightly muddy, full of every size and shape of fish. Covered partially with water lilies and gently undulating green leaves. The amazement of seeing powkauri birds, thin, long beaked, splayed feet, actually walking from leaf to leaf, and quickly picking up tiny fish and insects.

At night, shattering all night sounds—whispers, chirps, ripples, sighing—which are the gentlest lullabies, comes piercing croak of frog caught by water snake. Then for a long while, agonized croaks, farther and farther apart, less and less loud, keep me sweating even in the winter night as the snake inexorably swallows the frog bit by bit. All other sounds are also numbed into silence. The croaking dies. Slowly, hesitatingly, sounds start again. Tears dry up. Sleep, gentle sleep ends the agony.

Between the house and edge of pond, huge *jamun* tree, and on land tilting down into pond, dense, thorny bush. Every night, bush completely covered by hundreds of fireflies. Cold, winter night, whole colony asleep. Only one wonder-struck little boy sits on the verandah, exulting at the millions of stars twinkling in the clear night sky, and then at their reflection in the fireflies densely packed in the bush. Have fireflies come down from the skies, or have the fireflies ascended to the heavens, and swept to every corner of the night sky?

Delicious fish and crabs in the pond. The city bred boy never ceases to wonder at live fish pulled out at will from the pond. So many different ways, so many separate excitements! Sit for hours under shady tree in the still afternoon and hang out a small fishing rod, the hook baited with live earthworm freshly dug out of moist soil. Or persuade Dadu to cast the *khapla jaal*—small fishing net, twirled around first, and then an expert cast of a perfect circle. Sinks slowly, Dadu keeping a vigilant eye, and tight grip on the draw line, while the boy hops up and down in anticipation of the coming feast. Slowly, the net line is pulled in hand over hand until the net appears. Dozens of small fish, gills caught in the net, thrash around in a silver cascade. The net lands at our feet. Then the plucking of each fish carefully from the net. Slowly the ripples subside in the pond. But the biggest excitement is *pukur chancha jaal*—a big rectangular net, like the ones across a tennis court is dipped at one end of the pond by two burly men on opposite banks. Then slowly, with strong, measured, coordinated steps, they walk towards the other end, scraping the net right over the bottom with only the top edge sticking out of water. As the net approaches the other end, there is a furious churning just below the net top, as more and more fish get inexorably trapped. Then the bolder among them, refusing to be pushed forward, turn around and jump right back over the net. The air is filled with their silver sparks and flashes. At last, the net arrives at the other end, fully loaded with fish of every size, crabs, tiny shrimps, water snakes, frogs—a riot of water life desperately trying to escape. Everyone pitches in—long process of weeding out the smaller-sized fish and throwing them back in the water, keeping only the big shoal and pond fish for the grand feast ahead. Not just in our house, but in the true spirit of refugees who always share everything, fish portions are gifted to the entire neighborhood.

On the Road

Driving through South Orissa jungle. Dirt road snaking under canopy of tall trees. Hills, close enough to touch, rush by on both sides. Only sign of civilization, for miles, are the pylons on the hills and power line from Hirakud jumping from hill to hill. Evening gathering fast, but dappled sunlight still plays hide and seek with million leaves overhead. Driver stops to cool the engine and let us stretch our limbs. Sharp bend ahead. Foliage hides what is beyond, so I have to "discover" it. Walk forward beyond the bend and walk into an Amrita Sher-Gil painting of "Saanjha Choola." Small enclosure of pointed stakes in a miniature valley. Just five straw thatched tiny cottages. One huge banyan tree in middle. Underneath, four to five men and women, in dirty white dhotis, dark shadows in the dusk, sit absolutely still. No reaction at seeing me, no words, no movement—statues frozen in eternal disconnect. Even a few children seem to be playing in slow motion.

Who are they? What do they do? Think? Are they from the same country as me, just a 100 km away from the nearest town?

Santhal Paraganas—rolling sea of burnt red gravelly earth around sharply punctuated blocks of black granite and distant villages. Whole paraganas reverberating with maadol drum beats—some important tribal festival. Dildar's driving fast, tired, and eager to get to destination and cool shower and cooler beer. Kumar slouched next to him. I, as usual, stretched out on back seat.

Slightly ahead, right next to road, small Santhal village—neat, spotless, clean, picturesque. Circle of women, holding waists, swaying back-and-forth, side-by-side with three drummers swaying along.

Seeing our car at distance, whole group moves on to road. Dildar brakes hard, and starts honking furiously. Kumar waves a 10 rupee note. No reaction. Eyes half closed, drunken smile fixed on all faces, ecstasy in every undulation of statuesque bodies, they circle the car and keep dancing.

I understand. I persuade Dildar and Kumar to get out of the car, join the ring and dance for a while. The hosts are delighted. We are treated to pungent *handia* (rice beer) in cups stitched from sal leaves. Nearly knocks me down, but what joy! The swinging, the brushing of bodies in abandon, the earthy, heady smell of women—dance, dance, dance!

Kharagpur village, summer afternoon—paddy fields, ponds, trees blazing in summer heat. But one dirt road is a long, mysteriously shadowed, cool, cool tunnel because on both sides thick bamboo groves, which only a few persistent sunbeams can pierce, thrust against each other from two sides into a dense canopy over the road. The afternoon is still and airless, there is no sound anywhere—only the occasional mournful "ghoo!ghoo!" of the wood pigeons.

Nine-year-old boy, all alone, trudges through the tunnel. Forever the excited, eager, joyous discoverer of unknown lands—"what's round that bend? What strange lands are there over that hump?"

On the dirt road, thousands of bullock cart passages have left deep ruts on two side of a central humped spine. During monsoons, it all blends into thick slushy mud. Then gradually, the mud dries up, forming a hard layer, to be crushed and pulverized repeatedly into talcum, fine sandalwood colored dust. The ruts are now pools of dust, icy cold under the bamboo arches. The boy sloshes slowly through the dust right up to his knees, savoring every cold tingle of the caressing dust. Walks on, deeper into the tunnel—"what's round the next corner?" hasn't been answered yet—never will.

Assorted Animals

Till pretty late in life, until we moved into Delhi after Father's retirement, I can hardly remember when we two brothers—especially myself—were not engaged in a running battle with Ma to keep various types of animals as pets. Our argument was that God had created us and animals for an eternal relationship of love. Her argument was that she was anyway already up to her neck with taking care of the four of us. And any time a creature arrived, we would continue with the petting, but she always got the short end of the stick and had to be the food provider, cleaner, trainer, house breaker, etc., and she didn't want any more.

This obviously didn't stop us from smuggling in various species of fauna, chief among them being dogs. The first one, Buli, had a whopping pedigree. Our small town was ringed on three sides by green hills with a rich heritage of animal life. And preying on them were packs of hunter–killer indigenous dogs, much like the dhols of the Deccan Plateau. Buli's mother was a tiny pup that got separated from her mother, and a Santhal tribal picked her up, brought her to the market, and sold her to Mr Pai, or Pai uncle. As she grew up into a small but tough dog, her native ferocity bloomed fully, and she had to be restrained with two dog chains, and not one.

When she littered, after a brief dalliance with a mild mannered street dog, the pups, one felt, would have lost about half of their ferocity by dilution, but they were still ferocious enough. Pai uncle persuaded Father, over sustained protestations from Ma that a good guard dog is what every home needs. So on a Saturday morning, I went, with my heart beating wildly in pleasurable anticipation, to Pai uncle's house to select a pup of my choice. He escorted me to the room where Buli's new maid mother was lying down with five pups. The moment she saw me, she tried to snap her chains and go for my throat. I somehow pointed to the chubbiest of the pups whom Pai Uncle picked up and gave to me. By then the mother dog was berserk with fury, and I would have been killed if Pai uncle was not there.

Anyway, I proudly brought the pup home and we promptly christened her as "Buli," and made a makeshift bed for her in the empty chicken coop in the rear kitchen garden, Ma having firmly ruled against bringing Buli into any of the bedrooms.

Next morning, as soon as I woke up, I ran to the chicken coop to check on Buli. Imagine my consternation when I saw no Buli. I immediately set up a big howl. Ma came out to console me, smiled, and then looked at a small hole in the front wall which was blocked with a brick throughout the year, excepting in the monsoon to allow free flow of the rainwater that accumulated in the front garden and had to be drained out into the narrow drain connecting the bathroom to the backyard wall. The brick plug had been pushed inside with great violence.

Ma explained to me that it had been our mistake to bring in so tiny a pup which had still not been weaned. Buli's mother had broken the chains at night, tracked my body odor for more than a kilometer, come to our house, and lured Buli back with her. So once again I went to Pai uncle's house, where indeed I found Buli happily having a meal off her mother, who almost broke the chains again at seeing me. Anyway, I got Buli back, and every morning, I would take her for her morning milk to Pai uncle's house.

Then Buli started growing up by leaps and bounds. And as she grew, her wild genes started showing up in every muscle that rippled on her body. Very soon, she had become quite ferocious—a throw back to her hunter's lineage—and the entire colony was initially scared stiff, but soon realized that Buli was the ultimate guard for the whole colony. Thrice she foiled the nefarious plans of robber gangs, actually helping in apprehending quite a few of the gangsters. One of the most amusing sights was Buli's handling of various people who came on errands—the grocer's delivery man, postmen, milkmen, etc. To Buli, they appeared as a distinct group of shady people because they were always allowed to come up to the main doors, but were never allowed to come in any further. So they must be persona non grata to us, her beloved family, and so Buli singled them out for special treatment of attacks, furious barking, and occasional chasing across fields.

But the picture that will always endure in my mind is the one in which Buli would take care of my younger brother, who was quite younger to me. Now, even the most ferocious of dogs will be gentle with human infants. So, when, on a winter morning, Buli would be stretched out on the front verandah in warm sunlight, my toddler of a brother would approach her with a ladle or large steel spoon in his hand, crawl up to her, and then, slam, he would hit her flank very hard. Or he would hold her ear and twist it around, until she yelped with pain. If anyone else, including family members, tried such a thing, Buli would have bitten off chunks from them. But with my brother, she would merely whine for a while, although she was in great pain. The finale to these episodes would always be my brother lying down next to Buli, at right angles, using her broad side as a pillow. Then he would sleep off, like any other baby, in the warm winter sunlight, and even if he slept for two hours, Buli wouldn't even twitch. Such was the great love that she had for a human baby.

Then Buli grew up into a very attractive lady, and soon in the mating season, our house became the cynosure of all the young buck dogs of the neighborhood. Buli responded to the overtures of one of them, one thing led to another and in a few months, Buli gave birth to five puppies.

Unfortunately, she contracted some strange infection-related disease, and in less than a week, her babies died one by one.

Finally, Buli's heart was broken, and she, too, went off on the great journey. For the last two days, she didn't eat anything and kept following me with her bright, beautiful eyes. Finally those eyes closed forever.

It was one of the saddest blows that life served me when I was very young.

After Buli's sad demise, there was a gap of many years in which there were no more dogs. I had become a teenager and somehow life was too full to accommodate any pets. But the hunger remained subliminally to be actuated at the first opportunity.

More time passed. We had moved to Delhi. Sister moved out after her marriage. Father retired and the four of us, after a few rented homes, took up our residence in our own flat. Brother finished school and got into medical college.

Then, one summer, my parents announced their intention to do a religious-cum-tourism visit of the holy town of Puri. So off they went, leaving us two brothers to fend for ourselves. We took up the challenge bravely. One day, brother hesitatingly mentioned to me, "Now that the field is clear, how about bringing in a puppy to keep. Ma's not around to protest tooth and nail, and by the time she comes back, the puppy will be firmly established as a given!"

Now, I am as fond of dogs as Brother Babua. Against Ma's firm rejection of any plea for a resident puppy, he used to assuage his craving by going out every night to feed the dinner leftovers to assorted street dogs. Once he even got bitten by one, and had to go through the agony of rabies injections. But that couldn't deter him.

I found his puppy proposal to be excellent and agreed with alacrity. Within two days, Babua brought home a tiny, wriggling pup, long in the body with short legs, a big curving tail, and large ears. The coloring was mainly black, with a few blotches of white to relieve the monotony.

We, two, spent quite a few hours in fixing a good and appropriate name for her. We finally settled on "Krishnakumari" (black princess) or "KK" for short. She grew by leaps and bounds and by the time Ma came back, she was quite a handful. She became the center of our life, but was also a big nuisance because she created litter wherever she went and we were hard pressed to cope up with her to keep the house clean. Finally, when, courtesy a street boyfriend, she became pregnant, Ma put her foot down strongly because one KK was enough. We didn't need another litter. So she was successfully palmed off to one of the part-time maids who used to work in our house. So that was the end of the KK phenomenon. All our lives, we had been accustomed to the independent bungalow format of houses, with front and kitchen gardens, lawns, etc., where one could think of pets. But in the big city, compressed-together flats format, there was just no possibility of pets larger than caged birds.

But while it lasted, KK was good fun. One day, my cousin, who also was working in Delhi, came to visit us. Now he was very, very scared of dogs. And the moment a dog understands that it comes closer and closer to the scared person, trying to make friends with him. So KK jumped up on the sofa where my cousin was sitting, licked his hand with great relish, and then literally walked over his belly and chest like a mountaineer. Did the man shout and cry! My brother was laughing his guts out, holding his belly with one hand and KK with the other.

So that was the last dog that we brothers patronized.

Amit and His Children in the Hills
Source: Purnima Dutta Gupta.

Amit with Purnima
Source: Purnima Dutta Gupta.

Amit's Baba and Maa
Source: Purnima Dutta Gupta.

Random Musings

Random Memories

Getting up early in the morning during summer holidays, rounding up all friends, and off to the pristine sand banks of Khorkaai for at least an hour of vigorous games—kabaddi and dariabanda mainly. After that, back home, a refreshing bath, and a hearty breakfast, of homemade bread (roti) and fried vegetables. After that, out again for spending the whole morning practically on fruit trees of the neighborhood—Lalan uncle's blueberry tree was a favorite hunt. Every day, a fresh bunch of fruits would ripen, and I would climb the highest to get the best of them. Apart from this, my other favorites were our neighbor's mango tree and the guava tree at Mithu's house.

We'd get back home by lunch time, after which there was a mandatory three hours of studies. But as soon as the Steel Plant siren for 4:00 p.m. sounded, all of us would rush off for at least two hours of football. Back home for dinner and then convene again for a game of hide and seek among the houses of the colony and the service lane.

Vacation Time

Looking back right to my childhood days, I feel amazed as to how we had packed days of fun and activities, despite not having TV, Internet, mobile phones, and innumerable malls and cinema multiplexes. All we had was football, cricket, and a variety of local games very specific to that area.

The long-awaited summer vacation brought in two possibilities—either the pilgrimage like visit to mother's relatives in Jalpaiguri and Moynaguri, with Dida, my grandmother, or spending time at home.

Whenever it was the latter, despite the total absence of any of the above "modern" gadgets, we had a packed and fixed routine. The day began in summer as early as 4:30 in the morning. The sun would not come up for a while. Meanwhile, it was my responsibility to go from house to house in our colony, and wherever one had a friend of the gang, to call him up and get him to join me. Within half an hour, all of us would be ready as a group, and would walk off towards the sand bars of the summer—reduced Khorkaai's sand banks.

By the time we reached the river bed and marked out with the help of small stones, a kabaddi court, the first faint rays of the red, rising sun would strike the distant tree tops in the neighboring jungle. Now we were all equipped and ready, and the next two hours, would be spent in vigorous playing, shouting, and sweating as only a group of small children can. By 8 o'clock, the sun would be really hot, and we would bend our weary legs towards home.

A delightful bath on returning home. The bathroom shower felt like a cool, cool, mountain stream rushing down and drawing out the heat from head to toe, and leaving behind a glowing skin, cool to the touch with goose bumps.

The early morning exercise, and the invigorating bath after that would fuse together in imparting a massive hunger for breakfast, which Ma would keep ready. Instead of sitting on the dining table, it was always more delightful to sit in the kitchen with Ma, and eat the deliciously hot *luchi*s or *chapati*s as they came off straight from the clay ovens, fired by coal. Of course, no one had even heard of an LPG cylinder, leave alone seeing it.

Glorious were those simple but heartening breakfasts. I would sit on a small wooden platform, or *piri*, while mother first served the vegetables and pickles. Then would start a steady stream of puffed up *luchi*s or thin *chapati*s, Ma and I indulging in our own humorous race, as to who would beat the other person—would she fail to serve a fresh *luchi* while my plate was empty, or should I fail to clear my plate, when a new *luchi* was ready to be served?

By now, it was time to switch modes, from a hungry small boy at home to a champion tree climber and occasional (if the truth be told) fruit thief. After breakfast, Ma would make a feeble attempt to keep me confined to the home with books, but I wouldn't give up on sneaking out. What use was a vacation otherwise?

All the houses in our neighborhood were not multi-storied flats, but small bungalows with a liberal garden area in front and a nice enclosed courtyard at the back. These gardens were the habitat of some delightful types of fruit tree—three or four types of mango, lots of guava trees, papayas, jaam (a dark purple Indian berry, like cranberry), jackfruit, woodfruit, and even banana plants.

Of these, our main target was the huge jaam tree in one of the houses. In summer, the whole tree would be almost hidden by large clusters of jaam hanging over, ranging from raw green bunches to dark purple of the fully ripened fruits almost about to burst.

Every day, one new batch of fruits would ripen and get cleaned out by us. The only problem for everyone was that the fruit available in the lower branches would get consumed first, leaving new batches towards the top of the tree. But this was no problem at all for me because I was lightweight and an expert climber of trees. So when everyone gathered under the tree, I would jump up to catch the nearest branch and then climb up right to the top like a squirrel. The next two hours were spent in a dream of stuffing oneself with fat, ripe jaams. Worldly wisdom dictated that one would need to carry some of the best pieces home, for parents and sister and brother. This politically correct behavior would either help expiate some existing crime or remain as a credit entry against future crimes.

Since the houses were small bungalows, a long, common wall ran right across all courtyards, and an agile person could well run on top of the wall through the entire colony. This was the architectural wonder and heaven sent corridor that I ran on top of, to pluck and consume at will, unripe mangoes and ripe guavas. The mangoes would be taken home, the kernels thrown away, and the body diced properly and then shaken with a little mustard oil and salt to make a delightful snack to be relished. But the ripe guavas were picked and eaten right there. Of course, these habits were not necessarily liked by all neighbors, but since the colony was like one happy family, nobody really minded. Once in a while, my mother would be forced to listen to a slightly complaining, but largely amused complaint from a neighboring lady, but it was all in good fun. After all, they too had children who were no angels and who were certainly not averse to stealing a few of their neighbors' fruits.

So the morning hours were spent in all the young crowd becoming monkeys for a few hours. Left on our own, we would have continued so in the blazing afternoon. But all the ladies put their feet down and insisted that we take a nap, read story books, start on holiday homework—anything but run off again. So till about 4 o'clock, there was forced imprisonment.

But at 4:00 there was no holding us back from the playing grounds adjoining the new multi-storied colony for playing football in summer, and cricket in winter.

Thanks to the very rough, stone-infested hard ground that was typical of the town, coupled with remnants of slag dumping resulting in small, glass-like pieces with sharp edges, we had permanent cuts and bruises on our legs with new bandages replacing the old throughout the summer season. But that didn't deter us from playing on and on, generally for about three hours at a stretch. Our playing proficiency was not too high, but one stimulus always and invariably knocked up our game quality pretty high. That was the sight of the new colony girls, whom we didn't know like our playmates of the old colony. The girls would either gather in twos or threes on the rooftops of the multi-storied houses or the bolder among them also took walks along the road bordering our playing grounds. In both cases, the girls would pretend that they didn't care about us, feigning total indifference but in reality, they were as keen on seeing us as we were keen on seeing them. Our game would really peak and we would be really tired out.

The day had not ended still, although by the time we returned home, the sun would have just gone down. There would be as stimulating and energizing a bath as in the morning, followed by a good dinner to a ravished soul. Then, with due permission from parents, we would again run out and reconvene near the jaam tree for a round of "Gilot," the local version of "catch-as-you-can." The boys would be divided into two groups. One group would disperse and hide somewhere in the colony. The other bunch, after five minutes, would go out locating the first team. If they succeeded, they would shout "Gilot" loudly to notify everyone. If they failed, the first team would quietly slip back to the convention point and score one win.

After four or five such sessions, we'd be delightfully tired from the day-long activities. It would be time to go home, quietly change into night dress and lie down, looking at a broken moon, and the silver sprinkling of the stars till one fell asleep, asleep, asleep. One more day of the summer vacations, one more day towards the end of innocent joy, and return to regimentation of school.

The Picnic

No Bengali community existence is ever complete without an annual picnic, and the Government colony, though in a Jharkhand town, being essentially populated by Bengalis, the picnic rule applied here with full force.

The lead for this initiative, in the year that I remembered most vividly, was taken as usual by Babu da—lean, wiry, whippet like with oodles of enthusiasm, almost dripping from his sharp French goatee beard. He worked out, in just a couple of days' work, all the logistical issues of number of people translating to so many kilos of rice and mutton, the directions to the exact spot in Jadugorah that had been selected for the picnic, the contribution needed from each participant, etc., down to the last nauseating detail.

All this was meticulously written down in a plan document, for the final scrutiny and approval by Ghosh Kaku. While Babu da represented the brawn and application part of whatever happened in our little colony, it was Ghosh Kaku who represented the brains and authority part. Anyway, Babu da had done his homework well, with substantial secretarial help from me and could stand up to Ghosh Kaku's sharp and incisive scrutiny.

The moment it was known that the much dreamt about picnic was actually on, a ripple of excitement spread through the youngsters of the colony because, by design, only a handful of adults were invited—mainly to take care of the cooking—and the rest would all be the colony children, excluding only toddlers.

Finally the day, a Sunday, arrived. From our house, only I was participating because my sister and brother were too young. An open body truck had been organized. First, all the picnic ingredients—earthen ovens, firewood, provisions, and cutlery were carefully loaded towards the front and covered with thick cloth. Then we were asked to climb in, and did we climb in! It was like an avalanche of small children hitting the truck like a big tsunami wave.

Babu da did a frenzied last minute check that everyone was on board as per the list, hopped on, and signaled for the truck driver to push off. He did it with alacrity, and in a little while, we were out of the city limits. The rolling hills of the Chotanagpur Plateau, like small green mounds, kept nodding along, synchronized with the truck's jolts, and the earth turned from the well-groomed and grass covered city patches, to an angry yellow, carpeted with stones of every description, right up to boulders.

About two hours of driving into the wilderness brought us to destination picnic. It was right at the foot of the hills with a tiny brook of crystalline water flowing right by. The water was so clean and effervescent that all of us jumped down from the truck right to the river bank, bent over, and had our fill of the sparkling water.

As usual, I wanted to be alone by myself. I walked on along the river bank. At one point, the bank rose steeply and the river formed a deep pool against a big chunk of granite rock. I huffed and puffed up to the top of the granite rock, lay on my belly, and looked down at the hill stream. To my amazement, sheer wonder, and joy, I found that about a dozen fish, each a little less than a foot long, had swum out of the main stream and huddled together in the relatively calmer pool under the rock, where the stream didn't flow so fast and the pickings were better for the fish.

I slid back quietly and slowly to the ground, and ran off to let Babu da know of my wonderful discovery. He heard me out, grinned wolfishly, and putting a hand in his kurta pocket, he slowly pulled out a small brown paper packet and gave it to me with a, "brought this along, just in case." I unwrapped the packet, and lo and behold, two tiny fish hooks nestled there, along with about 2 m of strong twine.

In a jiffy, I broke off a small branch from a neighboring tree, tied the twine to one end, and the other to the fish hook. Then Babu da helped me in digging up a small stone from the moss-like moist bank of the stream. Sure enough, about half a dozen worms curled under the stone. I quickly picked up two of the fattest.

Back to the rock. I cautiously tore off the earthworms into bit-sized lengths. Carefully put the worm piece on the hook, hiding it completely. Then I lowered it slowly, so that it entered the water slightly upstream and was dragged by the stream gently into the pool without scaring the fish. I had to wait just for a few seconds. One of the largest fish started nibbling at the still squirming worm. Then it got bolder, and tried to swallow the worm in one gulp. Of course, that's exactly what I wanted because in this process, the hook got solidly stuck in the fish's mouth. It started thrashing about and all I had to do was to yank it out of the water.

The other fish were naturally upset by this commotion and fled back to the main stream. But it didn't take more than five minutes and not too much of patience before the fish slowly came back to the pool. It was so clear that I could see right down to the gravel bed.

So my fishing went on till I had six of them in a row, dangling from the fishing rod string. Now, six small fishes wouldn't go too long a way among 30 hungry children, but would be a good snack between the five people in my family. So the question was how to take the fish back without their getting spoilt.

I took the fish to the main cook and he volunteered to help. First, with a flint stone, he scraped off the scales of the fish. Then he made a small cut in the throat to pull out all the viscera from the fish's stomach. Then a little bit of oil was heated in the big picnic wok. As soon as the oil started sputtering angrily, the fish, with dead but protuberant eyes, were coated with salt and lowered into the oil. In five minutes they were deep fried. The cook wrapped them in a plantain leaf, tied it up, and kept it aside, asking me to remember to pick it up on our way home.

So engrossed was I with the fish, that I had not noticed where my friends were. Only the cooks and attendants for laying out lunch were there with three earthen ovens going full blast and the delicious aroma of food spread all over. Anyway, although I was ferociously hungry, there was no point in hanging around there because I was not going to be given an out-of-turn meal.

Brief queries elicited the information that all the children had walked across the shallow stream and had gone hill climbing. I followed suit immediately and quite soon I stumbled upon

Babu da and a teenaged girl who was related to one of our neighborhood friends. I didn't know her, but she had the wonderful ability to come across boldly and friendly, putting me at ease in five minutes—and to think that I didn't even know her name, in fact didn't know her at all till that day.

Shortly, it transpired that she was not only a very nice and simple girl who smiled all the while, but was also an accomplished singer. This of course was an invitation to Babu da and me to request her to sing a song. After a bit of shyness, she agreed. I thought that being a Bengali, she would sing the inevitable Rabindra Sangeet or Tagore's songs. But to my delight she sang *Naa jeyo naa, rojoni akhano baaki*, which roughly translates to "No, don't go away, the night is still young." The autumn sun, not too warm, playing hide and seek with stray clouds, the green hills all around, the magnificent old trees, the light breeze, and a clear teenager's voice rising and falling through sweet notes.

After that, the rest of the day was like a haze. The fun and frolic of everyone sitting and eating together, the short naps under the trees, the lazy afternoon, the delicious slumber-removing tea, and the quick truck ride home (with the fish not forgotten)—all images etched in memory. But dominating all was the memory of a slim, pretty girl, her bright pink dress, her smiling face, and delectable songs. End of picnic, end of a great day, and the beginning of a new chapter in life.

The Circus

When I was a small boy, cinema halls were a rarity. Our entire city probably had 8–10 of them. There was no sign of television, so piped entertainment was also nonexistent. The only device of mass entertainment was the large, outsized GE radio sets that ran on valves, not even transistors, and the total number of Indian channels was three.

While this forced greater interaction between humans, and not between humans and machines, building up close and caring communities, on the entertainment front it was sparse to the point of agony. So the annual visit of the "Great" circus companies was an eagerly awaited event.

"Great" because no circus company would announce its existence, and therefore name as anything "small." The medium itself was dramatic and given to hyperbolic excesses at every turn. Hence, the "Great Eastern" circus, the "Great National" circus, and many more of their ilk. Every year, shortly after winter, they would come into town in grand processions, and pitch their three main circus tents and other resident tents at a prefixed ground in Sakchi. Then every night, just for promotions, they would have two massive searchlights criss-cross their beams in the sky.

Needless to mention, by this time every kid in town would be in a state of frenzy, and they would hustle their parents every day beyond endurance for a visit to the circus.

The magic day would arrive and the family would trot off to the circus grounds in the prescribed single file mode—the patriarch of the family in the proud lead mode with me hanging on to his fingers and the little sister changing paces between a toddle and being carried.

Finally, the triumphant arrival at the circus doorsteps and standing in queue for the tickets. Then the entry into the magic seat stands in the main circus "ring." The atmosphere, aided by a loud live orchestra, was one of charm, intoxication, an attempt to transport you to a different, slightly unreal world of acrobats, midgets, yawning and cowering lions, trapeze artists, and charging stallions.

With a majestic flourish, the band would sign off with a roll of drums, paving the path for the circus manager to run in with a bevy of tightly garbed, pretty lady artists, and a bunch of comic artists—all traditionally midgets—who fooled around the most, but actually were most proficient in all the tricks.

The show very cleverly grew in intensity, as act after act was deliberately but subliminally unfolded with higher and higher levels of tension, thrills, and incredulity about how mere mortals could actually pull off these acts.

So, first there was a bevy of girls who got on a table and bent and twisted their bodies into crazy shapes. Looking at them, you wouldn't believe that they had any bones at all in their lissome bodies! They were transformed to U's and O's in a matter of minutes.

After this, came strongmen carrying long poles. While the strongmen stood with legs akimbo and poles held up, the girls swarmed over them and climbed up the poles. They gripped the poles with their legs and swung out like a bevy of birds in flight, spreading their arms like wings, while the men twirled the poles faster and faster, and even tossed them up in the air and caught them on the rebound. The audience broke out clapping in rapturous delight.

Now was the turn of the horse riders. First, a single stallion dashed into the ring with none of the usual stirrups, saddles, etc. A bareback riding specialist stood on the back of the horse as it galloped around. Then he started doing crazy things like going under the horse's stomach and climbing up from the other side. And going under the horse's forelegs, and coming up near the waist. He also did a handstand, first with two hands, and then with one on the bare back of the horse. While he presented the last part of his act, standing ramrod straight on the back of the horse, his arms spread out, an imperious look on his face, he continued to bow and bend his neck graciously to the applause as though condescending to allow lesser mortals like us to communicate with him through claps and cheers.

As the haughty horseman went off the ring towards the back, four more horsemen galloped in. This time the horses were properly equipped with saddles, and stirrups, and all kinds of finery including plumes on their heads. Their riders also were richly garbed, with shining top boots and top hats. The four horsemen presented breathtaking acts of riding in a line as a column, riding in twos, leaping in the air and quickly changing horses in mid-air by jumping and landing on the right saddle. Once again, the audience broke out into vigorous clapping, shrieks from small children and the ladies, and whistles from enthusiastic young men.

Just to give a little rest to everyone's adrenalin pumping equipment and to replace the grimaces by broad smiles and laughter, as soon as the horses took to the exit, in ran a group of six midgets, all with their faces painted in thick comic make up, highlighted eyes and eyebrows, and the classic red ball on their noses.

For 15 minutes, the "jokers" indulged in slapstick, acrobatics, and funny little skits, and tossing each other around. They regaled everyone, and the audience was in splits over their antics. They looked clumsy and disjointed, but actually were some of the best artists the circus had. In fact, one learnt later that quite often, they were the first teachers or experts for the young, fresh recruits. They drew a huge applause as they bowed, waved gracefully, and skipped their way out of the ring.

Immediately, all lights dimmed, except for two spotlights above, beaming down flat on to the ring floor. The orchestra drums started rolling, as a huge cannon was rolled in under one of the spotlights. At the same time, a safety net swung down from the roof, stopping in front of the cannon. The drums rolled on ominously, the loudspeakers heightened their sound. Softly, the ring master came in with a lighted taper. The drums rolled to a crescendo, and stopped abruptly. Simultaneously, the ring master applied the taper to the cannon, which roared and belched a thick white mushroom of smoke, and from the cannon mouth, one of the over-painted "jokers" was shot out straight into the net—a human cannon ball!

Even before one recovered from this thrill, a huge partition, made of 20 feet long rods strung together, was brought into the ring and stretched out into a circular barrier or ring-within-a-ring.

From the passageway, a series of cages were trundled in, interfaced to a small sliding door on the ring, and four huge tigers were prodded to leave their cages and jump into the ring. They were followed by the ringmaster wielding a long whip, which he kept cracking in the air just to keep reminding the tigers who the boss was, lest they forgot.

Then began a series of stunts played by the tigers. One by one they jumped up on small stools, crouching low, and growling low murmurs of protest. At the ring master's unseen by us subtle signals, the tigers jumped one by one through hoops held by the ringmaster. Then he bade one tiger to open its mouth into which he put his head without any fear. The whole audience burst out into rapturous cat calls, whistles, and clapping. The fact that some of the children—yours truly included—were actually also sniveling in fear—doesn't need to be elaborated! After all, the circus was supposed to provide the full range of emotions and thrills, wasn't it?

As the tigers got down one by one from their stools, and moved off in single file back to their cages, the orchestra suddenly piped up to high notes, building up tremendous tension and expectations. All the lights were dimmed simultaneously. Then the large foms lamp close to the ceiling started coming on one by one, and we could see two trapeze artists swing in mid air, two climbing platforms, and one safety net below. The time for performing the crème de la crème of all item numbers—the trapeze—had arrived.

Two artists each went up the climbing rope ladders to the top of the waiting stand. A long rope was tightly stretched between them. One of the performers, a young girl, started the tight rope walk nonchalantly, and she got across with just her outstretched arms for balancing. This apparently didn't look like too tough an act, until she started walking backwards all the way! There was pin drop silence in the audience, only the soft rolling of drums indicated any activity, and then a clash of cymbals just as she got back to her nest.

Then two artists, from both sides, started swinging in wider and wider arcs upside down by holding the swing rods under their legs. After some time, when they approached each other, one of them let go of his grip and flew out through the air with his arms outstretched. Promptly the other artist caught his hands and they swung out together for a while before letting go and falling on the safety nets, bowing to receive the thunderous applause.

That was the last act, and I returned home, thrilled to my gills as it were.

Bok-Khali

Summer in Kolkata, just before the onset of monsoons, was very much like being immersed, round the clock, in a tub of hot sugar syrup. The combination of high temperatures and near 100 percent humidity, this Turkish bath feeling would last the whole day, and only by early evening would there be a small breeze from the nearby sea which would at least help in drying up your sweat and bring some relief.

To add to this, was the agony of trying to sell computers in possibly the world's most computer-resistant city, thanks to the all pervading unions. Then, most of the decision making senior management levels in target companies had already happily left for summer holidays in idyllic hill resorts in India or abroad. So it was quite depressing to knock from door to door, only to find no takers in place. And finally, of course, there were the famous power cuts for anywhere from 12 to 18 hours a day, which left all of us lean and wiry as we shuffled up and down long staircases throughout the day.

It was a really frustrating experience, especially for people like me who were accustomed to the drier North Indian summers.

Finally, one day my patience snapped. I was just panting back to our 11th-floor office, after futile up and own trudge in a nearby office complex. I was hot, sweating like a rivulet, itchy, irritated, and at the end of my tether. I somehow managed to get back to the office, finding it pretty deserted with almost everyone in the field. But there sat Benu, friend of many moons, and now a fellow-suffering colleague. Benu was sitting and panting, and it looked like he too had just come back from a painful foray in the field. "Benu," I said in an agonized voice, "Isn't there any way in which we can escape this hellhole, even if it is for just a couple of days." "Or even less? Just one night out is what I would give my soul for."

Benu peered at me sharply, "Do you actually mean it, or is it just one of your usual excitements that dies out faster than it came?" "No, no," I said, "this time I mean it." So Benu thought for a while, and suddenly straightened up with a grin. "Let's go to Bok-Khali for one night!" "What or where is this Bok-Khali?" I asked. "It's a small resort, more a village right now, slowly on the way to becoming a resort like Digha. But right now, it is still quite pristine and unspoilt, so it would be a beautiful place to visit, and must be quite cheap too."

So, the Bok-Khali die was cast between two harried warriors to give them a chance to recharge the batteries. Fortunately, the day was Friday, so one could plan to leave after lunch on Saturday in order to do the roughly four hours' drive towards Diamond Harbor and the Bay of Bengal.

On Saturday, both of us turned up in the office with an overnighter sling bag each, since we had planned to leave straight from the office without going back home. I don't know how the wretched morning whizzed past. So delighted was I with the prospect of the escape that even two climbs to the office in the morning—thanks to load shedding—seemed like a non issue.

Finally, after lunch, we set off, enlightened by someone in the office that the bus left from a spot close to the monument.

We got to the spot and almost immediately, an old, rickety low-ceilinged bus which looked like it would fall apart any moment, coughed, and wheezed into position. It was immediately invaded by the waiting crowd and the two of us also managed to squeeze through, although we got standing room only. In a matter of minutes, the bus was packed to the brim, and yet, it refused to start because more people were now being stuffed in. Benu and I stood goggle-eyed at people still coming through.

Finally, the piece of cake was triumphantly earned by an old lady, wearing the usual Bengali widow's white sari, wiry as a whippet, standing quietly between two burly men, who, it transpired, were her sons. Suddenly, one of them barreled into the bus and squeezed his way through to the window which was where the lady stood outside. Without a word or signal, the man on the ground picked up the lady and squeezed her in, feet first, through the window. During this, she was stiff as a board with the same dull, resolute look. Once inside the bus, she was put into vertical mode by the other son, and amidst loud protests from the four people already occupying the seat, she wriggled and squeezed till her thin frame got accommodated.

It almost felt like an encore to a command performance of squeezing an incredible number of people into a small bus because shortly after this final assault, the bus started off, grunted, coughed, and jerked back and forth for a while, and then settled down to a weird combination of going up and down, swaying side to side, and shivering through the whole frame every few seconds.

All passengers had more or less settled down and squeezed in. Of course, for Benu and self there was no question of sitting down. Suddenly, from the forward area came a lament, "Why don't you remove your rear end from my face?" A typical configuration of a standing passenger, without wishing it, continuously bumping into a sitting passenger. The whole bus burst into laughter and everyone's frayed nerves soothed down a lot, as we rolled and rocked on our way to Bok-Khali.

Fortunately, half-way through, we came to halt for passengers to stretch out, get refreshments from road-side shops, and the bus also to cool down and take a fresh topping of radiator water.

Aching in every limb, we trudged into an open-air eatery where all the walls were half depth, and the thatched roof rested on poles sticking out of the thin walls, and going up to the roof. This created a beautiful open-air refreshment room. We had taken a seat close to the wall to get plenty of fresh air and tucked into a big plate of condiments and sweets, and glass each of tea, when I looked up. To my amazement I saw a young man, cleanly dressed in a kurta–pyjama outfit, walking towards us from a field with a loopy grin on his face. The amazing part was that he was carrying, across his chest, a fully grown street dog, much as one would carry one's favorite child.

By the time he reached the restaurant, two locals, who were sitting at the next table with tea, started muttering, "Oh no, here comes that mad man again." The dog lover had reached the wall. He stopped, and with a completely false smile, he leaned over the wall and said endearingly to the men, "Want a dog? Eh? Lovely, well-trained dog?" The men started shooing him off, asking him softly to go away. Suddenly, the young man started screaming at the top of his voice, "Hit my dog yesterday, did you? All of you want to torture him when I am not around, eh? Well, try touching him again, and I'll kill all of you."

Somehow, the fracas was brought under control. I told Benu to leave quietly without getting involved. The bus driver had also started honking the horn, asking passengers to get back into the bus. We filed back. Fortunately now the bus was considerably empty. The sun was setting slowly. We rambled off, without any more incidents. The road ended in a rickety bridge over a small canal. The bus trundled over it, rounded a corner, and we stopped at a cluster of stalls and huts—Bok-Khali! We had reached our destination, and now would have to find a place for sleep and dinner.

Before setting off from Kolkata, one had assumed Bok-Khali to be somewhere between a small town and a largish village. So it was quite daunting to see that actually it was more a tiny cluster of mud and thatched roof huts, scattered quite close to the restless waves of the Bay of Bengal. The only place superior to this was a hotel, under construction, which we were told was the State Guest House in the making where one would be able to book a proper room, with modern amenities, may be after six months.

This development was a bit depressing, but the escape from sweltering Kolkata, the beautiful cool breeze of the ocean, and the bleak and rugged appeal of the huts uplifted both of us to facing any unforeseen setback, and not treat it as a disaster. So it was not surprising at all that within 15 minutes of rummaging between the huts, we found two *charpai* beds in a room in a hut belonging to one ever smiling rustic. That was that, we dumped our overnighter bags, and responded with alacrity to mine host's suggestion of a refreshing bath with cool, cool water drawn from the well. That turned out to be a really exhilarating experience, and even in a five star hotel, I wonder if I had had the luxury of such an event.

It was so far so good. And then the boom came down with a thud. The bath had really set a fire of hunger in our bellies, and I was looking forward to a quick dinner, followed by a stroll along the beach. But our kindly host, with a lot of apologies and twisting of his clasped fingers, stated clearly that much as he would have loved to, unfortunately he wouldn't be able to serve any food. All the temporary shops, which were really stands to which the neighboring villagers brought their fresh produce, were unfortunately closed by lunch time, and since there was no prior notice of our arrival, there was no extra food for us either.

The sun had almost gone down, and the whole eastern sky on the horizon, where the waves blended into the sky, was aflame with the reflected lights from the sun going down on the other side. But appreciation of such opulent brilliance from nature was a bit tough to maintain while rats seemed to be running around in one's stomach from sheer hunger. In desperation I asked, "Do you have any fish?" "That we do sir, any amount, any time of the day." "Good," I said, "just fry a lot of fish for us and give it on a large plate. That'll be our dinner tonight." Everyone seemed very happy at this constructive development and the landlord got going.

One problem was solved, but how about the other—of securing a bottle of some respectable drink—whisky, rum, brandy, anything which was not illicit hooch for killing us. Back to the landlord, shy and sly grins, vigorous shaking of heads, quick transfer of money, and lo and behold, a bottle appeared magically from thin air.

Within the next half hour, the items were all ready—big plate of delicious fried fish, bottle of divine whisky, two glasses, and a sturdy lantern throwing its light for about 5 feet in every direction.

We walked towards the ocean. The sun had completely set, and for miles in every direction, it was pitch dark because it was the new moon night, when there was no moon in the sky. The slow moving lanterns among the huts were the only fireflies cruising around. With the help of our lantern, we walked over the soft sand towards the ocean and selected a spot as close to the water as possible.

After settling down, I took a deep breath and tried to soak in the ambience. The constant muted roar of the waves, the accompanying wind sighing through the leaves of the coconut trees, the soft voices of the villagers, a young girl singing a tune somewhere, distant sounds of a film song playing on a gramophone in a shanty on the main highway, and—oh yes—the clinking of our glasses, and gurgling of the drink as it fell into the glass, all put together in one glorious oeuvre of night sounds.

Forever in my memory, that magic night will keep reverberating like a beacon from that little lantern valiantly piercing the coal black darkness.

Next morning, we got up very early, a little before sunrise. We selected a spot under a coconut tree, facing the grey, hazy ocean, writhing like a vast animal with its own beat. Then, the magic of the sun coming up—first the coloring of the clouds in gentle shades of red and yellow. The gradual expansion and dilution of those colored bands. The faint, slightly formed arc of the tip of the sun, just barely visible. Then a fast progression of the sun's arc, ocean turning from slate grey to blue, the tree banks and huts gradually becoming visible. And then, magically, the sun leapt out of the water into the sky, and from red turned into glaring yellow which was difficult to stare at.

Having soaked it in, and with a quick "surya pranam" (obeisance to sun) chant from Benu, we went back to the hut to get the clothes for a bath in the ocean. We were warned that the declivity was very steep here, worse than even at Digha, so we shouldn't venture out too far. We heeded these good words and decided to bob up and down in the warm, engulfing water just a few feet from the shore.

A quick breakfast—rustic but wholesome—packing up and fond good-byes to the simple, wonderful people of Bok-Khali, and we had boarded the return bus to Kolkata. This time it was not eventful like the first journey, excepting another mad man (Bok-Khali seemed to have a large share of lunatics) sitting quietly, but continuously whispering slang to a fat acolyte from the Ramakrishna Mission, till he couldn't handle it anymore, and jumped up protesting. The mad man was unceremoniously kicked out, everyone sat back, and in no time (actually four hours), we were back at Kolkata.

Wonder how Bok-Khali looks now after all these years. I am sure, it has lost its pristine charm, however much the amenities have improved.

Humor

With everyone's existence getting violently buffeted by increasingly stressful urbanization, there is a desperate need today for a counterbalancing phenomenon that'll ensure the retention of sanity.

It's different strokes for different folks though. Many try out yoga and meditation, others take solace in music. Someone else in breaking convention and decorating their homes in apparently jarring motifs, which actually provide a lot of relief with every change.

I believe, however, that the one thing which we could practice with ease with no need for accessories, discipline regimens, or gurus, and is yet the most effective is plain old humor. Nothing takes away all the wrinkles and stressful premonitions than a breakout humorous session, even if it lasts only for a moment. It's like one sweating out the mind toxins that so corrode our peace.

The other great thing about humor is that it doesn't depend on the size of anyone's pocket to indulge in. It only calls for an ability to not just see, but actually observe and assimilate the ludicrous, the deviant, and the mirthful in an otherwise dull, prosaic, or indeed even a painful situation. And the quicker the response, the more productive it is.

There is, of course, a class system within different genres of humor. That which evokes loud, crude guffaws is no good—true humor is that which invokes a fleeting smile, not laughter, at the corner of the lips, illuminating the receiver with a flood of appreciation, and gone the next moment. That is true, artistic humor.

A small example might illustrate this important issue.

It was the 1930s, when India had not gained her freedom. A small bus was trundling along the famous GT Road. As buses went in those days, the roof of the bus was very low and if the road was too bumpy, or the shock absorbers were worn out, you ran the risk of hitting your head on the wooden cross beams above. So the passengers held on to whatever they could in order to keep sitting with some comfort.

One such person was a large sized gentleman with a lot of gravitas—a man of very few, but pithy words. So long as GT Road remained in British India, with reasonably good road maintenance, the ride was not too uncomfortable. But the road soon entered Chandan Nagar, a small town near Calcutta, which, along with Pondicherry in the South, had remained a French colony.

The road here was a grand mess—uncared for, full of large potholes, totally neglected. The bus fell into one such pothole, and moved so violently up—and—down, that our man flew up to the roof, and got a solid crack on his glistening bald head.

He just reacted with a loud "Ouch!" and then added, "thank God for Dupleix having lost!" This was a reference to the decisive battle in which the British Lord Clive defeated the French General Dupleix. If the latter had won, India would have been a French, not British, colony, and roads everywhere would have been in the same miserable shape and so, your head getting bumped would have been a constant, rather than occasional, phenomenon. The whole bus load erupted in laughter.

This is a very fine example of subtle humor, understated, indirect, and yet incisive in its impact. For a moment, the more appreciative cognoscenti would have completely forgotten all their stresses.

Of course, this class of humor is becoming rarer and rarer as each one of us struggles to find or create our own little island of sanity in a world gone mad. Most humor today has degenerated to the coarse, forcibly rib-tickling slapstick that really engulfs you from all sides and makes you feel sick after a while.

Yet, amidst all this darkness, as it were, one can still discover humor of a different sort. This genre, seemingly trying to evoke slapstick guffaws only, actually delves much deeper and cathartically purifies you because actually it is closely linked to pathos.

Not pathos of the kind which insists on barraging you continuously with fat man slips on banana peel kind of humor, leaving most people rolling with laughter, but not able to take away anything more from the session. But there is a rare breed that can blend true, systemic, universal pathos with humor in such a manner that even the most crass or apparently crude form of humor, while it is making you roll with uncontrollable laughter, suddenly jerks you up with one massive tug to your heart, and also head.

Charlie Chaplin was one such maestro, and his work will continue to be the benchmark against which every other film maker will have to be measured. A classic scene comes to mind as one thinks of hundreds of Chaplin scenes.

Charlie crushed and bent by a hard day's labor that is the fate of most poor men of the 1930s Americas, is hanging on for dear life, by the handle of the front door of a tram cab, which is jam packed. The tram stops at a point. A large man tries to enter the rear gate. Charlie implores him not to do so. The man is confused, because how can his getting into the back door be of any concern to Charlie?

So he pushes his way in, and the moment he does so, Charlie falls off the front door, so stuffed is the tram! The audience bursts out into laughter, until the camera zooms into the sad eyes of Charlie lying on the ground. No words are needed. Instantly you assimilate the pathos of the fringe existence of a worker—sad, almost hopeless, almost beaten, yet still defiant, still courageous. Within seconds you are transported over laughter, sorrow, and an indomitable zest for life. This is humor at its finest.

But there is a dark side to humor also, the underbelly of every society that has always expressed itself with brutal frankness, and without any bondages or barriers of more genteel societies. The greatest example of this phenomenon is graffiti, or literally, "writing on the wall." It's as old a practice as the civilization of Pompei, but today it proliferates mainly, in Britain, USA, Western

Europe, and a few off beats like Israel, and the English speaking world like Australia and New Zealand. Although graffiti occurs in major languages, English seems to be the lingua franca, since English, since the second half of the last century, has become the natural language for pop culture.

Traditionally, graffiti, or writing on the wall, has mainly been used for protest of the underdog against anything that represents the establishment in any form—government, organizations of authority against individuals, police and the indolent rich, statutory bodies, etc. So if there is any officious and slightly patronizing claim by such a body on a bill-board or sign, prompt comes an extension in the form of a witty rebuttal. Or, quite often, the graffiti artist himself takes the initiative to post a unilateral comment. No one is accepted—presidents, prime ministers, men and women of stature. All are grist to the graffito mill.

The next, most prevalent form of graffiti, of course, is sex. Every conceivable type of sexual indulgence is brought up for dissection, rebuttal, extension, and making ludicrous. Understandably, men's and women's separate toilets in universities and public places are the most usual playgrounds.

Conventionally, the pun is regarded as the worst form of humor. But to the graffiti artist, the pun is the most delicate scalpel used to make a telling point. Similarly, once upon a time, graffiti medium used to be only the building wall or bill board, but in the eternal fight between form and content, now graffiti has extended to messages on cars, posters, and even T-shirts. Graffiti really rules, OK!

Metamorphosis

Changing Times

Long, long ago, primitive man eked out his existence by foraging for whatever he could gather around himself. It could be fruits, berries, edible roots, whatever one could lay hands on. He was, essentially, a gatherer.

Then, over millennia, the transformation happened from gatherer to hunter to cultivator. Man learnt to settle down in fixed locations like villages and cities, and gave up his nomadic quests. Yet, the urge, to see new places and experience new events led to man's invention and perfection of different modes of transport. Initially, the invention of wheels, then navigation on rivers, and finally, the invention of airplanes completed the conquest of land, water, and air.

As different races came in contact with each other, there was a lot of healthy interchange—trade, food habits, apparel, ornaments, etc., but there was also a lot of strife—warfare, the invention and ghastly perfection of weaponry, the enslavement of many, and the spread of agony and sorrow. Perhaps, inevitably, there is an innate struggle between good and evil in man, every time change occurs in whatever the status quo is. From ancient classlessness, to the travails of modern, global capitalism, this built-in struggle has taken the best from opposing forces and moved forward. Thus "civilization." But it is still a moot point whether all such apparent moves forward have really been worthwhile.

One does not obviously, champion the cause of regression, of reversal back to a pastoral lifestyle, but the wholesale adoption of anything new also needs to be questioned.

Metamorphosis

When six of us contemplated the formation of our own IT company in 1988, little did we know about the twists and turns, and reshaping, that the company would go through in the next 20 odd years. At the times they happened, it seemed the most obvious reaction to circumstances, but later, one wondered whether we were either missing the bus or trying to create scenarios with a small minority, well before its time.

Well, as we geared up to come out of HCL, one severe blow that fell, almost dislocated us from not starting at all. It was the absurdly, untimely death—in his early 30s—of C.S. Patankar, undoubtedly the smartest and most competent of us. Even before the company registration, he proposed the name "Hindustan Office Products Limited." Then came the trauma of his fighting for life after a very serious brain aneurysm rupture, which the surgeons couldn't operate on. Unfortunately, that part of the brain controls breathing, so Patankar slowly went out over three days, never regaining consciousness. The supreme irony was that as life ebbed away on one side, new life was formed at the same time, as, on the last day, his wife gave birth to a daughter whom Patankar never saw.

This death almost grounded our project, with serious danger of it never taking off. But we somehow rallied on in his memory, five of us still got together and started the company (MP dropped out, though, so Nair brought in Dilip as the CTO). In Patankar's fond and precious memory, we retained the company name as he had visualized it, although we never did office products at all.

But one slight elaboration we did indulge in, though. If we left the Company name as is, there was a distinct possibility of people shortening it to HOP Ltd, which wouldn't have been elegant at all! So we added an E (Electronics? Enterprise? Take your pick, or give your own expansion) and made a logo HOPE. As expected, this gained currency fast, and everyone forgot Hindustan Office

Products. So after a few years, we went back to the Registrar of Companies, and filed for HOPE Technologies Ltd, which went through without any demur. The logo even got a pair of wings over the last letter E, and subliminally, at least, indicated that the time had come for us to take off. Business wise also, this was the time when things were indeed looking pretty good to us after many hiccups. So finally, everything was right and mature for us to change the logo into what our business was, and not how we generally felt about life! So the word "HOPE" was fused into a small geometric pattern, to announce to the world firmly about our being a CAD/CAM company, and CAD/CAM alone.

This served us well, and by 1998–1999, we were recognized as an organization that, along with its "virtual corporation" of 60 dedicated dealers all over India, stood for causing an eruption in PC-CAD usage in every segment, and in every corner of India. The principal driver was the full range of products from Autodesk, embellished neatly with third party software configured with AutoCAD to give a vastly effective solution in vertical engineering spaces.

Parallel with an aggressive engagement with corporates and government organizations for doing this, we also nurtured, in the background, a quiet operation for engineering colleges, AICTE, and World Bank–funded implementation agencies, to standardize our products as the de facto standard for technical education.

It took painstaking work for—three to four years to achieve this, but it created bedrock of patronage for today's students/tomorrow's practicing engineers. Till date, the education segment is a preferred hunting ground for us.

With this proliferation in both the commercial and the education segments, there was a steady and growing drumbeat of the name "HOPE." This is the time, as the 20th century moved towards its end, we decided to go beyond the shores of India, which is all that our product distribution agreements would allow.

With the aggressive thrust by Indian IT into global markets, why would we be left behind?

So, with the decision taken to fan out, a small services commando was created, and it established the flag firmly in US, Japan, Germany, and UK. It was a new and heady experience for us, and we were fairly gung-ho about global services business accelerating compared to product sales. Everything was falling in place. But unknown to us, a small dichotomy began to affect us negatively. IT was the very brand name, "HOPE," that we were so proud of. Unlike Indian customers who could relate emotionally to our company name, the global mind, especially the Western mind, would tend to be literal about the whole thing. "HOPE? Isn't that the name of a charity, or an NGO?"

One got quite tired explaining the whole genesis of our brand name. So we finally got fed up, and decided to change the company name. Broadly, it would have to be punchy, intellectual, and connote a capability which customers should feel immediately. After a lot of cogitation, we selected "Adroitec" (from "adroit" or "skillful"). For satisfying the registrar of companies, for whom the name would have to be explicitly descriptive of the nature of business, we added "Information Systems."

For the last few years, we have promoted this new brand name across all customers and market segments. Today it is well established, and only old timers mention "HOPE" with nostalgia.

What a roller coaster ride it has been!

Going Forward

Right now, we are at a business crossroad where some of the original assumptions have come round full circle, and after exactly 20 years of business practice, we have to do a very objective, incisive, and dispassionate self analysis.

Most successful Indian IT companies, including HCL Technologies, have started with some kind of product sales in India, and then gradually wheeled away into developing specific service competences, which they have taken to distant shores. Yet, product sales is still the bread and butter business, which ensures that Indian technology companies keep getting the basic technology building blocks with which to keep honing their global service efforts. Companies which have unabashedly done this are quite often at the head of the pack, albeit with low unit margins, but with huge volumes to make up for. Redington, with $3.5 billion sales, HCL Info Systems and hundreds of western technology suppliers with Indian distribution networks all over are ready examples of this market exploitation phenomenon.

The obvious market segment definition task begs us also to check whether these technology solutions are consumed only by other businesses, in service supplies, or whether there is also a lifestyle/aspirations market in a rapidly modernizing and explosively growing community of lay persons. Two examples would suffice—the rapid penetration by laptops, not as a development platform, but rather as a communication, entertainment, and self-learning device. The other, mind-boggling, phenomenon, of course, is the phenomenon of mobile phones, now ubiquitously ranging up and down all social strata, and across all geographical nooks and crannies. For a technology product sales company—witness HCL Info Systems—such a product can become the company's lifeline.

So, the importance of technology products vis-a-vis services is not the debate. Question is, can both coexist under the same roof, and management structure? The answer ranges from a vociferous "no way" to a hesitant, unsure, "not very sure about that. Could mean too much toggling for the mind set." Whichever end you look at, the consensus seems to be that you can't do both things together. Again witness how Redington steers clear of services, and has built up a $3.5 billion business, which is just not Indian only in scope, but is truly global—supply side and demand side. Or the deliberate bifurcation created in the HCL group—with HCL Technologies being the completely outward facing global services organization, and HCL Infrastructure being the totally Indian product supply business.

That said, the moot point that emerges is that if you have competences in both, and want to do both of them, then you better plan a restructure that creates clearly etched and distinct business units. This is the key derivative also for the tiny Adroitec, which, on one hand, has built up a small but definite practice of Mechanical and AEC services, and has also been highly successful with products like ZWCAD, PTC family, and now, Primavera and Map Info. The services on one hand and product sales on the other need to be enveloped in separate group companies, which would be held in majority stakes by the parent Adroitec. This would replace the present everything pell mell under the same-roof divisional structure. This would certainly eradicate the present customer confusion.

Of course, clear business plans would have to be drawn up for each candidate company. Of particular importance would be questions about working capital requirements, intercompany transfer pricing norms, extents of stock options for key personnel, roles of the parent holding company, etc. Once this dust settles, we can go to the market with may be seven young, exuberant horses pulling the chariot instead of one confused old horse trying to do his best with tongue hanging out!

Of Soft Drinks and Softwares

I consider myself extremely fortunate in having had a ringside seat, keenly observing, and actively participating in, the evolution and maturing of two huge, live-wire industries—soft drinks and IT.

This happened in the 1970–1977 period during my stint with the Coca-Cola Export Corporation, and with HCL during 1977–1988.

On the face of it, there can't be two industries which are as different from each other than these. Yet, as I look back, there were, indeed, amusing similarities and challenges!

When I joined Coke, it was available in a maximum of 20 towns. By the time I left, it was doing merry business in more than 2,000 towns. When HCL started, there were less than 100 computers in India. By 1988, computers were working in more than 300 towns. Both of these things happened because a bunch of young people fanatically believed that you had to take the product to the market, and not sit pretty expecting the market to come to the product.

The IT business lends itself to a lot of segmentation of the market place by usage—industry, government, education, leisure, etc. So does, strange as it might seem, the soft-drink industry—the classic eating house, pan shop, stores, institutional, home, etc., by place of consumption, just as there are consumption occasions—parties, get together, friends lazing out, with food, etc. It took me a while to figure all this out, and then to attempt precisely formulated market penetration/expansion plans by different segments. The rewards were really gratifying.

In the initial periods, when the market was still small and unformed, a lot of the likely success in a new foray depended on successfully giving the potential customer a taste of the product's deliverables, instead of "educating" him through ads, brochures, and lectures. In case of soft drinks, this was best done through "free sampling" exercises in schools, colleges and during breaks at cinema halls. In case of computers, HCL was the first company to work out taking the machine directly to the market—mainly targeting SMEs—in the form of "road shows." And believe it or not, the first ever road show in India was held in Ludhiana, and not one of the metros. Participation by the local business community was wildly beyond all expectation. The rest is history—of how the computer got out of elite corporates in metros, and quickly proliferated through 300 smaller towns, sometimes with only one installation in that town.

As one grows older and moves towards hanging up one's boots, there is great nostalgia about these events and phenomena, and a yearning to take a shot at yet another industry launch and nurturing.

Coke Marketing

I spent seven and a half years from 1970 onwards, establishing Coca-Cola, Fanta Orange, and Fanta Soda all over eastern India, and then also in other parts like Bangalore, Meerut, Madurai, etc. I would set off with the bottling plant people in the factory car, and light out for all the small towns, since the larger towns already had distributors.

On reaching the target town, we would home in on the local ITC, or other well-known consumer brands' distributor, because they understood product distribution very well. We would then casually introduce our product and ask him if he could recommend anyone in the town. If he was interested himself, he would, of course, ask about terms with equal casualness. Else he would anyway recommend another good person to us. So we benefited either way.

Working in this mode, we travelled from town to town appointing new distributors. Our maximum work was presummer, so that we could reap the benefit of peak sales in the April–June period. Once the distributor was in place, we started appointing dealers, or retail outlets, which could be stores, corner tobacco shops, restaurants, etc., with ice boxes, and later, electric bottle coolers. The latter, however, were a big pain—especially the ones from Blue Star, because their local Indian compressors kept going out of order, especially in the Durgapur—Dhanbad—Sindhri area, where electric supply voltages were extremely erratic.

The Border Town

One of the big problems in Coke marketing was the fact that because of different sales tax rates in different states, the rates to the distributors and dealers used to vary from state to state. So we had to maintain vigilance, so that lower priced product didn't get smuggled to higher price border towns. So when I found that one town in Orissa, on the Bihar–Orissa border, had unusually high sales, I suspected the usual smuggling racket, and prioritized a visit there.

The distributor had a large grocery store on the crossing of the two main, perpendicular roads of the town. When I confronted him with the abnormally high sales data, he smiled and said, "Sir, I don't smuggle products to Bihar. Small dealers with small grocery stores in 50 neighboring villages pick up their grocery from my shop, and they also pick up Coke, which has become a prestigious item to serve on occasions like weddings." "How do they chill the coke then," I asked, since no ice reached the remote villages. "Simple, Sir!" said the man, "they dig large holes in the ground, put the coke bottles in, cover them with fine sand, over which they keep pouring water. As the water evaporates, the bottles get absolutely chilled." For me, it was a lesson in high school Physics, learnt all over again.

The Melting Pot

Somewhere in the 1960s, the great scientist and sci-fi writer, Arthur Clark, wrote that what man had created by way of science and technology from time immemorial till 1900 was nothing compared to what he had garnered from 1900 to the time of his writing. IF Clark were to write again today, in 2010, what he postulated could very well be applied to the period 1960–2010, especially 2000–2010, more than swamping man's achievements from 1960 to 2000.

The impact of this constant acceleration has obviously become manifest in every aspect of human life. But it is as a social animal that man has altered his society most profoundly. The term being used is "global village," which in turn, has two aspects. One is the crashing of distances, literally, and symbolically. The other, more profound, aspect is the rapid dissolution of intersociety prejudices, narrow jingoisms, ignorance of each other's social behavior patterns, and a corresponding amount of intolerance. This leveling of attitudes and social behavior, into a "melting pot," was initially restricted to some pockets of affluent and modern societies, which attracted a lot of immigrants from all over the world. But now, this phenomenon itself is progressing laterally across geographies, so that you need not look only at, say, San Francisco to exemplify the melting pot, but even the humble Jhumri Tillaia has transformed to a melting pot of sorts.

In this pot, language, the arts, social interaction, modes of food, clothing, entertainment—all are getting stirred together, first maintaining the idiosyncrasies of different constituent cultures, but then quickly sublimating to one uniform, super culture which borrows from the best—and alas, sometimes worst—aspects of cultures. And the ripple effect goes on spreading all over.

The immediate impact of this is the rapid leveling of cultural differentials. In India, the graded cultural slope between villages, small towns, and large cities, has now become practically flat owing to rapid communication, far-reaching penetration of vocations (BPOs' centers in villages), a certain minimum level of available education, and quick adaptation of new ways of life. This transformation is so radical as to make cultural recognition of the same place almost impossible after every decade.

There are many drivers to this exciting and magnificent phenomenon. But of all of them, possibly the biggest, the most pervasive, and the most explosively growing is information technology (IT). Up to the 1980s, IT's proliferation was in low per capita, too disparate with little standardization, and with usability interfaces which were too tough for the lay users to go through.

Within a decade though, all that changed dramatically, with ubiquitous, standardized PCs which can now be used by a 5-year-old and an 85-year-old with the same ease. Once a critical mass was in place, at least in advanced society, networking, and the Internet exploded the whole phenomenon, with IT creating an upheaval which was mutually fuelling. It made the machines come alive, not just in commerce, but in every walk of life. That fanned the demand for individual stations. That in turn called for more networking, and so on, ad infinitum.

I witnessed firsthand how IT can expedite cultural change-overs. Somewhere in the mid-1980s, I visited Sunnyvale in the Silicon Valley for the weekend, hosted by two HCL R&D boys who had been posted there for interactions with a few potential customers on their requirements. Since all computer systems were non-standard, it took our deeply embedded R&D people, and not today's computer science system engineers, to ferret out customer needs.

Anyway, they almost stuck out like sore thumbs in an alien society that didn't care much for "outsourcing." Indians were there, in the whole valley, as an almost negligible percentage.

On Saturday morning, my hosts, who had planned for a day's tourist schedule for me, were very excited for some reason. Queries revealed that very recently, an NRI professor at Berkley had chucked up his prestigious and rock-steady career, in order to open and manage an Indian restaurant! And he was successful too. Already two more outlets had been opened. But his was the only foray known till then. So, with as much curiosity as hunger, I trotted off to the Sunnyvale restaurant, which just had space for about a dozen people to sit, to enjoy a typical Indian breakfast. The whole experience was exotic and exceptional.

Towards the end of the decade, I happened to be in Sunnyvale again. We went out for dinner, and well before I reached the market, I could hear Tamil, Hindi, Guajarati, and Telugu songs being broadcast full blast. Coming close, one found that in less than 10 years, that lone multi-region restaurant of the Berkley professor had proliferated into specialist shops for different areas. Their patronage was justified by 60 percent of Sunnyvale's population having become Indians, compared to the initial handful. And all the new people were almost inevitably from the IT profession, who could now afford the luxury of "home" food, not just from India, but even from their own "home" state.

So Indian presence, driven by IT, had crossed the critical mass level. But the interesting question was whether these NRI had maintained their own provincialism, or had developed a common, melting pot culture. It was gratifying to see that just as their vocational expertise had reached standardization of tools, their socio-cultural make-up was also moving towards standards. And by the time children started appearing, and growing up, the cultural shift to Americanism was complete. The children knew nothing of India, and probably couldn't care less, being products of local American culture completely.

But the sublimation of one's persona into the melting pot of a standardized culture has not been easy or smooth either. The unhealthy aspects of an alien culture have extracted their toll, especially from sensitive immigrants, who have not necessarily visualized their self-actualization only from material objects around them. It is these lost souls, as it were, whom I have always found to be the most interesting people to relate to.

It is completely different for those people who came to the US with only dollars in mind, and who wallow in accumulating more and more, and immerse themselves in goodies. Interestingly they come in thousands to USA and Europe not just from A cities of India, but also from B and C category smaller towns. To start with, there are obvious cultural differentials owing to these origins, but very soon the melting pot of American life flattens those differences out. It goes on and on, this churn, first between the local indigents and the immigrants, and also within the groups of immigrants. The world is indeed getting to become a small melting pot.

The Nineteenth Century

In many more senses than one, the 19th century is one of the greatest watershed eras in the history of modern India, and more so, of Bengal. This largely owes to the fact that the fate of contemporary India was molded largely by the British rule of over two centuries, and well into the 20th. Also, Bengal happened to be the location for most of the foundational impact of British rule, until the focus shifted to the whole country, with Delhi as the titular capital.

Not surprisingly, the 19th century of Bengal is filled with a rich tapestry of characters, events, idiosyncrasies, and impacts. So we homed on to this in Natyakaal, and the material for several of our plays was the outcome of exhaustive research on the era, the people, and the major events that were turning points, or crossroads in history.

To understand this, we went back to the fag end of the previous, i.e., the 18th century—in fact to 1793, during the rule of Lord Cornwallis. In one stroke of his pen, he devastated rural, agrarian India like no flood, drought or famine had been able to wreak in its history. He enacted the Permanent Settlement Act. Prior to this, throughout Indian history, revenue to the state from agriculture was proportionate in a year to the actual crop production that year. So whether it was the Hindu kingdoms or Muslim, if there was a bad year, everyone shared the burden, and the farmer paid a fixed fraction of his production as land tax. So there was perfect equitability.

More critically, land was inalienable, which means that a farmer always owned his own land. Even the King did not have that right. He could collect taxes from that land, but he still didn't own the land. So if, as historical romantic stories project, a King "donated" 10 villages to someone as a boon, he merely gave that person the right to collect taxes from those villages on his behalf, and not have the right to physically own the land.

The Permanent Settlement Act changed all that. Firstly, it didn't bother about the amount of crop produced in a particular year. It fixed an amount of money to be paid as tax definitely. Secondly, in case of failure to pay, for the first time in Indian history, land became alienable. The farmer could be evicted, his land forfeited and sold off to fill the gap in taxation.

This, as can be easily visualized, threw out thousands of landless farmers. Having no roof above their heads any more, and with nothing to eat, they migrated like locusts to nearby, towns, which were few, or became easy prey of the touts enslaving thousands for tea and coffee plantations, and distant colonies like Mauritius. In one single century, there were more famines and deaths in India, than in all the other centuries put together.

This aspect of Indian history became rich material for our plays, where starting with satirical songs on Cornwallis, to pathetic pleas of beggars for a little rice, we projected this momentous era to spell-bound audiences all over.

Another major happening of the early 19th century—1832 to be precise—was the introduction of public education by Lord Macaulay. This single instrument has probably had the most far-reaching impact on India's problems—festering till date—relating to conflicts between majority Hindus and the minority religions, especially that of Muslims.

Lord Macaulay's introduction to the Public Education Policy document is an eye-opener on long-range politics. Although it may be assumed to posture to be egalitarian and sympathetic, it states, without mincing words "The object of this public education is to create between us, and those whom we rule, a body of people who would be Indian by color, but completely British in their values, beliefs, and allegiances."

On the introduction of the scheme, there was a hue and cry across the country about "low-class" English education being a religious transgression and despoiler. Initially, both Hindu pundits of traditional *pathashalas*, and Muslim Mullahs rejected the new system outright. Then Derozio's followers—the Young Bengal—ensured that sense prevailed, and Hindu boys (girls weren't allowed to school those days) slowly started going to early institutions like Hindu College, Sanskrit College, etc.

More than the educational content, this opened up for Hindus all the opportunities of professional jobs—doctors, teachers, lawyers, administrators—which, as per Macaulay's foresight were badly required for successful British rule. The Muslims, however, refused to leave their traditional scholastic system, and were thus left out of the professional cadres. This malaise continued well into the next century, and in some senses, exists even today. So in any given geographic area, even with majority population of Muslims, most professional jobs still belong to non Muslims (Hindus mainly), and Muslims are still predominantly engaged in "menial" jobs down the social spectrum. A lot of Hindu—Muslim tension even today can be attributed to this "profession divide" that had denied an equal footing to Muslims, whose forefathers had committed the cardinal sin of exclusion in 1832.

Night drive to Saeger town from Jersey

City: Snowing throughout night.

Morning: Robert Frost's poem comes alive in miles of countryside around.

Only flaw sound of gunshot—hunter after deer.

Why can't life freeze—frame forever on that winter morning?

Huge wide rolling grounds covered with snow right up to the horizon.

The pine stands bent double and splotched with ice streamers. The river under the old stone bridge frozen solid.

Occasional isolated houses dotting the landscape, almost indistinguishable from the wide white carpet.

And right in front of me, as I sit in the modern auto instead of on a horse, the small pine forest from Frost's poem.

About the Editors

Arjun Malhotra

Orbiculsris oculi is the muscle that makes you smile—and this is a muscle that gets overworked after a session with Arjun.

In his very accomplished career, Arjun has played a role of entrepreneur, philanthropist, board member, technician, counselor, referee, salesperson, and organizer, but never a role of a disciplinarian.

Arjun has amazing capacity for networking and mind-boggling capacity for remembering names, dates, and incidences. He communicates with thousands of connections, globally, on a daily basis through emails/phone, Facebook, and Linked-in. If not on a flight you can be assured of a response to your SMS, phone message, or email within few hours.

"To receive the full value of success you must have someone to share it with"—Arjun believes and has practiced this during his long string of entrepreneurial successes.

Arjun co-founded the HCL group in 1975, taking it from six-person "garage operation" to one of India's largest Information Technology corporations. Arjun took over HCL's US operation in 1989 and in 1992 he ran the HCL-HP joint venture in India.

Arjun later founded TechSpan in 1998 with funding from Goldman Sachs and Walden International. In 2003, TechSpan merged with Headstrong and Arjun served as CEO and Chairman of Headstrong's Board of Directors before its acquisition for $550m by Genpact in May 2011.

Arjun did his schooling from Doon School (Dehradun) and graduated from IIT with B.Tech. (Hons.) in Electronics & Electrical Communication Engineering and received the Dr B.C. Roy Gold Medal. In 1985, he attended the Advanced Management Program at Harvard Business School. He founded the Prof. G.S. Sanyal School of Telecommunications at IIT Kharagpur through a personal endowment. Arjun was declared Life Fellow of IIT Kharagpur in February 2003 and was awarded Doctor of Science (Honoris Causa) in September 2012.

Arjun is one of the founding members of SPIC-MACAY, the Society for Promotion of Indian Classical Music and Culture amongst Youth, and is presently on their Advisory Board. He is also on the Board of Governors of a number of Educational institutions like ISB Hyderabad, IIM Udaipur, IIM Shillong, and the Doon School.

Sushmita Sengupta

The area between the eyes is known as "agna" the seat of wisdom—the point where all thoughts are gathered in total concentration. This is what grabs your attention when you first meet Calcutta-born Sushmita and could have influenced the comment from one of her clients—"I have personally seen the power of her mind when she designed a strategy for us to stall disinvestment in coal."

Sushmita is presently the Founder and Managing Partner of Confab Communications.

For the past 20 years Sushmita has made Delhi her home and has successfully made strategic planning and business development her core competency, experienced by her colleagues with comment in Linked-in profile—"I believe her strength lies in being able to think strategically AND implement effectively."

She has worked in organizations like DCM DataSystems, Xerox and Times of India and has consulted with Hitachi Cables & Wires Ltd to develop "go-to-market" strategies as Principal Advisor for emerging market (Indian Railways and Metro Rails). Sushmita has conceptualized management seminars with speakers and participants like Sam Pitroda, F.C. Kohli, Sunil Mittal, Ajay Chowdhry, Nandan Nilekani, Russi Mody, Alyque Padamsee.

This book is her tribute to her mentor Amit Dutta Gupta.